W9-BRH-443

# IT ONLY HURTS WHEN I LAUGH

# IT ONLY HURTS WHEN I LAUGH

*Stan Freberg*

Times BOOKS

 Published in the United States by Times Books, a division of Random House, Inc., New York, and simultaneously in Canada by Random House of Canada Limited, Toronto.

Grateful acknowledgment is made to Freberg Music Corporation for permission to reprint lyrics from "Take an Indian to Lunch This Week" and "A Man Can't Be Too Careful What He Signs These Days" from *Stan Freberg Presents the United States of America*. Copyright © 1988 by Freberg Music Corp.

Library of Congress Cataloging-in-Publication Data
Freberg, Stan.
It only hurts when I laugh/by Stan Freberg.
p. cm.
ISBN 0-8129-1297-7
1. Freberg, Stan. 2. Comedians—United States—Biography.
3. Radio broadcasters—United States—Biography. I. Title.
PN2287.F678A3 1988
792.7'028'0924—dc19
[B] 88-12197

Manufactured in the United States of America
9 8 7 6 5 4 3 2
FIRST EDITION

For Donna, with love.
And for all those people in the world who,
in spite of everything, have managed
to hang on to their sense of humor.
Including myself.

# ACKNOWLEDGMENTS ✍

I WOULD LIKE TO THANK EVERYONE WHO HELPED IN making this book a reality. Especially my editor, Jonathan Segal, editor in chief of Times Books, for his editorial expertise and faith in me, and my literary agent, Don Congdon, for his continued support and enthusiasm. And both of them for their nagging about this, my first book.

I would also like to acknowledge Donna Freberg, my co-producer and wife (although not necessarily in that order), who also serves as my primary editor in all that I write, and Bill Andresen, VP for business affairs at Freberg, Ltd., for their advice, extraordinary hard work, and patience with my various careers. Especially the patience part. Donna and Bill have been my right and left hands, respectively, working with me over the past three decades.

And with much love to the other two members of my humor support group: my daughter, Donna, a talented writer, and my son, Donavan, a fine young actor, who have always understood just what it is I am up to. They have been a constant source of love, devotion, and material.

I also thank my parents, the Reverend and Mrs. Victor Freberg, for always believing that I could be whatever I wanted to be, and especially my dad for not forcing me into the traditional form of ministering.

Many people, of course, are always scattered back over the mosaic of one's life in some minor but important capacity to help shape what we end up being, for better or worse. But if I acknowledge positive influences like Hazel Reynolds, my high school drama teacher, who encouraged me as an actor and helped my voice become what it is by showing me how to speak "from the diaphram!" and to "hit the back wall of the theater!," I would also have to mention a "creative writing" teacher whose name I have managed to block but who gave me no encouragement whatsoever. She's the one who told me my humor was "too bombastic" and that I should give up any thoughts of being a writer. This advice, which initially discouraged me, eventually had the opposite effect. And of course the first time I heard an audience laughing at what I had written, the thought crossed my mind that the woman was full of art-gum erasers.

At any rate, the other influences in my life may crop up in the following pages, which, I hope, will prove entertaining and at least semibombastic.

# CONTENTS ✍

CONTENTS

# *And Now . . .*
# *a Word from the Author*

I AM NOT A MAN WHO ZEROES IN ON AN IMMEDIATE decision, when multiple choices exist.

In the restaurants of the world, when a dazzling dessert cart of possibilities has been wheeled up to me—say twenty minutes ago—I have observed large veins of frustration pulsating on the foreheads of headwaiters, ready to snap. So it will not surprise anyone to learn that I have spent a great deal of time over the years staring at that tiny space on those printed forms that are always being thrust at me, reading, OCCUPATION.

In my head, I compose several possibilities.

Writer-director-entertainer-composer-lyricist?

No good.

Producer-satirist-advertising person?

Forget it.

Not in a space designed to contain one Bufferin tablet and a caraway seed.

Using a magnifying glass and a fine-point pen, I have, a few times, settled on "Guerrilla-satirist."

Let 'em think about that for a while.

Actually, that is a fairly accurate, if distilled, summation of what it is I do.

A story in *The New York Times* once referred to me as "the Che Guevara of advertising." Not too far off the mark, except for two important distinctions: (1) I don't have a beard, and (2) the only weapon I have ever carried is the stiletto of satire.

My critics along Madison Avenue, whom you can count on the fingers of . . . the Mormon Tabernacle Choir, probably expected this book to be mainly about advertising.

That would be right. It *did* start out to be mostly about advertising, detailing my lifelong hostility as a consumer toward the dumb and boring quality of most commercials. And how I was suddenly, in the mid-fifties, given the opportunity to do something about it: to create *my* kind of advertising directed at all the disgruntled people who felt the same way I did. Okay so far. But then my editor—the man who asked me to write this book in the first place—said in essence: You're not telling us how your particular sense of humor was shaped. Go back to your childhood, and fill in the blanks. What was it that made Freberg what he is? Tell us how you happened to break into radio and then television, and became a record star, before you ever got to the advertising part of your life . . . then go on from there.

So I did. But the next thing I knew, memories of my early life were unleashed like a fountain of Slinky toys, springing out of my head and into my word processor.

There was no glossing over these events. Before I knew it, I had filled in about a thousand more blanks than my editor had in mind, I'm sure. A journalist friend of mine, Shana Alexander, in a *Life* magazine story on Burt Lancaster, once tried to convey how it was drawing out the apparently closemouthed Lancaster. "At best," she said, "he gives you what might be described as 'long shrift.' "

Would that I could have given my early life breaking into radio, television, and the record business "long shrift," but that's the way it's always been with me. I always write more than I intended to. For Butter-nut coffee, as you will read later on, a one-minute radio commercial ended up over six times as long as it needed to be. What to do with it? What else? Simply record the six-and-a-half minute commercial, walk it through the mine-field of resistance, and somehow get it on the air. Not so easy with a book, unless you are willing to have it end up roughly the weight of *The Random House Encyclopedia.* So that this would not, from all appearances, seem to be a more humorous *War and Peace,* I have cut this book off, barely skimming the world of advertising as I have known it. My intention is, as soon as the book fairy whisks this off to my publisher, to pick up immediately in the next book where I left off here, with me up to my sinus cavities in advertising. This second volume is about half done, as we speak. (We are speaking, aren't we?)

In case you couldn't care less about the strange, warped events of my early life, which led me into the entertainment business, and simply want a whole book dealing with *nothing* but advertising, I'm sorry.

On the other hand, in case you picked this up in the bookstore a little too quickly, thinking that you had whisked home *An Introduction to Accounting,* hang in there. You may enjoy this more.

Stan Freberg
*Beverly Hills*
FEBRUARY 1988

# IT ONLY HURTS WHEN I LAUGH

# I

# *Playing with Fire*

I WAS STANDING IN THE LONG, DARK TUNNEL OF A stadium in Sydney, Australia, when the orchestra hit a suspense chord.

In my hand was an Olympic torch. The year was 1956. The 19,000 people who had filled the stadium didn't know how I would make my entrance, but this being the year of the Olympics, they certainly didn't expect me to lampoon the games that were sacred to them. For days now, the papers had tracked the progress of the relay runners who held the burning torch high, as they ran toward Melbourne, where the giant flame would at last be ignited. Each night the evening paper showed a ten-inch-wide picture of the breathless athlete who brought the torch nearer. RUNNER NEARS CANBERRA! the headline cried. And the next night, RUNNER NEARS MELBOURNE!

I heard my name echoing through the stadium

speakers as I was finally introduced, and the band began to play my entrance music. A young Australian assistant leaned over the torch and ignited it with a match. *Whoom!* The flames burst up in an orange ball of fire, filling the dark tunnel with light. I started running in my dark blue suit. The first thing the audience saw was a kind of unnatural eerie glow spreading out of the darkness. Then this tall, lanky man exploded out of the tunnel carrying what appeared to be . . . an Olympic torch? I perceived as I ran that for a moment the cheering almost stopped, as 19,000 mental computers assessed new and outrageous information. This American upstart actually had the gall to kid around with the games they had waited countless decades to take place in *their* country for a change? My life seemed to hang in the balance as I jogged up the aisle toward the stage.

The silver metal torch was starting to heat up seriously in my hand. Then a giant laugh burst out of the game Australian crowd. The laugh grew into applause and cheers. Perhaps I would not be torn limb from limb after all. But wait! Before I had come on, I had carefully rehearsed the MC who introduced me to put an unlighted cigar in his mouth. After that he was to slap all his pockets for a match, to no avail. I told him to shrug then and put the cigar back into his breast pocket. Now, as I climbed the steps to the stage, torch blazing, the man replaced the cigar in his mouth. As I loped toward him, he leaned forward at a ninety-degree angle, the cigar jutting out. Then I actually took that sacred torch and shoved it toward him until his stogie was well lit, and glowing. Outrage! Freberg had turned that holy flame into an Olympic cigar lighter! And yet, the sound that now burst forth from all those throats was like the roar of the ocean.

Was it actually approval? It was hard to tell. Added now to the cheering was a giant rumbling sound, which was nothing I could identify. The earthquakelike quality was coming from a *footroll!*—the ultimate Australian tribute, I found out. Thousands of people pumping their feet up and down on the wood floor of the stadium in approval. The American comedian they had paid good money to see, mainly because of the way he had parodied the excesses of the pop-music business on his records, had unexpectedly lampooned something near and dear to *them.* I would find out later that they were mainly applauding my guts. As I came backstage after the show that first night, an unrecognizable form rushed toward me. Then I placed him as the young Australian who had lit my torch for me. But he looked somehow . . . different. He had no eyebrows, and the front part of his hair had disappeared. He also had only half a mustache, and in the garish dressing room lights, his entire head gleamed with Vaseline.

But his admiration for the show I had just finished shone in his star-struck eyes. "You *beaut* you!" he cried, hurling his young arms around me. It was such a beautiful moment. In each city of my tour I repeated the Olympic entrance to the same crowd hysteria, but I made my torch lighter stand well back and use longer matches.

The torch opening was hard for me to follow. However, I went on to perform my Capitol comedy records, all of which had been hits in Australia, for over an hour. (Three out of the top ten records in the country at that moment were mine—the Australian people loving humor as they do.) My takeoffs on hit records like "Sh-boom," "The Great Pretender," and Elvis's "Heartbreak Hotel" were as big down under as they had been in America. For an encore I performed my biggest single, a takeoff of the *Dragnet* TV show: "St. George and the Dragonet." "Just the facts!" they cried out from the audience, egging me on. That was really strange because they barely had television in Australia in 1956, and the *Dragnet* show had not yet arrived. Amazing. The record was funny to them without ever knowing the television show I was spoofing, something I never would have believed possible.

Three years later, in 1959, I returned to Australia to perform again, this time as a guest star with Frank Sinatra. By this time *Dragnet* had arrived and was a hit. A reporter from the Sydney *Morning Herald* ran up to me at the airport with his breathless news:

"Mr. Freberg!" he shouted. "Some bloke has gone and built a whole television show around your record!"

THE CHANCE I TOOK USING THE OLYMPIC TORCH IN front of a crowd who could just as easily have ended up burning me at the stake was typical of the unorthodox approach to things I seem to have favored all my life: the way I broke into radio in my teens, the way I entered the record business, and absolutely the way I backed into advertising. But I'm getting ahead of myself.

# 2

# *Pardon Me, You're Standing on My Roots*

MY PATERNAL GRANDFATHER, PAUL ANDREW JOHNSON, landed on Ellis Island in 1893 with a boatload of wide-eyed Swedes. He had made the long trip from Skana, in the southern part of Sweden, near the border of Norway. If anybody had told this young Scandinavian bachelor that once he settled down in America, one of his sons, Victor, would grow up to be a Baptist minister and that Victor's son Stanley would grow up to be a satirist, he would have thought the person had put away too much aquavit. Paul Johnson, like millions of other immigrants, wondered if things would ever again be the same, now that he had landed in this glorious but confusing new country.

One thing that never *would* be the same was his name.

The immigration officer said to my grandfather: "What? Not another Johnson! Do you know how many thousands of Swedes I've logged in here with the name of Johnson? Forget it! Why don't you change it to something else?" My grandfather's young brow must have furrowed at that startling suggestion as he twisted his cap in his big Swedish hands.

"Come on, you're holding up the line. What name do you want me to put down on your papers?" the man persisted.

My grandfather's mother's maiden name had been Elna Friberg. "Friberg. Paul Johnson Friberg," my grandfather told him. After my grandfather spelled it for the officer, the man said: "Fry-berg? *Fry*-berg?" The new Paul Friberg explained it patiently. "The *i* is pronounced *e* in Swedish. Freeeeeeeberg!"

"OK, Freberg," the immigration man sighed, stamping my grandfather's papers. "*Anything* has to be better than another Johnson."

MY GRANDFATHER SETTLED SOME THREE THOUSAND miles away from Ellis Island, in a little hole in the map called Ferndale, Washington, outside of Bellingham, near the Canadian border. The government gave him sixty acres of land free, as they did to any new settler in the wild Northwest, if he would develop and improve the land. And he did.

Living alone there in the woods, up to his beard in wilderness, he was startled to see an enormous grizzly bear appear one night at his cabin window. So he went outside and simply shot the bear. Later, he decided to take part of the bear meat to the Lofgrens, a family of Swedes who were his nearest neighbors, a few miles away. As he rode up on horseback with his bear-meat gift, he noticed a beautiful young woman whom he had not met before. Her name was Amanda Lofgren, and she bowled the young Paul Freberg over. She would not only become my grandmother, but would cause my grandfather to eventually become a born-again Christian, a thought that had never previously crossed his mind. Her father (*my* great-grandfather) Nils Otto Lofgren had come from the northern part of Sweden, in Sundsvall, and more or less looked down on infidel Swedes from the South like Paul Freberg. Nevertheless, love triumphed. And so did the Lord.

Eventually, they married and had three sons, Gunner, Victor, and Rudy, as they developed the Freberg land into a thriving farm. The oldest son, Victor Richard Freberg, being raised a Christian boy, felt the call from God, and his father Paul put aside the money for him to travel to a theological seminary, the Bible Institute of Los Angeles (BIOLA) in Southern California.

It was there that he met a beautiful seventeen-year-old girl with dark brown hair named Evelyn Conner, who would later become my mother. She was the daughter of two ordained Baptist ministers of Irish and English parentage named Carrie and William Wilmer Conner—W.W. to his friends. The Reverend Mr. Conner had been pastor of the First Baptist Church of Oxnard, California —near Santa Barbara—until he was invited to move down to L.A. and work on the staff of BIOLA. After my father was ordained four years later, he and Evelyn were married, with W.W. presiding in a long black frock coat like Billy Sunday used to wear.

A year later, I waltzed into the world, a few months before another Swede with an *h* on the end of his berg—Charles Lindbergh—became the first person to wing it solo across the Atlantic.

My father's dream had been to become a missionary

to Africa, until another missionary warned him that with his pale Scandinavian skin he could never endure the broiling sun of Africa.

"How about if I wear long sleeves, a pith helmet, and lots of sunscreen ointment?" my dad asked.

"Forget it, Vic," the missionary told my strawberry-blond-haired dad. "The Lord doesn't expect you to be stupid. You have to wear short sleeves in that heat. You'll run out of sunscreen, and some Watusi warrior will borrow your pith helmet."

My father said he'd think it over. He never made it to Léopoldville, but he named me after Stanley, the *New York Herald* correspondent who found Dr. Livingstone, the famous missionary who had been given up as lost, deep in the Belgian Congo. I think my father always secretly wished me to become a missionary, but I hadn't read the script and somehow turned into a humorist instead. All I know about Stanley and Livingstone is that Spencer Tracy played my part.

About the time my sister Gwennie came along, two years after me, my father became the pastor of the First Baptist Church of San Dimas, California. No problem. Except that we were living in South Pasadena at the time. This was not just around the corner from San Dimas, believe me. It was fifty miles away in those prefreeway days, forcing a long commute for my dad two or three times a week in his used Ford sedan. We could have lived for free in the parsonage next to the church and saved my dad all those hours on the highway. But my mother, a stubbornly independent woman with a fiery Irish temper, didn't want to move away from my grandparents, who lived in the duplex next door in South Pasadena. You can see the problem.

My father, who was paid his meager pittance partially in money, but mostly in fruits and vegetables from the various farms of his San Dimas congregation, used up much of his pastor's salary on gas and car repairs. Not a great economic gameplan. But he felt he had been "called" to that church, and he was doing the Lord's work. In those Depression days, long before the era of highly paid TV evangelists, preachers were poorly paid. Like most churches, the San Dimas Baptist Board of Deacons paid their minister only once a month and told him he was lucky to get that. My father would drive the long road home on payday, the bulk of his perishable salary stacked in paper and burlap sacks in the backseat.

He told me recently that a couple of times he was able to trade a sack of sweet potatoes for five gallons of Rio Grande gas as he limped into Pomona, or a crate of corn for a lube job. But he found that it was tough to make a phone call with an avocado. Produce didn't make it down at the gas company either, when the bill was overdue. On the other hand, my family radiated rosy good health in those days. We had been turned into vegetarians, but not by choice. Coming home with his nonnegotiable nectarines, his unbankable zucchini squashes, may have put food on the table. But he was forced to moonlight as a Health-Mor vacuum cleaner salesman to create cash flow.

He soon became a top salesman, which is really all that a good preacher is anyhow. After being invited to demonstrate his vacuum in some spotless Pasadena living room, and before the woman of the house could protest, he would empty a brown paper bag of soot and other unrecognizable gunk onto her beige wall-to-wall carpeting. Before the woman stopped screaming, he would have it vacuumed up spotless again. Then he would stride briskly to the dining room to repeat the amazing demo on her Oriental rug as she grabbed her head in horror. Now that he had her attention, he would extoll the marvels of the Health-Mor vacuum, which also released positive ions into the air if you reversed the suction after the floor was clean. Finally, the woman would buy the vacuum plus all the attachments just to get my father out of the house. But not before he had pressed a few Christian tracts and a Gospel of John into her hand as a parting gift. If all this seems a bit extreme, remember those were tough times for a Depression-era preacher. In between vacuums he sold insurance for the National Life & Accident Company on the days when he wasn't writing his sermon or logging thousands of miles to conduct Wednesday-night prayer meeting, Baptist Young Peoples Union gatherings, and two services on Sunday.

Once he managed to sell a million dollars worth of accident insurance to an entire family of circus high-wire aerialists. The Huustrai Troop from Europe, who were frequently accident prone, had been mostly unable to get insurance until my dad accosted them as they were passing through Los Angeles with Ringling Brothers. They happily paid the year's premium in advance.

Later, the district manager for National Life & Accident, impressed with a sale of five policies to one family, made my dad salesman of the month. My father told me that at their usual morning motivational meeting the manager proudly told what my dad had done to the roomful of salesmen, and they all cheered him. "What line of work is Mr. Huustrai in, Vic?" the sales manager asked him.

"He's a circus aerialist," Dad replied. "The whole family is. They all work in the same high-wire act. I sold a policy to each one of them."

"High-wire act???" the man gasped. "You sold all

those policies to people who teeter around on a high wire? What if they miss the net?"

"Oh, they work mostly without a net," my dad told him. "That's why they're so highly paid. I saw their act when I took my children to the circus. That's what gave me the idea to sell them accident policies. They came riding out on the high wire on two bicycles, see? On top of the two bike riders' shoulders is a long pole . . . " He had everyone's rapt attention by now. "On top of the pole are two chairs with two other people sitting in them, and on their shoulders is the daughter upside down doing a handstand in the air. All this and no net! Can you imagine? They gave me a picture. Autographed!"

Nobody spoke for a while. My dad figured they were pretty impressed, so he told them his other piece of good news: "I sold them a Health-Mor vacuum, too. Their trailer really needed one. Sawdust all over the place."

# 3 ✍

## *The Magic of Childhood*

THE MOST EXCITING DAY OF MY CHILDHOOD WAS THE day my uncle the magician moved in with us. But *not* to my father. We were about halfway through the Great Depression, and to my dad—a struggling Baptist minister trying to feed a family of five—this was not what the doctor ordered. My uncle's name was Raymond Conner, but his business card read CONRAY THE MAGICIAN! Into our small South Pasadena house came trunks of magic paraphernalia and illusions brought by the movers. Then suddenly—Conray himself! He materialized in the doorway, smiling his wide charismatic smile, and before my nine-year-old eyes a large brass bowl of bright feather flowers burst from under his coat, followed by a cage full of live white doves. My sister Gwennie and I applauded, but my dad just sort of breathed a deep sigh.

"Anymore, ahhh, baggage outside, Raymond?" he asked, trying to peer beyond him into the twilight.

"Just a couple more, Vic. What have we here?" my uncle said, pulling a quarter from behind my father's ear. I remember my mother's line at that point. "Well, it's going to come in very handy having somebody in the house who can produce money for a change," she said, snatching the quarter from my uncle and handing it to me. "Run down to Mr. Freedle's, Stanley, and get another box of Kraft's macaroni dinner."

My uncle was my mother's brother, who had just separated from his wife Leah. "Uncle Raymond will be staying with us for a while until he gets on his feet," she announced to my sister and me. Then I was off down the alley, streaking to Mr. Freedle's grocery store in my black high-top Keds. A real magician living in our house! Sleeping on our couch! I could hardly believe it. Neither could my father.

By now we had moved out of the duplex into a slightly larger house in South Pasadena, on Monterey Road. It was near the rim of the scenic Arroyo Seco Canyon through which bulldozers were digging, far down below, what would become the Pasadena Freeway, the first freeway in America. The California-style bungalow was pleasant, but with the four of us—plus my mother's mother Carrie Conner, the Baptist minister now in her late seventies, who lived with us now that my grandfather W.W. had died—it was a well-populated little house *before* my uncle settled in. It meant that I had to move out of my room in the sleeping porch and onto the living-room couch, to make room for my uncle, who now settled in with his cages of white doves. But I didn't care. The best part of that house was the sycamore tree in the backyard, into which I built a tree house for Gwennie and me, and the big garage with room for me to raise my pet rabbit and guinea pigs.

No alarm clock was necessary in those days. At the first glow of daylight, whether we liked it or not, the sound of my uncle's white doves cooing loudly from under their useless bird-cage covers would rudely awaken everyone in our house, plus the distraught people in the houses on either side. Later, I heard that this "dove alarm" was the final straw for my aunt Leah. The apartment they shared with their pretty young daughter Carolyn was so small, he had kept the dove cages in the kitchen, so that an occasional white feather would drift unnoticed into their Cream of Wheat. She finally gave Raymond an ultimatum: "Take your pick, the doves or me." Since he needed them for his act, he opted for the doves.

The main image I have of my uncle's living with us was mostly this: My father, a conservative Baptist preacher who disdained all gambling and card playing, would be followed around the house by my uncle, who begged him to "pick a card, *any* card." My father would decline, of course, and turn away. Whereupon my uncle would thrust the fanned-out cards at him from a different angle. "Come on, Vic, how can I keep in practice if you don't pick a card?"

Finally, my father, a kindly man who aimed to please, would, against his better judgment, reach toward those cardboard instruments of the devil and select one. "It has little red heart-shaped things on it, and the number six," my father would say. Or: "There are little black three-leaf clovers and . . ."

"No, no!" My uncle Raymond would shout. "Don't *tell* me what it is. Just keep it to yourself, and put it back in the deck. And that's called a club, Vic. A club."

As it turned out, I made a better assistant to my uncle than my father. My uncle promptly commandeered my pet rabbit for his act. As he worked occasional one-nighters in the Los Angeles area, I accompanied him after school, and on weekends, in his Graham sedan bursting with magic paraphernalia and small stage pieces. Before the audience came in, it was my job to help him load his coat: to carefully place the live dove in its tiny compartment in the collapsible dove cage hanging under his coat, then reassure my rabbit as he was placed in a deep pocket on the other side. Then it was down into the empty theater and walking all over the house, to see if any "gimmicks" could be seen from the audience. "I see a wire under the table with the water pitcher," I would yell. Or "I see the dove pan when you point with your right hand."

The large poster outside the front doors would declare: A LIVE RABBIT WILL BE GIVEN AWAY TODAY TO SOME LUCKY BOY OR GIRL! Then at some point during the performance, Conray would ask for a volunteer.

"Can I have some little boy or girl come up and help me?" he would ask, and a forest of arms would grow out of the audience. "There, the little blond boy on the end," my uncle would say, pointing at me. Up I would go, smiling sweetly, to tell him my name. "Stanley? Well, all right then Stanley, tell me if you see anything in this hat," he would say, handing me his silk top hat.

"It's empty," I would announce, for indeed it was at that point. Sometimes out of my peripheral vision I would see my rabbit kicking deep inside the trick pocket, creating a kind of mohair goiter in the side of my uncle's coat. *Be still*, I would silently pray. Then in a flash the rabbit was in the hat, and my uncle was pulling him out to great applause. After he gave me the rabbit, I returned to the audience and left a bit early. At the stage door my uncle would discreetly let me and the rabbit back in.

As time went on, the ethical aspects of this, combined with lectures from my father, moved my uncle to buy a second rabbit so that after a short interval a series of small bunnies could *actually* be given away. As the Depression wore on, and bookings dried up, I found *myself* giving rabbits away to neighborhood children. The low point in my uncle's magic career came when he had to hock his tall silk hat and make do with his soft felt everyday hat. The main problem came in scrunching a large kicking white rabbit down into a six-and-three-eighths gray fedora. "Ohhhh, my. This is ridiculous," my uncle would sigh. "I'll bet Blackstone doesn't have to work like this." The solution was to get that rabbit into that hat and back out again at high speed. The whole thing came off as a kind of white and gray blur, while my uncle maintained his nonstop smile under a forehead beaded with perspiration. It was indeed a far cry from the Great Blackstone, but he was "making do," he told me gamely. "We just have to make do, until my big break, and I can get my hat out of hock."

Previously, my multitalented uncle had been a fine musician who played first violin with the Los Angeles Symphony and later the WPA Orchestra. Eventually, his interest in magic made him determined to try for a more interesting and lucrative line of work. That he would choose magic as the Depression arrived and vaudeville departed was a career move unfathomable to his wife and my family. After a while he supplemented his meager magic dates with violin lessons, which he gave to a handful of private students. Conray the Magician inked in a small change on his cards: CONRAY THE MUSICIAN, it now read.

# 4 ✍

## *Radiohead*

THERE MUST BE SOME WAY I COULD GET MY UNCLE'S top hat out of hock, I thought. My friend Buzzie Hagerman had offered to sell me his paper route. "You can earn enough money to get a Louisville Slugger," he told me. I decided to take him up on it. But I wasn't buying any bat with the money.

Sports, as a matter of fact, has always bored me. When the other kids ran out to play baseball, I ran *in* to play the radio. I have been a radio buff for as long as I can remember. Longer, actually. According to my mother, there was a table-model Philco dragged into the delivery room by a nurse who hated to miss *Young Dr. Malone*. I was born on August 7 between the NBC chimes and a Rinso commercial, which makes me a Leo, with Lever Brothers as my rising sign.

As a child, I'd lie on the living-room floor in that pretelevision cocoon of sound, while giant radio waves washed over me, enveloped me, thrilled me far beyond anything else my childhood had to offer.

Radio changed forever the life of this introverted South Pasadena kid. It educated and inspired me—for this was the Golden Age of Radio. It brought a world I never knew existed into my living room and simultaneously transported me *out* of my house on the wings of sound *into* that world.

I remember my parents trying to get me to spend more time on my homework and less time lying on the floor with my ear jammed up against our big console-model Atwater Kent. But it was useless. The radio had become my electronic fraternal twin. I still remember the dusty smell of the golden grill cloth in between the ornate carved wood of the speaker as the voices flowed:

*Burns and Allen*: "Say goodnight, Gracie . . ." "*The March of Time*!" "From Hollywood, *The Jack Benny Program*!" "*The Witch's Tale* . . . " (a cackling laugh!).

*Sound*: marching feet, machine guns, sirens wail . . . "*Gang Busters*!" (The term "coming on like gangbusters" sprung from the way that radio show came on.) *The Amos and Andy Show*: "Kingfish, does you reazalize . . ." A frantic Morse code key tapping and then the hysterical voice of Walter Winchell, "Good evening, Mr. and Mrs. North and South America and all the ships at sea. Let's go to press! Flash!" "*Jack Armstrong, the Allll-American Boy*!" "*Little Orphan Annie*!" ("Who's that little chatterbox?") The soothing voice of F.D.R., "My fellow Americans . . ." "Ladies and gentlemen, *Easy Aces*." "Lights out! Everybody!" *Inner Sanctum Mysteries*, with that terrifying creaking door. *Big Town*, starring Edward G. Robinson. *The Edgar Bergen and Charlie McCarthy Show*: "So help me, Bergen, I'll mow 'em down!" *Fibber McGee and Molly*: "Don't open that closet, McGee!"

*Sound*: Horses hooves. "From out of the past come

the thundering hoofbeats of the great horse Silver. The Lone Ranger rides again!" *Buck Rogers in the Twenty-Fifth Century*! "Who knows what evil lurks in the hearts of men? The Shadow knows!" (A fiendish laugh.) "This is Bob 'Pepsodent' Hope . . ." "This is Cecil B. De Mille in Holly–wood . . ." (Static sounds.) "This is Edward R. Murrow . . . in London."

I was barely twelve years old when I first heard the voice of Orson Welles broadcasting his famous "War of the Worlds" show on CBS (the Columbia Broadcasting System). I heard it not from some old tape, but *live*, coming out of a radio in a diner called The Root Beer Barrel on Fair Oaks Avenue in South Pasadena. It was October 30, 1938, and the first time I had ever eaten out by myself. My mom had given me the money to stop at the Barrel and grab a cheeseburger and a root beer. As I sat down at the counter, I saw that the radio was playing up on a shelf next to the pumpkin pie. I had no idea I was going to have such an exciting evening.

The "War of the Worlds" drama by H. G. Wells was just part of Orson Welles's weekly *Mercury Theater* series, but somehow I hadn't heard the show before. It featured such actors as Joseph Cotton, Everett Sloan, and Agnes Moorehead. Welles and the scriptwriter, Howard Koch, had designed it to sound like the regular show kept getting interrupted by CBS newsflashes announcing that martians had actually landed in New Jersey. It appeared to be the real thing, and believe me, it brought everything to a screeching stop in that diner. A number of customers left their half-eaten bowls of chili and fled out the door, as did thousands of other panicky people across America. Finally, the waitress, who was worried about this gangling kid staring up at the radio with his mouth open in awe, patted my arm.

"Don't worry, honey, it's just a radio program," she

reassured me. But I knew it wasn't for real. I realized it was just another marvelous use of radio, by someone who signed off the show saying, "Until next week, this is your obedient servant, Orson Welles."*

A multitude of radio images are engraved forever on my built-in interior random-access memory disc. But whenever I look back and punch up RADIO, the names of two creative geniuses leap out above all the rest: Fred Allen and Norman Corwin.

Fred Allen. The acid-tongued wit who first opened my mind to the possibilities of satire in the medium of radio, and who first taught me respect for The Word: the precisely correct statement in a sentence of humor.

Allen on my native state: "California is a great place to live, if you're an orange."

Allen on Hollywood: "You could fit all the sincerity of Hollywood into a flea's navel and still have room left over for two caraway seeds and an agent's heart."

As a young boy, I couldn't appreciate the bittersweet truth of that observation. That was to come later. But I knew when I heard it that the comedic construction of such a line was perfection, a verbal jewel. As the great humorist James Thurber once said, "You can count on the thumb of one hand the American who is at once a comedian, a humorist, a wit, and a satirist, and his name is Fred Allen."

He was also very unusual in that he was the only radio comedian who wrote almost all of his own scripts. He sat bleary-eyed batting out his weekly monologues and sketches, while people like Bob Hope and Jack Benny, funny as they were, relied on stables of writers.

* As an adult, one of my greatest thrills was when Ray Bradbury finally introduced me to Orson Welles, and it turned out that by then Orson was a fan of *mine*.

Allen had a lot of trouble with advertising agency people, as I would come to appreciate later.

Allen on advertising men: "A vice president in an advertising agency is a 'molehill man.' A molehill man is a pseudo-busy executive who comes to work at nine A.M. and finds a molehill on his desk. He has until five P.M. to make this molehill into a mountain. An accomplished molehill man will often have his mountain even before lunch."

I knew one thing—I knew I wanted to stand at a network-radio mike someday and be able to write just the right line to skewer some of the absurdities I was already observing in the world: the Pasadena rich kids looking down their noses at people they decided weren't worthy of being included in the "in" group; the other boys treating sports with such deadly seriousness; some of my father's overly pious church members with their tight mouths all squinched up to ward off any possibility of "fun" in this world; along with the pompous attitudes I detected in the voices of politicians and public figures on the radio. I knew I wanted to write and perform someday, as my idol Fred Allen did, taking potshots at the pretensions and nonsense all around us.

Years later, on an airplane to New York, I looked across the aisle, and there, with every bag in place under his eyes, was Fred Allen, sitting with his wife and costar Portland Hoffa. I had just finished writing an article for *Colliers* magazine and had an advance copy with me. Since I had mentioned in the piece that Allen influenced me, I leaned over in the aisle, introduced myself, and asked if he'd like to read the article. To my everlasting joy, he not only knew who I was, but said he'd be delighted to read it. For the next half hour I was thrilled to hear that famous nasal laugh, as he chortled through my writing, occasionally reading passages to Portland. Approval from one of my idols! Something I would never have believed possible as I lay on the living-room floor, chin in hands, listening to *The Fred Allen Show*.

Sunday evening was comedy night at the Freberg house. My minister father believed that God intended us to find humor where we could in this overserious world and laughed along with me. Much to my sister Gwennie's dismay, I tied up the radio for an hour and a half every Sunday evening. First, Jack Benny, broadcasting from Hollywood on CBS, followed by Fred Allen for one hour, coming in from the NBC studios in New York. It was heaven. As the theme of *The Manhattan Merry-Go-Round,* with its supersonic xylophone player driving the orchestra, finally swept the brilliant Allen show away for another week, my sister would wrench the dial away, searching for the young Frank Sinatra.

As I approached my thirteenth birthday, radio, my dearest friend, was always there to comfort me. By now I had my own small bedside model. At night, I could put out the lights and still see my Philco, its friendly dial glowing beside me. I could scare myself to sleep with *The Witch's Tale* or *Lights Out!*—Arch Obeler's marvelous fright show.

One day, home from school with a cold, I lay propped up having my lunch in bed. I heard a few drippy soaps; flipping from one network to another, all of a sudden a little program came on that I had never heard. It was called *Vic and Sade,* and it was so strange and lovely that I can't imagine how it got on. I was so enchanted, I almost choked on my chicken noodle soup and buttered crackers. I was hooked forever. The dry wit and throwaway delivery of this show was a revelation. I started feigning a cold so I could stay home just to hear it. A lot of my sense of humor was shaped not only by Fred Allen, but by *Vic and Sade*.

There was another idol who gradually seized control of my cars, followed by my head.

I began to discover that the radio dramas that moved me most were somehow all written and directed by somebody named Norman Corwin, that brilliant weaver of audio tapestries. He did for the dramatic line what Fred Allen had done for the comedy line. The perfect word, once again. The perfect sentence, flowing into another perfect sentence, designed not just to fill up a few minutes of air time, but to reach out and stop you cold, to shake your sensibilities.

Corwin performed a spectacular feat in radio, not unlike Fred Allen. He single-handedly wrote a new play each week. He cast it, rehearsed it, and directed it *live* over CBS. I, along with millions of other grateful listeners, including my good friend Ray Bradbury, were the recipients of this awesome creative outpouring that so influenced us. Mostly via a show called *Columbia Presents Corwin*.

He was the most brilliant audiomagician ever to spring full blown from the brow of radio. Through his artistry, I learned that there were no limits on imagination, no restrictions when creating for the theater of the mind. He also reinforced that sense of morality instilled in me by my father, for Corwin was nothing if not sweetly moral in all of his dramas. The man played a listener like a human synthesizer, producing one shimmering emotion after another. He did this with the combined forces of an orchestra, chorus of singers, sound effects, actors, and a narrator. But mostly he did it with his writing, rich in those sweeping Corwinesque rhythms until, lying there in my living room, my young goose bumps would bang into each other like crash cymbals.

Meanwhile, in the real world of my childhood, I had problems. The news that the Freberg kid, who couldn't connect the bat with the ball if his life were on the line, was not even available as a last-resort backup hitter because he was in the house listening to some sissy radio program was not well received in the neighborhood. He doesn't like baseball? What is he, some kind of weirdo? It was okay to closet myself with Amazing Tales and Superman comic books while turning into some kind of radio junkie, but not to hang out with the jocks, well, that was the kiss of death. They would make me conform.

One day at dawn, as I sat folding newspapers for my morning route, a little bit apart from the other paperboys, it suddenly got very quiet. The next thing I knew, I had been grabbed from behind and tied to a tree. It was very early in the morning, and nobody was around to hear me cry and yell in the middle of the deserted vacant lot. A couple of hours later, a friendly fireman came to my rescue and untied me. When he did, he noticed that one of the kids had slashed me across the knee with a knife for good measure and that I had lost a lot of blood. He took me to the emergency room at the hospital, where they stitched up my knee.

When I look at the scar on my knee today, it reminds me that I have been a nonconformist for a long time now and that basically nothing has changed. The guys in the dark suits still wonder why I won't play ball. *"You're out of line, Freberg!"* a brand manager at H. J. Heinz once snarled at me.

By God, I hope so.

# 5

## *My First Audience*

LITTLE DID I REALIZE WHILE I WAS GROWING UP that I was on a trajectory headed toward radio, not just as a listener, but as a performer. When it didn't look like vaudeville was coming back, my uncle Raymond the magician put his magic act in mothballs for a while and took a series of colorful jobs.

Like the great detective story writer Raymond Chandler, he, too, worked for a while in Hollywood for Nick Harris Detectives. He was still living with us (the other Raymond, not Chandler) and would hold me enthralled with tales of stakeouts and the shadowing of suspicious suspects. My father the minister was grateful that Raymond no longer followed him around begging him to "pick a card—any card," but now, it would appear, the magician at the dining-room table had been replaced by a man with a shoulder holster. Sometimes if he were in a hurry, he would slip it on and sit down across from me at the breakfast table without yet sliding into his coat. There, to my joy, the handle of his snub-nosed .38 could be seen jutting out—adding a note of high drama just above my cornflakes bowl. This was bad form for a detective, but my uncle was still a magician at heart. The weapon was just another prop to him. "Do you have to wear that thing at the table, Raymond?" my mother would comment. "It's just not right." It was also occasionally awkward. On at least one occasion he dribbled orange marmalade on his gun.

"I'm dressed for work, Evelyn," he would say, opening his arms in a wide shrug. "I'm running late." Then he would hunch into his nondescript tweed jacket, adjust his gray snap-brim low over his eye like Humphrey Bogart in *The Big Sleep,* pluck a fifty-cent piece from behind my ear, and slink out the door. It was heaven for a thirteen-year-old boy. Two years later, my uncle left Nick Harris Detectives for a job as a security guard at CBS radio in Hollywood. The Japanese had just attacked Pearl Harbor, and we were now in the war for sure. Apparently, a big concern was that saboteurs would attempt to break into a radio network and disable it.

My uncle Raymond's job was to sit in the master control room at CBS from midnight until dawn, trying to keep himself awake with a pot of coffee, his hand never far from his trusty Smith & Wesson. The most significant thing fate had yet done for me was to place my uncle in close proximity to the wastebaskets of CBS radio. A couple of times a night he would walk stealthily around the studio, testing locked doors and looking for Oriental people in the shrubbery by the lobby doors. As he passed through the studios themselves, he would frequently find radio scripts in perfect condition tossed into the wastebaskets. He would snatch them out before the cleaning crew arrived and bring them home to me. Ecstasy!

In the evenings I would head for the garage, clutching the well-thumbed scripts to my breast as though they were precious jewels. After I fed my cages of white rabbits and guinea pigs their dinner, I would perform the scripts for their benefit. "I'm going to read this script for you guys," I would announce to the rabbits.

"Do you mind being sort of like . . . guinea pigs?" I would ask my guinea pigs. Silence, as my animals all stared at me. Then I would cue myself and start.

"From Hollywood!" I would cry. "*The Jack Benny Program!* With Mary Livingstone, Dennis Day, Rochester, Phil Harris and the orchestra, and yours truly, Don Wilson." I even sang the theme song, "Love in Bloom."

As I read through the script, playing all the parts, there was no applause from my garage audience. Just the gentle crunching of lettuce leaves.

"Stanleyyyy!" my mother's voice would cry from the house firmly. "What *are* you doing out there?"

Later, as I discovered books, my thirst for the well-honed comedy line would lead me to Robert Benchley, James Thurber, H. Allen Smith, and S. J. Perelman, the greatest humor writer of them all. But I was young and not yet into eye-contact education found in the wonders of books. I was into *ear* contact. Radio was my first library.

By the time I got to high school, I had managed to avoid the throwing, kicking, punting, or touching of any and all sports equipment. I did, however, win a letter in debate. As a speech and drama major, I managed to win three different California State Championship trophies simultaneously, while writing, directing, and starring in a Freberg-produced school variety show. The preparation of all this caused me to skip one PE class after another, using my gym time at the typewriter. This made me a track star, inadvertently. To avoid my flunking gym, the coach gave me laps to make up. Hundreds of laps. To get them over with so I could get back up to the school auditorium and my rehearsals, I began to run faster and faster.

One afternoon, as I streaked past the stadium, the coach stepped out briskly, hitting his stopwatch. "Freberg!" he yelled at me with amazement. "You've just broken the Southern California record for the half mile." Fine. Whatever. Can I get back to my typewriter now?

Running for student office in my senior year, I promised to install an eighty-foot picture window in the girls' locker room and turn the principal's office into an automatic car wash. I was elected in a landslide but found it hard to deliver on my campaign promises. My main responsibility was to organize all student entertainment, assemblies, and dances, but I had no budget. No matter. After buying tickets to a sock hop supposedly featuring trumpet star Harry James and his orchestra, the senior class cheered when the curtain went up on the appointed night to the strains of James's theme song, "Chirri Chirri Bin." Then they groaned. The only thing on stage was what appeared to be a trained gorilla pumping money into a brightly glowing jukebox, full of Harry James records. A sign around the gorilla's neck read HAIRY JAMES. The girls were not amused, but most of the guys laughed. Finally, approval of sorts from my peers.

Since I had been elected to be the commissioner of forensics, a student office making me in charge of student assemblies, I got up my nerve one afternoon and talked the vice principal into allowing me to put on an assembly in which I would be the only entertainment. I had written a comedy radio script, and I read a little for him. He smiled at my nerve, I remember, and finally said okay. I had not yet heard the word *chutzpah,* but somehow I seem to have developed a lot of it growing up, as a means of self-defense. Years later, at a dinner party in San Francisco, a lady on my left commented to me in the middle of a story, "I don't suppose you know the meaning of the word *chutzpah*?" "Know the meaning?" I said to her, "my dear lady, I am the Southern California distributor."

Anyhow, back at high school I performed as a kind of one-man show in an assembly a few days later. I played all the parts in my script, standing by a huge sound-effects door, cuing other sounds and background music from a turntable, while enacting the entire cast of an original Freberg radio show. It wasn't exactly Corwin, or Fred Allen, but the kids laughed and cheered me on, climaxing with a standing ovation. I was hooked. *Now, if I could only turn this into an actual occupation,* I thought that afternoon, riding home on the big red streetcar.

# 6

## *What Do You Think, I Just Got Off the Bus?*

BECAUSE OF MY SPEECH CHAMPIONSHIPS, I WAS awarded a scholarship by both Redlands University and Stanford. My parents were thrilled, and I looked forward to my college years. In the meantime, though, I thought: *What would it hurt to knock on a few doors in Hollywood? See if I could break into radio.* That was the summer of 1944, just after I graduated from high school.

"Stanley—you don't just get off the bus and step right into a job," my mother told me.

"Hollywood is a bad place to walk around," my dad warned me. "A lot of strange characters. Go there if you want to, but take the bus back home before dark."

I promised I would. My mother packed me a sandwich, and I boarded the big orange-top Asbury bus from Pasadena to Hollywood. Later, as it tooled down Hollywood Boulevard, I wondered, *Where should I get off?* I wasn't too sure where any radio studios were. Why hadn't I asked my uncle Raymond better directions to

CBS? Finally, I asked the bus driver, "Where's the middle of Hollywood?"

"Right here," he told me.

"Right here is the middle?" I persisted.

The driver was checking me out in his rearview mirror. "Where do you want to get off?"

"Just, sort of, in the middle of Hollywood," I explained. The bus pulled over; then with a great *whoosh* the doors opened. Something must have told him this seventeen-year-old gangling boy needed a lot of help.

"This is as middle as it gets, kid. Don't lose your return ticket, okay?" he told me.

As the bus pulled away in a cloud of carbon monoxide, I looked up at the corner street sign: Cherokee and Hollywood Boulevard. Hollywood! I was here! But where to start? Across the street a red, fifty-foot-high Coca-Cola sign peered down at me. Cars rushed behind me, honking. And a group of sailors almost capsized me. There was definitely more action here than in Pasadena. I now examined the building right in front of me. It was a kind of dingy-looking two-story Spanish structure. I stepped past the Orange Julius stand on the ground floor and into the tiny foyer at the corner to get out of the hot sun. I checked out the names on the lobby wall: a cut-rate dentist, a chiropractor, an invisible weaving lady, and then the words STARS OF TOMORROW, TALENT AGENTS. SECOND FLOOR. My heart was beating wildly. An actual talent agent. Incredible! Should I just walk in and introduce myself? What if they laughed at me? I went out and had an Orange Julius while I thought it over. Then I walked back in, checked out my hair in the glass over the lobby directory, and took the world's oldest elevator to the second floor. Then down a threadbare hall to a frosted door with the words STARS OF TOMORROW on it. I opened the door offhandedly, smiling for the benefit of an empty reception desk. After a while I called out to the furniture. "Hello? Stars of Tomorrow?"

A door opened from an inner office, and two agent types stared at me: a jaded-looking older man with a cigar and a pretty, forceful lady, who looked a lot like Eve Arden. She walked toward me, holding out her hand and smiling. I remember a white silk suit with Joan Crawford shoulders and exotic perfume. Everything is a kind of blur after that except for the highlights. After telling them my name and how I wanted to be an actor, I launched into a cavalcade of voices and impersonations. The next thing I knew, the woman was saying, "Let's all hold hands and pray for this talented young man. Lord, help Stan . . . what was your last name again?"

"Freberg," I said, clearing it up for the Lord.

". . . Freberg to become a true star of tomorrow," she prayed, clutching my hand and raising her closed eyes heavenward. "Direct him into the right job, oh Lord, in Jesus' name. Amen! Now," she said, clapping her hands, "where is the best place to hit first? There's radio of course, but what about cartoons? Why couldn't you do cartoon voices?" she asked me. Why not indeed? The thought had never occurred to me. She stepped briskly to the phone, and as God is my witness, she set up an interview for the next afternoon at Warner Brothers Cartoons. I took the bus back to Pasadena, while visions of loony tunes danced in my head. I remember rehearsing in the back of the bus for an appreciative wino, while an old lady with two shopping bags moved away from the crazy kid talking to himself.

I stayed up half the night writing new material for all the voices I would do. The next afternoon, I was back on the Asbury bus to Hollywood. The lady agent from Stars of Tomorrow drove me to the Warner Brothers Cartoons building on Van Ness, on the same lot where

Al Jolson had filmed *The Jazz Singer* the year I was born. VITAPHONE, it said on a tall water tower. Inside I was introduced not to some world-weary executive who would give me short shrift but to one of the sweetest men I would ever meet. His name was John Burton, and he ran the studio for Leon Schlesinger, the head of Warner Brothers Cartoons. Sitting there in the chair by his desk, I gave him a few voices. After only a minute or two, he held up his hand for me to stop. "Terrific," he smiled. "Could you come back tomorrow and do some of these voices for a couple of our directors?"

Back in Pasadena, my folks were thrilled that I was going to audition for Warner Brothers Cartoons, though my dad wasn't a very big moviegoer in those days, motion pictures being a kind of iffy entertainment, not far removed from playing cards in the Baptist view. He wasn't too sure what a Warner Brothers cartoon *was*. Nevertheless, he gave me a hug and his full support. Especially when I told him the story of the Stars of Tomorrow lady praying over me before I had gone to the studio.

"That settles it," my dad told me. "It's predestination." I lay awake breathlessly all night. *Looney Tunes!* I thought. *Merrie Melodies!* This wasn't just being funny in front of an auditorium of high-school kids. This was the cartoon big time.

The next afternoon I was back on the bus to Hollywood and the Warner Brothers Cartoons building. John Burton led me back through the halls, where I could see dozens of artists in small cubicles inking and painting Bugs Bunny and Daffy Duck on thousands of individual animation "cels." Then he led me into a screening room and asked me to stand at a mike behind a black curtain. In a minute my ears told me the room was filling up with people. From behind the curtain I heard Burton say my name as he told me to go ahead. I was terrified, but I launched into a series of voices. Almost immediately, I heard laughter. I did everybody from Jimmy Durante to Peter Lorre, F.D.R., and Eleanor Roosevelt. I also did a few original voices. At the end everybody applauded me warmly, and John Burton led his exhilarated teenage actor out from behind the curtain. Several directors stepped up instantly. The first man was Chuck Jones, the creator of the brilliant Coyote and Road Runner cartoons. (He is considered one of the "fathers" of Bugs Bunny.) He said he would think of a way to use me, and he did. A couple of other directors who saw me that day were Bob McKimson and Bob Clampett. Clampett would enter my life a few years later with a children's television show, *Time For Beany*. But that day he told me he had a cartoon in the works that I would be perfect for. One of the main characters was a Scotty dog just like Fala, the president's dog. Clampett said that, as he had listened to me, he had decided to have the dog talk like Roosevelt.

"You do a great F.D.R.," said Clampett. "Could you possibly record day after tomorrow?"

I said, "I think I could work it in."

Another man stepped up and shook my hand—a short man with a mustache. His name was Friz Freleng, a legendary Warners cartoon director who would later create the Pink Panther series.

"Why haven't we heard of you before, Stan?" Freleng asked.

"Beats me," I shrugged. "I've been around, you know."

"Oh well, of course," he said in all sincerity. "I didn't mean that the way it sounded. I'm sure you didn't just get off the bus."

# 7

## *Other Voices, Other Studios*

TWO DAYS LATER, MY NEW SCREEN ACTORS GUILD card in my wallet, I was standing in Warner Brothers' main studio in Burbank, recording the sound track for the Bob Clampett cartoon.

The location of my first professional Hollywood job was odd indeed. The only stage set up for sound that afternoon turned out to be the set of a Humphrey Bogart movie, *The Big Sleep.* The stars were out on location that day, which is why Warners' cartoon division could borrow their set. But I didn't know that, and the sound engineer had to keep telling me, "Stay in the mike, Stan," as I kept looking over my shoulder waiting for Lauren Bacall to walk in. She never did.

When I finished recording, I went to sink in a plush chair on the set.

"Don't sit on the furniture!" everybody yelled at the green kid. "This is a hot set!"—the term used to describe a set that will be used again any time, and which is not to be disturbed in any way. The Warner Brothers cartoon studios were located on Van Ness Avenue in Hollywood but were not equipped to record the sound track on film. So whenever we recorded the track, which always came first—so that the animation could follow—we had to drive over the hill to Warner Brothers' main studios in Burbank.

Frequently the most available sound setup was on the stage of some Warner Brothers movie being shot, and the cartoon directors would simply work around the movie's shooting schedule. I recorded cartoon characters in bedrooms, in courtrooms, on shipboard, wherever the boom mike was handy.

Over the next few years, I did dozens of voices for Warner Brothers, Walt Disney, United Productions of America—the "nearsighted Mr. Magoo" studio—Paramount, Walter Lantz, and MGM, where I worked for the great cartoon director Tex Avery. But mostly I worked for Chuck Jones, Friz Freleng, and other animation directors at Warner Brothers. Mel Blanc, the voice of Bugs Bunny, Porky Pig, Sylvester the Cat, and most of the other main characters, would stand on one side of the mike, while I would fill in various characters on the other side. As the Goofy Gophers, Mel would do one very polite gopher, and I did the other: "After *you!*" "No, after *you*. I insist!" We did a whole series of these gopher cartoons for directors Friz Freleng and Bob McKimson. They had wonderfully wacky titles like "Gopher Broke," and "Lumber Jerks." Mel and I were also another pair of wise-guy mice: Hubie and Bertie, in cartoons like "Mouse Wreckers" and "Hypo-Chondri-Cat," in which we drove a cat up the wall. After pulling some dastardly stunt, they would laugh behind their paws:

"Riot! Riot!" and then, "Come on, Boitie!"—"Sure, sure, Hubie!"

In "The Abominable Snow Rabbit," I did a takeoff on Lenny in *Of Mice and Men* ("I will hug him and pet him, and hold him and squeeze him") while Mel did Bugs. Chuck Jones cast me as the voice of the huge seven-foot-tall baby bear in a series of Three Bears cartoons: "Bear Feat," and "A Bear for Punishment" are a couple I remember. And as Chester, a small dog yapping at a huge lazy bulldog, I would goad him into battle with cats and other dogs. "Attaboy, Spike! Go get 'em, Spike!" I would cry, jumping and leaping over and under the big peaceful dog. But according to Warner Brothers Cartoons people in Burbank, the question that is most asked of them today is "Which cartoon was Pete Puma in?" It was a Bugs Bunny picture that had Bugs teaching his small nephew rabbit how to catch a puma, and it was called "Rabbit's Kin." I did the voice of Pete Puma. As Bugs and his little nephew bunny sat down to tea with the puma, they would politely offer him the sugar. "One lump or two, doc?" Bugs would ask, a huge mallet behind his back. I would then reply, "Gimme a lotta lumps. I want a whooooole lotta lumps!" Then Bugs would clobber him, of course. Poor Pete Puma would be suckered in again and again as the cartoon lumps kept adding up on his head. That was the great thing about cartoon violence. You laughed at the violence, but you knew that it was just a cartoon. Would that life were merely one long Warner Brothers cartoon.

This was the same period of time celebrated in the Steven Spielberg/Robert Zemeckis tribute to cartoon animation, *Who Framed Roger Rabbit*. But in 1944–46, I was walking around "Toontown" for real, as the voices of many "Toons," and riding around the big red street-cars featured in the movie.*

Early in 1945, the Stars of Tomorrow Agency folded their tent unexpectedly and disappeared into thin air. Then my father, of all people, introduced me to a theatrical agent. It was still wartime, and my dad was working as an inspector of aircraft parts at a defense plant. This agent was the father of a girl who worked for my dad.

"Rosemary says he's a big agent," my dad told me. The man's name was Bosty Pizzo. At our first meeting, he had what he called his "principal attraction" in tow. We met in Coffee Dan's restaurant in Hollywood, and the principal attraction sat across from me. The attraction's name was Willy the Whiz. As I stared at him, I realized he was doing something unusual with the cigar in his mouth. He was eating it.

"Is that what he does? Eats cigars?" I asked.

"No, no, stop that, Willy!" Bosty said, taking the cigar out of the man's mouth. "Willy is a mathematical genius."

It turned out that he was indeed. Willy raced adding machines and calculators as they added up long lists of figures, which he could do in his head with the speed of light. Willy usually won, cigars down.

After he took me on, Bosty Pizzo had two clients in his stable: Willie the Whiz and me. One day he booked the two of us on a popular Los Angeles radio show on KFWB called *Stuart Hamblen and His Lucky Stars.* Hamblen, the writer of hit songs like "This Ole House" and

* Over the years, I have continued to do animation voices. I was the voice of the beaver in *The Lady and the Tramp* for Disney and, more recently, on television, of the father in "The Family Dog," the only animated episode of *Amazing Stories,* which was produced by Spielberg.

"It Is No Secret What God Can Do" was basically a country and western personality who was on radio every day with a live band.

Before the show, I auditioned for Hamblen's three-hundred-pound bass player, a man named Cliffie Stone. He also acted as a talent coordinator for the show and eventually led me into the record business. But that day I only knew him as a smiling face giving me terrific encouragement. The band played Willy the Whiz's theme song, "The Stars and Stripes Forever." Then the Whiz ambled out and did his act, beating a frustrated accountant at an adding machine. Bosty gave him a cigar and led him off. Then I was introduced. I did my impressions of Mr. and Mrs. Roosevelt and Jimmy Durante and finished with a harmonica solo. I played "Deep Purple" on my 64 Chromatic, with the band supporting me, and got a big hand from the studio audience.

Afterward, Cliffie Stone put his arm around me and asked if I'd like to be on a new radio show he had just started doing every day. It was an early morning audience-participation show over KRLA, a Pasadena radio station.

"What luck!" I told him. "I live in Pasadena."

"No, we do it live from downtown Hollywood. It's a remote," Stone told me. "I'm on five days a week. Can you start tomorrow?"

The next morning I got off the Asbury Rapid Transit bus at the corner where Cliffie told me, "Look for the big red Coca-Cola sign and walk up a long flight of stairs over Manning's Coffee Shop. You'll hear us rehearsing in the studio." I was amazed. It was right across the street from where I had first got off the bus weeks before.

The show, which was called *Coffee Time at Harmony*

*Homestead,* went on the air at 8 A.M. When I walked in at 7:45, I saw a small country and western band on a small stage. In the band were musicians who became famous later in the country music field. People like Merle Travis, Tennessee Ernie Ford (who doubled as staff announcer at the station), Porky Freeman, and a pretty young singer named Coleen Summers. (She later changed her name to Mary Ford and married the famous guitar innovator Les Paul.) Then I noticed there was no audience in the seats. Ladies in crisp white uniforms stood by big coffee urns of Manning's coffee—the sponsor—and huge trays of doughnuts for an audience that wasn't there. Stone suddenly thrust a handful of show tickets at me.

"Quick, Stanley, run downstairs to the street and see if you can give away these free tickets. We've had a tough time getting an audience. Okay? Don't come back without an audience!"

I ran downstairs to the street. I stood there in my new blue and gray checked sportcoat, holding my free tickets in the drizzly California air. The problem was, there isn't ever anyone on Hollywood Boulevard at that hour but winos and derelicts. At three minutes to eight I dashed back up the stairs with the useless free tickets and gave Cliffie the bad news.

"How about I interview you from time to time and you can play different people?" he said.

Before I could answer, the band kicked it off and Tennessee Ernie Ford was saying, "From Hollywood . . . Manning's coffee presents *Coffee Time at Harmony Homestead!*" A great cheer of audience reaction suddenly materialized. I was flabbergasted. Then I understood. A thin, wiry engineer was playing a sound-effects record of audience cheers, whistles, and applause.

Then Cliffie was saying to the empty room, "Let me just get down here into the audience of friends and neighbors who have dropped by our studio this morning . . . pardon me . . . if I can just squeeze through . . . excuse me . . . this gentleman here in the green windbreaker . . . where are you from, sir?" He thrust his hand mike at me.

"Well, I'm out here from East Sandusky, Ohio," I whined in a kind of midwestern voice. "Sure is a thrill to be on a real radio program like this."

"Is this your wife?" Cliffie suddenly asked.

"Yah-us, say hi, Ethel," I answered. Then, without missing a beat, I switched to a high falsetto giggle.

"Heh heh heh . . . wellll golly, I'd just like to say hello to all the family back in Ohio, Aunt Judy . . . my sister Laverne. . . ." Then Cliffie cued the applause record and the band took it away. A few minutes later with an audience "hubbub" in the background I played a dentist from South Carolina, attending a cavity seminar. And a Viennese poet, seeking asylum in America, who read terrible poems.

I either ad-libbed or wrote the material during the musical numbers. That's the way it went for the many months I was on the show. I was forced to develop more voices and accents and routines than I would have thought possible. The experience was terrific. The money wasn't. Cliffie had no salary for me on this low-budget show, but he would slip me ten bucks every few days, and bought me a book of Asbury bus tickets.

When I offered Bosty Pizzo 10 percent of my bus tickets, he thought it over for a moment, then disgustedly rejected it. "I ain't in this business for the bus tickets," he said and dropped me as a client.

When the show went off the air at nine o'clock,

Cliffie would frequently buy me breakfast downstairs and then drop me in front of CBS. Working for Warner Brothers Cartoons, plus being on this show, such as it was, gave me enough confidence to work my way around the radio networks, trying to get hired as a radio actor. I would write my name on the mimeographed lists secretaries put out for the various shows. Under the section "Special Skills," I would check off every dialect known to man. Serbian? Lithuanian? No problem. I figured I'd fake my way. One afternoon I was standing in the lobby of the CBS radio network building on Sunset Boulevard, asking the receptionist if there were any auditions that day. Suddenly, an anxious-looking man with a pencil mustache burst out of a studio door. He squinted across the lobby at me, then tentatively walked over.

"You're the guy who does animals, right?"

I had never laid eyes on this man in my life. To this day, I don't know if he had me confused with another actor or not. Whatever. I was young, desperate, and my chutzpah knew no bounds. "Right," I smiled.

"Okay, so what kind of animals do you do mainly?" he asked.

I stalled briefly. Could this guy be looking for *real* animal voices? Not dogs that talked like F.D.R., but *real* dogs or horses?

"What do you need?" I hedged.

"My name is Ralph Rose," he explained. "I'm a CBS producer. I do a network show called *Tell It Again*. We dramatize a different classic children's story each week, and this Sunday we're doing 'Toby Tyler at the Circus.' I need a monkey badly, but I don't like any of the recorded monkeys. Do you do monkeys?"

"You're in luck," I assured him. "Monkeys are my specialty."

"Okay, so let's hear a little monkey." He closed his eyes, waiting.

"Wait a minute," I sparred. "Can you be more specific? Are we talking about a gorilla here?"

"Too big," Rose said. "I hear something smaller."

"Chimpanzee?" I offered.

"Mmmmmmmm, maybe even smaller."

"Okay," I said, warming to the subject. "Now we're talking orangutans, spider monkeys, marmoset . . ."

"Marmoset!" Rose begged. "Lemme hear a little marmoset!"

And now, would we have the moment of truth? Not a chance.

"I'm a little rusty on my marmoset," I told him. "Let me take a quick run up to the Griffith Park Zoo and check out the . . ."

"That won't be necessary. Please." Rose waved his hand, but I was already on my way out the door.

"Be back in forty-five minutes," I called. "I'm sorry, but I'm a perfectionist."

Two hours and four buses later, I was standing back in front of Rose's desk, sweaty from my run at the Griffith Park monkey cages and very out of breath. "Lay a little marmoset on me," said the anxious Rose, checking his watch, then closing his eyes in anticipation.

I gave him a variety of monkey noises, chattering like an idiot. I must have given him what he imagined to be the perfect marmoset, because I got the job instantly. Three days later, I did my monkey along with a studio full of fine actors: Marvin Miller, Peter Leeds, Vic Perrin, Parley Baer, and Lurene Tuttle. The two sound men accepted me like I was an old pro, and at last my voice was heard, so to speak, on CBS radio.

A pattern to the job was established early. As I finished all the whinnies for "Black Beauty," say, Rose would give me my assignment for the next show. ("A medium-sized fox terrier and a lion.") Up to the zoo, check out the lion pit, and back to CBS. I wondered, *Is this what they mean by on-the-job training?*

I was with the show for a year, performing all the animal parts until the series went off. Gradually, I got more work as a network radio actor. I worked shows like *The CBS Radio Workshop,* and the Armed Forces Radio Network show *Jubilee.* At eighteen, I was the last actor in America to impersonate the voice of President Roosevelt before he died. In those days you had to get permission from the White House to imitate the president on the air. (Rich Little would have had some sweet time getting an okay every time he performed.) CBS rushed a recording of me doing F.D.R. to the White House, some military officer approved it, and the next thing I knew I was standing at a CBS radio network mike, right next to Chet Huntley, impersonating Roosevelt on a wartime CBS documentary called *Destination Tomorrow.* Two weeks later, F.D.R. was dead, and Harry Truman became president.

My draft board was getting so desperate they were getting ready to call nearsighted guys like me whose eyes were 20/400. Before that happened, though, I performed on a couple of other network shows that were memorable to me. One was *The Henry Morgan Show* on the ABC radio network. I walked out in front of the huge Bernie Green Orchestra and placed my music on a music stand by the mike. Morgan announced me deadpan. "And now, a young musician named Stanley Freberg will give a rather unusual concert," he said.

I gave the nod to Green, and the orchestra crashed into the opening bars of a familiar Rimsky-Korsakov melody. Suddenly, the audience screamed with laughter. They were laughing because I was playing "Flight of the Bumblebee" on my mouth using only my lips and my index finger.

One of the last things I did before I went into the army was to appear on a show starring one of my idols, Jack Benny. A dream come true. At the dress rehearsal I saw that my small part was coming up fast. In order to be at the mike in time, I leapt out of my chair on stage and hurried toward the other side of the star's diamond-shaped mike. Too late I realized I had walked on his punch line.

"Young man!" Benny bellowed. *"What's your name?"*

The studio became deadly still. Mary Livingstone, Rochester, Dennis Day, and Phil Harris's entire orchestra stared at me. I swallowed hard. "Stan Freberg, Mr. Benny."

"Well, let me tell you something, Stan Freberg. Don't you ever dare walk on my punch line again." He said it with that great Benny inflection, but believe me, nobody was laughing. My mouth seemed to be full of cotton balls.

"I . . . have the next line after your punch line, Mr. Benny," I stammered. "I wanted to be sure I got to the mike in time."

Benny glared at me over his reading glasses. In that pedantic delivery he was famous for, he laid it out for me with precise enunciation. "Wellll, leave *later* . . . and walk *faster*."

I never again walked, moved, or breathed on anybody's punch line.

# 8 ✍

## *Uncle Sam Wants Me?*

I WAS SO ENCOURAGED BY THE WORK I WAS GETTING on radio, and the checks that were now coming in, I decided to put college off for another semester. Working alongside top radio actors on network shows was teaching me mike technique, comedy timing, and an appreciation of things like sound effects. Listening to radio shows at home had given me only half the picture. Now I was standing on the other side, working in the actual studio, learning how it was done. Believe me, I paid very close attention to how a radio production came together. All of it went into my mental file.

Then suddenly, my acting career came to a dead stop.

Until August 7, 1945, I always thought of that day as my birthday. Ever since then, I think of it as the day after we dropped the atom bomb on Hiroshima, and just coincidentally, my birthday. As Japan surrendered to

General MacArthur in the terrible aftermath of that devastation, I thought surely my draft board would have no further need of a nineteen-year-old 4-F with thick glasses.

Wrong. With my mother fighting back the tears, and my dad giving me a long checklist of things to look out for, they put me on the train to Fort MacArthur in San Pedro, California. There I was inducted into the army and given an ill-fitting olive drab uniform with a Fifth Army patch on the sleeve. "Could I see something in a forty-two long?" I asked the supply sergeant. He looked like he was about to give me a forty-two long *head*. "You know," I continued, "if General Patton walks up to me, I want to look nice for him. Otherwise it'd be a reflection on you." I remember the supply sergeant blinking hard while he thought that over. Then he went back into the shelves and rooted around. The new uniform he thrust at me fit perfectly.

We were all waiting to be shipped overseas, but I was anxious to get into a branch of the army called Special Services, an entertainment division, in which at least my basic talents could be utilized entertaining the troops. After a few days of ridiculous marching and climbing ropes, I walked into the captain's office on the base. I saluted and handed him a sheaf of letters of recommendation from Warner Brothers Cartoons, CBS, and others testifying to my ability as a funny young man. He read them carefully. "Very impressive, private," he said.

"Yes sir! I thought maybe I'd be of greater use to the United States Army in Special Services," I said to him. He was already dialing his phone.

"Sergeant Brown," I heard him say. "I think we've got the man you've been looking for." Pause. "Freberg. He's on his way." He hung up and wrote down the number of a building for me and told me to report there. I thanked him profusely. Then I saluted and did an about-face, putting my right foot back the way I'd seen Van Johnson do it in *Thirty Seconds over Tokyo*. I almost fell on my face.

Once outside, I detoured to my barracks. I wanted to do a good audition, so I raced to my footlocker and grabbed a few props: my Eleanor Roosevelt false teeth; a woman's floppy white hat; my Jimmy Durante nose; and last, a colored scarf tucked into a false finger my uncle Raymond had given me.

Building 18 sure didn't look like a theater. It didn't smell like one either. *What is that odor?* I thought as I walked in. All around me were men in white hats and aprons. Then I recognized the sweet, warm aroma. It was bread! Home-baked bread! A large man weighing about 280 pounds was towering over me. His name was Master Sergeant "Tiger" Brown.

"I took a chance on your head size. You *are* Freberg, right?" he was saying, thrusting a baker's hat at me. "I'm Tiger Brown, but you can call me sergeant. Understood?" I stood there flabbergasted, with my jaw open. "You ever been a baker?" he asked.

"Ah, not exactly," I told him.

"You are now. Here's your apron. I'll see you at four A.M. sharp. Repeat, four A.M. What's that stuff you're lugging around there?"

"Oh, nothing," I mumbled.

"Whata we got here? Funny teeth? A cardboard condom?"

"Nose," I corrected him. "A cardboard nose. Like Jimmy Durante."

He shook his head slowly. "That ain't gonna help you bake bread." Actually, the man was right.

The entire company of men shipped out to Germany a week later, but not me. I learned to bake not just bread, but how to make terrific omelettes. The only problem is I only know how to make one for 150 men. (First you crack three hundred eggs . . . )

From time to time, I would entertain the men in the bakery. This got me into a lot of trouble. Once in the middle of playing "The Flight of the Bumblebee" on my mouth, a giant doughnut machine went out of control. Since the men were all gathered around watching me, the machine had been left unattended, and hundreds of doughnuts were piling up in the huge vat of grease. As the men laughed and applauded, the doughnuts cascaded over the side, bouncing and rolling all over the bakery. Tiger Brown was far from amused. I was put on extra duty scrubbing the decks outside at three A.M. in the freezing San Pedro Harbor air. By this time I was somehow writing a newspaper column each week as well for the *Fort MacArthur Alert.* My editor was Sergeant Forrest J Ackerman, who later became a famous science-fiction editor.

I finally became sick from lack of sleep and exposure to the chilling harbor air. But Tiger Brown refused to let me report to sick bay. "Goldbrick," he taunted me. "If your nose is blue out there, put on your Jimmy Durante nose. Keep scrubbing."

Finally, my ears began aching badly. I threw down my scrub brush and staggered up the hill to the base hospital. A doctor there, a major, informed me I had a temperature of 104 and pneumonia. After a few days in bed it was determined that I also had a mastoid infection in my left ear.

"Why didn't you report to the hospital if you were this sick, private?" he demanded. When I told him why, he became very angry. Later, I understood that Tiger Brown was severely disciplined. Sometimes, there is justice.

It was determined that my ear had to be operated on at a bigger, better-equipped hospital. An ambulance drove me to McCornack General Hospital, the closest army facility in, of all places, Pasadena. After my operation, during which my eardrum had to be punctured, I recuperated for a couple of weeks in the hospital. Even though my home was nearby, I was afraid to remind anybody for fear the army would ship me to Greenland, just to be perverse. (Later, I would quietly walk home on an occasional weekend pass.) Meanwhile, as soon as I was ambulatory, I found my way to the Special Services officer at the base. She was a Wac, First Lieutenant Laura Mack. She looked over my letters of recommendation from Warner Brothers, CBS, and others, and smiled. But I was on to the system now. Any minute I knew I would be sent to the kitchen to cook or the motor pool to become an ambulance mechanic. Fate, however, once again intervened.

"I just lost a good assistant. He was discharged yesterday," she told me. "I think you're just the man I need. I'll have your gear shipped up from Fort MacArthur." I drew myself up in my maroon bathrobe and saluted. "Yes, sir. Ma'am! You won't be sorry."

"Oh, one more thing. This job calls for a corporal. You won't mind a little upgrade, will you, private?"

I was soon launched into my new duties, one of which was associate editor of the base newspaper, *The Needle*. But mainly I tried to help keep the hundreds of hospitalized men entertained. This was a plastic-surgery center, filled mainly with wounded men from the Pacific theater of war. Their disfigured limbs and faces were in various stages of plastic surgery, and their morale was in the basement. I toured the wards entertaining and helped cast the men in little theater productions like the classic farce *Room Service* to help bring the men out of their shells.

Once, while I was doing a stand-up routine in the psycho ward, one of the inmates grabbed the MP's keys and shoved him out the door, locking us all in. I was trapped in there for seven hours. I went through every routine I knew to keep them preoccupied, until a doctor outside finally talked the man into unlocking the door. It was like a scene from *One Flew Over the Cuckoo's Nest,* and it was very nerve-racking. One thing was very clear: These men laughed not at the punch lines but at the straight lines. Try to figure *that* out.

Each week I would drive a staff car to Hollywood to pick up free radio tickets and accompanied different groups of men to see the network shows.

One afternoon, just before Harpo Marx was coming to entertain at the hospital, I drove a weapons-carrier truck and a couple of men to his home in Beverly Hills and stood by while he lovingly selected the joke props from his storage room behind his house. I was amazed. He could actually talk! But not much. "Here," he said, handing me a long coat. A few minutes later, "Take this," as he handed me a blonde wig. Then a cane with a bulb horn attached. He tested it. *Honkkkk!* it went. Harpo smiled that sweet smile of his as though the bulb horn had been a Stradivarius. I noticed that he was taking his good old time, rummaging around his props, rejecting a joke cigar here, settling on a shapely plaster woman's leg there. Then he handed me a heavy bag of silverware. Silverware? Mine was not to question. He presented a huge pair of scissors to me as though he were an officer surrendering his sword. "Will you be bringing your harp I hope, Mr. Marx?" I asked. He nodded silently. Then he led us back into his house, where his harp was already in its case. He pointed to the harp, and we put it on a dolly. Now, one more word from Harpo: "Careful," he said to us.

An endearing detail remains. When Harpo answered his front door, I had noticed a faint imprint of someone's lipstick on his cheek. It remained there unbeknownst to him (or was it?), all through the hour that it took him to select his props. I kept hoping to see the owner of the lipstick, but she never appeared.

That night, backstage in the hospital auditorium, I once again helped someone load his trick coat. "Pour that bag of silverware in here," Harpo told me, pointing to a huge concealed pocket under his armpit. Later, after Harpo had concluded his hilarious stage show, during which he had, of course, never spoken a word, he closed with a virtuoso performance on his beautiful golden harp. As the audience cheered, the commanding general came up on stage to thank Harpo. Harpo put out his hand, and the general shook it warmly. Suddenly, a spoon fell out of Harpo's sleeve and clattered to the stage. Then a fork, and two knives. The general looked down, confused. He tried to pull his hand away, but Harpo had a death grip on him. The audience started to laugh. Harpo had to all appearances stolen some silverware from the general's hospital dining room. More spoons. A complete place setting. Finally, as Harpo continued to pump the general's hand, an avalanche of silverware rained to the stage, with a tremendous crash. The audience cheered for two minutes while Harpo just smiled that sweet smile of the innocent, and the general stared at the mountain of cutlery at his feet.

It was a great moment for me. I realized the value of the elaborately planned joke in the face of authority, if it was done properly.

After I got out of the army two years later, I continued to work in radio, and my friends at Warners Cartoons welcomed me back. On a few three-day passes I had managed to do an occasional cartoon voice, standing next to Mel Blanc in my army uniform. Now Blanc peered at me from the corner of his eye. What kind of uniform was the Freberg kid wearing *now?* It was white, and the name over my pocket was stitched in red: DAINTY DIDY SERVICE, it read. To support myself between acting jobs, I was driving a delivery truck for a baby laundry, Pampers not yet having been invented. I often left the truck piled high with customers' fresh clean diapers outside the studio while I recorded. Dozens of frantic mothers called the Dainty Didy company to find out where that guy was with their diapers.

Once Blanc questioned my strange uniform.

"I'm on a picture," I told him. "I play the part of a diaper delivery man."

"But weren't you wearing that the last time we worked? A month ago?" Blanc said, boring in like a prosecuting attorney.

"Yeah, it's been a good part," I told him. "I've been on it about six weeks now. Matter of fact, I have to really scoot."

"What studio?" Blanc called, as I pushed the big stage door open.

"Independent production," I yelled, running off toward my truck.

# 9

## *Play the Guitar!*
## *Amaze Your Friends!*

MY CAREER AS A DIAPER MAN WAS FORTUNATELY short-lived. I lost so much business for the Dainty Didy Service, using their truck to drive to readings for jobs, I did the only decent thing: I quit before they fired me.

Shortly after that, I nailed down a permanent job with a small comedy orchestra called Red Fox and his Musical Hounds. (Not *the* Redd Foxx, by the way.) I had answered an ad for a comedian in *Daily Variety* and auditioned for Fox. He said, "That's great. We do two floor shows a night, so I hope you have enough comedy material. By the way, what instrument do you play?" This was a new wrinkle.

"Instrument?" I said.

"Of course. I can't afford to just carry a comedian. We all have to play. I'm a drummer. What do you play?"

"What do you need?" I said, stretching and yawning nonchalantly.

"Guitar. I don't have a full rhythm section," he told me. "You're not a guitar man, by any chance?"

"What luck!" I informed him.

As his front door closed behind me, I was on my way to Music City. I bought a guitar, a book of instructions, and six Nick Lucas guitar picks.

At the first rehearsal, holding my new Gibson F hole guitar, I knew I was going to last about thirty seconds, once we started playing. "One, two, three and . . ." Fox called, kicking off the first musical number. Violent sound exploded all around me. It turned out to be a poor man's Spike Jones orchestra. Fox was using sticks, socking the cymbals hard as the trumpet player growled loudly. Standing over me, Fox fired blank cartridges from a pistol every few bars. It was bedlam. I was saved! Nobody could have heard my guitar if I *had* been playing.

Next thing I knew, we were on the road. I stroked with my pick, deliberately missing the strings by about a half inch. When everybody else turned the music pages, I did, too. Fortunately, I was knocking 'em dead during the floor show as a stand-up comic. Fox played, among other bizarre instruments, a musical tree. The branches, complete with leaves, were tuned up the scale chromatically. When he hit the top branch, a small explosion blew a birdhouse apart on top and a ladies brassiere jumped out on a long spring. This was truly a class act.

Of course the musical tree wasn't employed during the dance music, which is what we played for most of the evening. During these "straight" sets, the five of us sat in maroon cardigan blazers, white shirts, and black knit ties, as the Red Fox Orchestra. Very straight. Sort of like a shrunken Stan Kenton band. But then twice a night, we would go backstage and slip into these outrageous outfits—late Spike Jones or early Alice Cooper.

***Stan Freberg*** ✍

Rick Fay was a terrific clarinet and sax man who today is a writer and also has his own band in the new Grand Floridian Hotel at Disney World in Orlando. At the time he hated the woman's flowered housecoat, blond wig, and cigar that Fox made him wear every night. Jack Coons, the trumpet player, sometimes put on a gorilla head if he could get the mouthpiece through the King Kong lips. Jack today is considered one of the top Dixieland trumpet and flügelhorn players and is currently with the Abalone Stompers in Monterey, California. At any rate, Red Fox, the leader, would change into a clown nose, huge horn-rimmed glasses, and an enormous plaid jacket. Twice a night we would creep out in the dark and take our positions, while George Howard, the piano player, who had changed into formal tails, flipped the little Red Fox Orchestra sign over. It now read, RED FOX AND HIS MUSICAL HOUNDS. Then we would hit a big fanfare as Red kicked the spotlight on from the floor switch down by his bass drum. It was *showtime!* The opening musical number usually moved at the speed of light, featuring Red on drums, slide whistle, and exquisitely timed gunshots. Rick Fay and I would alternate as musical tree soloist. In the middle of the floor show, I would do a few minutes of stand-up comedy. I ran through my repertoire of impressions, interspersed with fake radio commercials for products I had made up.

"And now a *brief* word from our sponsor!" I would announce at the mike, as I released the ten-foot-long rolled-up script I was holding, which cascaded down, hit the stage, and flowed over the edge onto the dance floor.

"The *Lox* Radio Theatre, brought to you by the makers of Lox soap," I would say, holding up a small bar of soap in the shape of a salmon. "Remember . . . Lox is the only soap that swims up-tub."

Eventually I would launch into a routine I had written called "John and Marsha." It was a satire of soap operas, and I played the parts of both John and Marsha. As the audience waited expectantly for the real dialogue to begin, I simply repeated the characters' names, over and over, as the laughs built. I ended up bending the mike over backward on one knee as I spoke the final "Mar-shaaaaaaaa!" Then I leapt to my feet and said "Be with us again tomorrow, for another thrilling episode of John and Marsha!" That was the biggest laugh, as the audience realized that the soap opera was over and nothing other than *John* and *Marsha* had been spoken.

To close, I played "The Flight of the Bumblebee" on my mouth with the band backing me in a somewhat less than classical arrangement. The audience loved it, but I'm sure that, wherever he was, Rimsky-Korsakov was not cheering. Or was he? Hard to tell.

The name of the comedy band caused some unique problems. Once Red wired ahead to the only motel in the middle of some godforsaken stretch of desert, in between dates. "Please reserve rooms Monday night. Signed—Red Fox and His Musical Hounds." When we finally arrived shivering and exhausted on that rain-soaked night, the old motel manager had only one room left.

"I saved the last room for you and Mrs. Fox," he said, "and I've fixed up a nice kennel out back for the dogs."

The fact that I was a big hit each night as a comedian in the floor show saved my job. But as a straight musician on the dance sets, I left something to be desired.

Fox kept asking me, "How come you don't have an amplifier on that guitar? Sometimes I can hardly hear you."

"No way," I told him. I like the true guitar sound. Like Segovia. I'm a purist."

"Freddie Green with Count Basie plays an unamplified guitar, too," he told me. "But at least you can hear him. Try and drive us a little harder."

I promised I would, and indeed, every night in my hotel room I was woodshedding with a book of instructions, *Play the Guitar! Amaze Your Friends!* I kept practicing until my fingers bled, trying to build up my calluses. The big problem, as I've said, was that in between the bedlam we had to play the straight dance sets. I was getting better but was still reluctant actually to play on stage. Once again, I appreciated the black humor thought: *Is this what they mean by on-the-job training?* You have to understand that Fox had obtained a Musicians Union card for me, so that my guilt knew no bounds.

One night, at a supper club in South Bend, Indiana, on a slow night, in the middle of "Honeysuckle Rose," Red Fox yelled, "Hold it! Everybody lay out, except Freberg!"

The silence was deafening. "Play us a little something," he said to me.

I sat back and crossed my knee. "What would you like to hear?" I asked, bluffing it out to the end. But it was no good.

"You can't play, can you?" Fox said to me gently.

"Noooo," I admitted, "but I'm learning."

As the band stared at me, Red gave us a five. Then he headed for the bar to get himself smashed.

As the band filed off the stand, I heard the clarinet player Rick Fay say to Jack Coons, "Wow, man. I thought he was playing awfully soft."

By the time I left the band a year later, not only was I playing guitar, but I had added an amplifier. I even picked up enough banjo to help on the Dixie stuff. I also started writing songs.

I left the band with mixed emotions. I liked the road, believe it or not, mainly because I enjoyed palling around with Rick Fay and Jack Coons. During the day, we would either find the nearest place to shoot pool, or spend hours in some record store listening to Django Reinhardt and Stéphane Grappelli and their Quintette of the Hot Club of France till it was time to rush back and get dressed for the job. My tastes for jazz were formed on the road, listening to everyone from the Benny Goodman Quintet with the great Red Norvo, to Charlie "Bird" Parker, to Art Tatum. But the reason I finally left was not because I wasn't having a good time. It was to get in on the ground floor of television. As we worked our way back home from Salt Lake City to Eugene, Oregon, to San Francisco and finally to a date in Los Angeles, I had no idea that a phone call awaiting me from my old friend the cartoon director Bob Clampett would change my life radically over the next five years.

Red Fox begged me not to leave the band. "I need you," he said. "You want more money? Is that it?"

"That's not it," I told him. "I have a chance to get into television, and I think I should take it."

"Television!" Fox snorted. "They've been trying to get that off the ground for years. Believe me, it's just a passing fad."

# 10

## *You're Sure This Is the Ground Floor of Television?*

IN LATE 1949 BOB CLAMPETT, WHO HAD LEFT WARner Brothers Cartoons, wanted to get in on the ground floor of television. He had a very rough idea for a children's puppet show about a little kid with a beanie on his head. He asked me if I would help write it and do some of the voices. He asked the same thing of a brilliant young actor named Daws Butler. He had brought in Wilder Wiley from Edgar Bergen's stable of writers, and an art director, Bill Oberlin. After a couple of weeks, Wiley left the group, due to differences with Clampett, and Daws and I had to take over the writing.

We tried to pull together the first script, which featured the main characters, Beany and "Uncle Captain" Huffenpuff, who talked from the deck of a little boat. At one end of Clampett's garage, behind his house on Formosa Street in Hollywood, Oberlin had constructed a hand-puppet stage above our heads up into which the puppets would be thrust.

"Where are the puppeteers?" we asked Clampett.

"You're the puppeteers," he told us. Daws and I looked at each other and shrugged. We thought we had been merely hired as voice actors, while puppet people would operate all of the puppets.

We walked back to pull the puppets on our arms, and I gave Daws a nudge: "It's called 'on-the-job training,' " I said. By now, we had added the additional characters of a villain, Dishonest John, and a friendly sea serpent, Cecil, who at first terrified Uncle Captain.

Over the next week, representatives from several television stations walked into our garage theater with their entourage. They sat and laughed at the unique little children's show with adult overtones and said they'd think it over. Then at the end of the week a lone man walked in. His name was Klaus Landsberg. He was the head of independent station KTLA, the first Los Angeles commercial television station. After he finished applauding us, he just said one thing: "This is Friday. Can you start Monday?" We could, and we did.

We performed it live, five days a week, fifty-two weeks a year, including Christmas and New Year's, for the next five years. We managed to become the number-one children's show, while appealing to adults as well. Whole families would gather before their TV sets each evening to watch *Time for Beany*. (A 70 share of the audience was not unusual.)

With mikes on our chests and both arms holding various puppets in the air, Butler and I literally had our hands full. We would perform all the characters, walking one hand out of camera range, only to have an assistant pull off the Chinese cook Hopalong Wong and put Tear-along the Dotted Lion on one of our hands so we could walk him back in as the three cameras shot above our heads. Daws's main characters were Beany and Uncle

Captain; mine were Cecil the Seasick Sea Serpent and Dishonest John. Cecil had been made by Daws's wife, Myrtis, out of the arm from one of Daws's old sweatshirts. His nostrils were made from small suction cups.

It was difficult enough for us to hold both our arms in the air and read a script below the stage, but how would we turn the pages? The first night on the air we tried out Clampett's "ingenious" script solution. He had us type out our lines on index cards, numbered 1 through 30, and the thick wad of cards was held by one large metal clip. A stagehand would crouch down below, Clampett told us, and pull the cards off one by one as we finished reading. It *sounded* good, but the man in question was a highly nervous person, and as we peeked through a hole in the set, waiting for the red light on the camera to go on, we could see he was trembling. Suddenly, we were on. This was *live* television, mind you. As Daws and I held our four arms up into camera range, reading down to the end of the first card, nothing happened. Why wasn't the man pulling the first index card off so we could go on with the script? He was crouching down below between us, doing *something,* but what? I nudged him with my elbow, having no other appendage free at the moment. Daws now signaled him with a bump of his hip. Up above, the puppets were stalling, trying to send a hint to the man, who obviously had forgotten when to pull the first card.

"You sure are a *card,* Cecil," Daws was ad-libbing.

"Yeah," I said. "I never know what's coming *next.*"

Suddenly, as the stagehand, who had been having difficulty pulling off the first card, lost his balance and fell to the floor, the entire wad of cards came out of the clip. We looked down and the cards were raining around him like five-by-seven snowflakes.

"Let's see, seven . . . fourteen . . . uh, twenty-seven," we heard him mumbling.

Daws and I had to ad-lib the rest of the show. For a finish, I crashed Cecil through a cardboard brick wall, and the whole set started to fall over. I turned him into the camera. As I looked up, I noticed that half his nose had fallen off when he hit the brick wall.

"I seem to have gained a laugh and lost a nostril," I ad-libbed. Daws put Beany's arm around Cecil's long neck and reassured his wounded friend.

"No problem," Daws said. "We'll just have to run down and make a withdrawal from the Nostril Bank."

We told the audience goodnight and faded to black.

Down below, the nervous man had reassembled the index cards. "I think I got 'em all in order now," he smiled up from his knees.

"Forget it, Ralph," I said. "Thanks anyhow."

Clampett had rushed out of the booth and was now coming around the corner of the puppet stage.

Stan! Daws!" he was yelling angrily, waving his legal pad of notes. "Please! Stick to the script!"

By the next night we had devised a way for the pages of the script to be taped together into a continuous sheet attached to rollers, so it would move down in front of our eyes, operated by the same nervous man. We had invented the first crude TelePrompTer, but we were so busy doing the show, we forgot to patent it. It turned out later that the best lines often came from the ad-libs Daws and I would inspire each other to toss off, as we worked side by side, night after night,—our four arms in the air, like a well-oiled machine.

In other ways we were the odd couple indeed: Butler at about five feet tall and Freberg about six foot one. At first, the problems caused by the difference in our heights seemed insurmountable. The top of my head was always showing in the shot, and nobody could figure out what to do. Finally Klaus Landsberg, the man who had hired us, made a suggestion in his faint German accent.

"Simple," he said. "Ve just take an air hammer and dig a trench in the concrete studio floor. Daws valks along the edge, and Stan valks down in the trench. Now you're both the same height. Okay?"

"Not okay," Daws said. "I'll fall in the trench and break my leg."

"Vatch vere you're valking then," Klaus said.

"I can't watch where I'm walking," Daws told him. "I've got my puppets in the air, and I'm looking up. I'll walk right off the edge into the hole and break my leg, I tell you. Forget the trench."

Klaus was not a man used to people telling him no. "If I'm villing to cut a trench in my studio floor, you should be villing to vatch vere you're valking," he said. But Daws held out, and we killed the trench idea. For Klaus, an electronic genius who pioneered early television and who later televised the first atom-bomb blast from Yucca Flats when the networks couldn't manage to get their acts together in time to cover it, the "trench plan" was the only bad idea I ever knew him to have.

The solution eventually was for Daws to wear a special pair of paratrooper boots with built-up soles and for me to slump to keep my head out of the camera shots. After five years of that, Daws pulled tendons in his arms from stretching upward, and I tend to be round-shouldered from slouching over to this day.

In the beginning, since we went on the air so fast and nobody had written any scripts in advance, Daws and I would do the show, and then, dripping wet from the unbearably hot early lights of television, retire to

Oblath's Cafe on the corner, across from the Paramount gate, while we cooled off. After a quick bite to eat, we would sit in the restaurant booth and write the next day's Beany show into a portable typewriter. By about eight P.M. the Oblaths would have to lock up their cafe, and we would have to leave. Clampett would then take us on a prowl of the adjacent streets to find a few hours of office space. As we walked down the little block shared by KTLA and Paramount, typewriter under my arm, Clampett would open the door of a car parked there. After cautiously looking left and right, he would say, "Get in, boys."

"What?" we would say. "Whose car is this?"

"Friend of mine," Clampett said. "I told him we might be using his car to write in for a while."

Fine. We would sit there typing in the California twilight until darkness fell, when we would be forced to turn on the car owner's dome light to see the typewriter keys. Finally, footsteps would approach.

"Hey!" a startled voice would yell. "What are you doing in my car?"

"Isn't this Mike Maltese's car?" Clampett would protest. "I'm awfully sorry, we must have the wrong car."

As we piled out with our typewriter, the man would be left staring at us. "You turned on my dome light? You ran my battery down?" his voice would be fading, as we hurried around the corner.

The next night we would be suckered in again by Clampett.

"This time I really do have the right car," he would assure us. "Producer friend of mine from Paramount. Get in."

"How come he doesn't park on the Paramount lot?" we'd ask.

"Lot's full. Too many pictures going at once, so Bernie told me we could use his convertible around the corner on Marathon Street here. You sit in front, Stan, with the typewriter, Daws and I in the back with Bill."

Oberlin, the art director, was only there in self-defense. "Can you just give me a rough idea whether you're gonna be in the hold of the ship or on a desert island, or in Close Shave Cave for the whole show, so I know what sets to build?" he would beg. "I gotta get this stuff done by tomorrow night." It was a continuing dilemma.

We could see a little better with the top down, but eventually I would have to type by the feeble light from the open glove compartment. Daws and I would toss the lines back and forth. By now, Clampett was attuned to the sudden approach of footsteps.

"Bernie?" he would call out as we all scrambled out, slamming the glove compartment shut. "Just leaving, okay? Sure appreciate the use of the hall. Heh, heh."

With five shows a week to grind out, a writer named Charlie Shows soon came aboard. I had known Charlie from a couple of years earlier, when I did some of the voices, along with June Foray, for a series of Paramount theatrical short subjects called *Speaking of Animals.* Charlie wrote all the lines that came out of real animals whose lips were animated to match our voices. Charlie was a flexible writer but wasn't sure he wanted to get into television *that* much.

"How come we have to write in restaurants and cars?" Charlie asked from the back of a two-toned Chevy Club Coupe one night.

"A lot of writers would like this chance, Charlie," Clampett told him, sitting in the dark in his sunglasses. (For reasons best known to him, Clampett preferred to be incognito and walked around in sunglasses, day and night.)

"Doesn't everybody write this way?" I asked Shows.

"Where's your sense of high adventure?" Daws asked.

"But why can't we write in bigger cars then?" Charlie asked.

"As a matter of fact," Clampett told us as we moved quickly down the street at the sound of stiletto high heels approaching the car, "I've just rented a beautiful office. Call me in the morning, and I'll give you the exact address." Then he was gone, disappearing up an alley like Dracula in horn-rimmed sunglasses.

The next morning, we all stood staring up at an apartment building on Van Ness Avenue. A sign read, THIS BUILDING CONDEMNED. The structure seemed to be up off the ground on blocks. We studied the address on a piece of paper, then stared back at the building. Obviously, a mistake. We walked to a phone booth and called Clampett at home.

"No mistake," he told us. "I've made arrangements with the owner. We can use it until the building is moved."

Back in our condemned new office we stared at a card table Clampett had set up for a desk, a couple of folding chairs, and a ratty sofa. It was ridiculous, but better than a cramped backseat. The plumbing was still connected somehow, and we were grateful for that, but there was no electricity or heat. We had to finish writing by darkness or type by romantic candlelight. As soon as we had agreed on the scenery, Oberlin would run down the stairs at a gallop, leap off the front steps, which dangled in the air, and race two blocks to the television station to start painting the miniature sets for that night's live show. While we were creating five shows a week under these abnormal conditions, millions of people were glued to their sets watching *Beany*. They must have thought these charming little shows were put together in comfortable modern offices, weeks in advance, by a staff of maybe twenty-five or thirty people. Eventually, Bill Oberlin left the show and Bob Dahlquist took over as art director.

During the early years of *Beany,* I began to write novelty songs and "special material" for comedians. I wrote a song for Scatman Crothers, which he performed in the Universal movie *Meet Me at the Fair,* starring Dan Dailey. Crothers, who was later recognized as a great character actor in Stanley Kubrick's *The Shining,* had an enormous mouth full of gold teeth. The song I wrote for him at that time was called "I've Got the Shiniest Mouth in Town."

This was also the time when 3-D movies first burst on the scene, giving everyone migraine headaches from peering through crude red and green glasses. I wrote a song about it for the comedienne Rose Marie, which she introduced in the main room at the Flamingo Hotel in Las Vegas. The song was called "Third Dimension Is a Pain in the Eyes to Me."

I wrote all kinds of songs. I was even invited by the great movie composer Victor Young to put a straight lyric to a melody that he had woven into the theme music he had composed for a Paramount movie. The song was called "Theme for Love," but the romantic lyric I wrote changed it to "This Is Forever."

Young sat at his Steinway in his Beverly Hills living room and played while I sang my lyrics. As I finished, he turned to me with tears in his eyes. "This is the lyric I had hoped could be written," he told me. "Several writers have tried, but you're the only one who wrote what I had in mind." It was published by Victor Young Music, but we never were able to get a record on it. No matter.

Very soon after that I started writing and recording my own songs on Capitol records. But not just yet.

As I began to write more songs, I was encouraged by one of my idols, Johnny Mercer, who was one of the founders of Capitol Records. He urged me to join the American Society of Composers, Authors, and Publishers (ASCAP) and said he would provide one of the recommendations for membership. Mercer was the composer of countless hit songs, such as "Ac-cent-tchuate the Positive," "Moon River," "Atchison Topeka & the Santa Fe," "Too Marvelous for Words," "Laura," and many more. His encouragement meant more than anyone's. He invited me many times to spend the weekend with him and his wife Ginger at his home in Balboa Beach. Once, as we sat looking out the window at the ocean, Johnny asked me what I wanted to do in life. I told him, "Among other things, I'd like to be a really good lyricist some day." His answer was a terrific inspiration. He said to me, "You're a damn good lyricist right now."

Mercer had suggested me to the producers of a local Los Angeles television show called *Musical Chairs*. He wanted me to be part of a musical panel along with him and songwriter Bobby Troup, composer of such hits as "Get Your Kicks on Route 66." On the air we would be given four extraneous lines by the studio audience. Then, as the Bobby Troup Trio vamped, Mercer, Troup, and I would build them into a musical stanza. Not only did it have to rhyme; hopefully, it was funny, and we had to do it in about three minutes. We did it every week, and looking back, the stress hurts my head even now.

Once a week, as I came off the *Beany* show, I would race down Sunset to CBS, where *Musical Chairs* started only fifteen minutes later. A parking guy would grab my car in the CBS lot at Vine Street, and as I ran toward the studio, a makeup person ran alongside me, making me up. As I slid into my chair next to Mercer, in the nick of time, the crew would applaud another hair's breadth arrival. I did both of these shows for the last two years of *Beany*'s five-year run.

About that time I was called out to 20th Century–Fox. A producer named Sol Siegel, who had produced such pictures as *Call Me Madam* and *Gentlemen Prefer Blondes,* wondered if I'd like to write the lyrics for a musical he was producing for Fox called *Pink Tights,* to star Marilyn Monroe. I would be working with the great movie composer Jule Styne. Siegel told me that obviously there was no way I could do a daily television show and still work on the score at Fox every day. I asked Clampett for a leave of absence, but he refused.

Finally, I decided to quit *Beany* so I could do the picture. Clampett said he'd bring suit against me for breach of contract, and my agent at the time suggested that I had to pass on the picture, which I did to my everlasting regret.

Four years later, I became an ASCAP writer and ASCAP publisher as well, establishing the Freberg Music Corporation. As long as I could work around the *Beany* show, I was allowed to do a couple of movies as an actor. As the popularity of the show grew, two Paramount producers called me. They were Norman Panama and Mel Frank, the team responsible for several hit movies, including a couple of Bob Hope/Bing Crosby pictures, like *The Road to Utopia.*

They had a small part for me in a film they were about to shoot called *Callaway Went Thataway* at MGM. It starred Fred MacMurray, Howard Keel, and Dorothy McGuire. Clampett reluctantly allowed me to do the picture for a week, providing I left Culver City by 5:00 every day to race back to a fast dress rehearsal of *Beany,* before we went on the air live at 6:30. As I stood on the set at MGM with MacMurray and McGuire late each day, Norman Panama, the director, would start looking at his watch with some irritation. The crew all knew of my arrangement. Finally, from high on a catwalk, an electrician or a grip would call down "It's *Time for Beany!*" and Panama would release me as I shot out the door.

One day a letter came in from Lionel Barrymore's chauffeur. He told of racing toward Encino one evening in an effort to get the great actor home in time to watch *Time for Beany.* "Faster! Faster!" Barrymore called from the backseat, prodding the driver with his cane. As he realized that they wouldn't make it, he commanded the chauffeur to pull over to the nearest house with a TV antenna on the roof. At this time in his life the actor was confined to a wheelchair, so he waited in the car while his driver went up to the door and asked if he could watch the show. The family graciously let the chauffeur watch *Beany* with them, after which he thanked them and left. All the way home Barrymore leaned forward while his driver recounted the adventures of Beany and Cecil.

"And then what did Cecil say to that?" he asked. "And then what did Beany say to Dishonest John? Tell me everything."

As summer moved into winter, our condemned office became freezing cold. We were taking turns typing in mackinaws and warm scarves. One day, as Charlie Shows sat at the typewriter in a long tweed overcoat, typing in gloves and swearing at the mistakes they were causing, the house suddenly groaned and listed to one side.

"Earthquake!" we all yelled, and ran to the window. Down below, two giant bulldozers were pulling the house onto a wide trailer.

"Hey!" we called down. "What do you think you're doing?"

A foreman in a hard hat craned his head to locate our voices. He peered up at us.

"Hold it, guys!" he called to his crew. "There's *people* in the building, for God's sake!"

Then he called up to us. "This building is condemned! Can't you read the signs?"

"But this is our office," we cried. "Bob Clampett, the creator/producer of *Time for Beany,* made a special arrangement for us to write here."

"Are you kidding?" the man yelled. "Get outa there!"

"I'm telling you these are the executive offices of *Time for Beany!*" I shouted down. "We're in the middle of a television script!"

"And I'm telling you, you gotta get out of that building!"

Our pleading fell on deaf ears, and the man gave us fifteen minutes to vacate the premises. A short time later, Charlie, Daws, and I were on the sidewalk, carrying our typewriter, watching as our temporary office crawled slowly toward Melrose Avenue. Eventually, Clampett anted up the money for actual offices across the street from the station.

The show won three Emmys and a Peabody and proved that a successful program does not necessarily have to be geared to a specific demographic audience or age group. If you do it right, it can reach almost everybody at the same time. Every time I hear some broadcasting or advertising whiz start to explain "demographics" to me, I smile to myself and remember this: One day the show received a letter from a nuclear physicist at the California Institute of Technology, who told us of a meeting he had attended at which Dr. Albert Einstein was present. As the time approached for our "children's show," Einstein pulled out a gold pocket watch, studied it for a minute, and stood up.

"You vill haf to excuse me, gentlemen," he said, shuffling toward the door. "It's time for Beany."

# 11 ✍

# *It Only Hurts When I Laugh*

WHILE I WAS FIRST DOING THE *BEANY* TELEVISION shows, a call came in 1950 from my old friend Cliffie Stone, who was then an independent producer of country and western records. He had heard my "John and Marsha" routine, which of course I had perfected night after night on the road with Red Fox the year before, and he thought it would make an interesting novelty record. I made a rough recording of it, which he then took to an A&R man at Capitol Records, Ken Nelson.

"John and Marsha," as previously noted, was simply a satire on soap operas. I thought it would be funny if a man and a woman (I played both parts) ran the gamut of soap-opera-like emotions yet never said anything but each other's names over and over. Nelson, a gentle and supportive man, loved it. "This is a very strange record," he told me, "but I think it could be a hit."

On the strength of that demo, he signed me to a

Capitol Records contract. Then he took me into the studio, where we redid the record and, at his suggestion, added a syrupy orchestral underscore to make it more like a soap opera. Standing at the Capitol mike, I was so thrilled I could hardly contain myself. Little did I know that over the next few days, I almost never became a recording star at all.

Once a week, the Capitol executives held a staff meeting to review new releases. When Nelson played them "John and Marsha," it was greeted with a stunned silence. What *was* this thing? It wasn't any kind of record *they* could relate to. One man asked, "Don't they *ever* say anything but 'John' and 'Marsha'?" "That's the idea," Nelson said. The head of sales, a close-minded, humorless man named Hal Cook, turned beet red, according to Nelson, and snarled, "What the hell are you wasting the company's money for?" Nelson told him, "How do *you* know what people will think is funny? This could be a big hit."

Fortunately, the president of Capitol, Glenn Wallichs, was also in that meeting. He later became one of my greatest fans. Wallichs had founded Capitol with songwriters B. G. DeSylva and Johnny Mercer. The record brains in that meeting all wanted to write it off as a loss and throw "John and Marsha" down the garbage chute, but Wallichs, on a hunch, ordered them to insert it into a group of new unreleased records about to be tested.

Two days later, an audience was herded into a theater and told to respond to the various records by squeezing a rubber bulb fastened to their seat arm if they liked what they heard and to do nothing if they did *not*. No artists' names were mentioned; the records were simply identified by numbers 1 through 10. Nat King Cole's

"Nature Boy" was in slot number 3, "John and Marsha" slot number 7.

After it was over, the testing people told Capitol that while some had gotten a fair response, only two records had gotten a positive enough reaction to be judged as potential hits. Number 3, the Nat Cole selection, and number 7, "John and Marsha."

"I don't know what the heck this 'John and Marsha' thing is supposed to be," the testing maven told Capitol, "But the reaction went through the ceiling. The audience went bananas. They almost broke our bulbs!"

Both records were released immediately and were runaway hits. Nat Cole's "Nature Boy" and "John and Marsha" zoomed up the charts, and my career was launched as a recording artist. Hal Cook, the beet-faced prophet who had said my first record had "no chance," later left Capitol to become publisher of *Billboard* magazine, the magazine that chronicles the weekly rise and fall of hit records. It makes you wonder.

Aline Mosby, a reporter with Associated Press, filed a wire-service story on the comedy phenomenon. "Soap opera nothing," she wrote, getting me banned on radio stations in Boston. "Freberg put a tape recorder under somebody's bed, and he can't tell me otherwise." Capitol printed bumper stickers, which restaurant owners the world over immediately cut in half. The JOHN part they taped up over the men's room and MARSHA over the ladies'. It seems I had unwittingly created a new medium to advertise records: restrooms. To this day, joke-weary women named Marsha approach me and say they don't know whether to kiss me or slug me.

The niche I had carved out for myself in the record business was the perfect place for me to operate, as a satirist. When something rankled me enough, I leapt to my typewriter and knocked out a record on the absurdity. My next big record after "John and Marsha" was a send-up of Johnny Ray, the sobbing vocalist who recorded "Little White Cloud that Cried" and "Cry" and had teenage girls screaming all over America at his tearful concerts. It was such a dead-on parody that it had some girls thinking it was the real thing.

The song I had written for the occasion was called "Try." ("You too can be un-happy if you ta-ryyyy!") I wrote the lyrics, and Ruby Raksin did the music. Within days of its release the record was a smash hit, and *Time* magazine did its first story on me.

"Everytime I turned on the radio I was up to my hips in tears," I told *Time*. "I thought the country was in danger of turning into one big wailing wall." (The *Time* reporter who wrote the story was Jim Murray, who later became a Pulitzer Prize–winning sports columnist for the *Los Angeles Times*.) After the success of "John and Marsha" and "Try," Glenn Wallichs and Ken Nelson felt greatly vindicated. The Capitol sales-department executives now beamed and patted me on the back as I passed them in the hall. Everybody but the legal department seemed happy to have me on the label.

This was my first involvement with the kind of nervous, paranoid "corporate" lawyers at big companies. Some are less paranoid than others, but I have never met a corporate lawyer yet who had a sense of humor. In all fairness, these people are paid to protect the interests of the company that is signing their checks, and when in doubt, the easiest way out is to just say no. This may put their company in a nice safe position, but it sure binds and gags a working satirist. Time and again, the lawyers would hamstring me while insisting that I get clearances. Much of the time Nelson ignored them. Here is the way it would work: When I wanted to record, I would simply go in to the Capitol Tower, sit down with Nelson, and tell him roughly what I wanted to do. In all those years he never once told me no, even if he didn't understand exactly what the record was going to sound like in the end. Sometimes he would run it past legal first, and other times he would pick up the phone and reserve the studio for my use. We went ahead and made the record, because he knew they'd never get its significance from the script. They got it *then* all right, and the legal department held up some of my masters while they attempted to get approval from the individuals I was satirizing.

After discovering this, I stormed into the Capitol Tower and told the head of legal (a wiry, nervous man named Robert Karp), "Hey, listen! A political cartoonist with the L.A. *Times* or the *Washington Post* doesn't ask the target of his political cartoon if it will be all right if he satirizes them. It doesn't work that way."

"Maybe not," he fired back, "but that's the way it's going to work around here as long as I'm in the legal department."

Records roasting Arthur Godfrey and Ed Sullivan were held up while Karp sent each of them tapes for their approval. The Sullivan spoof was especially savage, making fun of the way Sullivan introduced the acts on his television variety show as though his mouth were full of marbles. I had Sullivan go to a voice coach, and by the end of the record, not only didn't it help any, but the voice coach talked like Sullivan. As I listened to Godfrey babbling along on his daily radio show, it seemed to me that he was often oblivious to the fact that while he was a very rich man, his audience wasn't necessarily in the same income bracket. We had him commenting to the audience while his sidekick Tony Marvin (who served the same function Ed McMahon does with Johnny Carson) agreed with everything Godfrey said.

**GODFREY:** Sayyy, you folks ought to go out and buy your own airplane, just like I did. Help you relax.
**MARVIN:** That's right, Arthur.
**GODFREY:** I see where the Douglas Aircraft Company is havin' a one-cent sale. You buy one DC-3 for five million dollars, you get another one for a penny. You folks should take advantage of that.
**MARVIN:** That's right, Arthur.

Godfrey was firing people left and right at the time, and he had just axed the singer Julius La Rosa. People working for Godfrey trembled in their boots for fear of being the next to go. We had Godfrey tell some feeble joke, followed by the sound of gargling.

**SOUND:** GARGLING
**GODFREY:** What's that noise?
**MARVIN:** It was me, Arthur. I was drinking a glass of water when you told that last joke. I wasn't able to laugh in time, so I did the next best thing: I gargled.
**GODFREY:** Sayyy, that's thinkin' on your feet. Hyuk, hyuk, hyuk. Only the quick thinkers stay with me!
**MARVIN:** That's right, Arthur.

The record was called "That's Right, Arthur." After a few days Capitol heard from the lawyers of Sullivan and Godfrey. They both said no, of course. The masters were locked up in the Capitol vaults, where they reside to this day. That is why I once said in a magazine article I wrote on censorship: "My records are not released . . . they escape."

• • •

*Stan Freberg* ✍

A BOOK CAME OUT THAT CAUSED A FLURRY OF NAtional attention. It was called *The Search for Bridey Murphy,* a supposedly true account of a woman in Colorado who had regressed back in time through hypnosis. Out of these sessions came the discovery that she had lived a whole other life one hundred years earlier in Ireland as a woman named Bridey Murphy. A recording of the woman's sessions with her hypnotist came out as an album, complete with a lot of "Look deep into my candle" talk while the woman breathed heavily and eventually started talking in an Irish brogue. The woman claimed later that she had never (in this lifetime) been to Ireland and knew no one who had. The whole phenomenon seemed ripe for parody, so I went into the studio and recorded what I had called "The Quest for Bridey Murphy." The funniest line to me was when my woman under hypnosis heard a harp glissando in the background for an eerie effect and said, deep into her trance, "Who's blowing harp, man?" The legal pundit once again jumped all over me.

"Don't you think it's funny?" I asked Karp.

"Funny?" he said. "What's funny got to do with it? You've used the same title as the real book and record."

"I changed 'search' to 'quest,' " I told him. "It's called 'The *Quest* for Bridey Murphy.' "

Karp leaned across his desk. "You think changing 'search' to 'quest' pulls Capitol's chestnuts out of the fire? It's the woman's name I'm worried about. You think we want Bridey Murphy's lawyers serving us with a subpoena? Oh, she'd *like* us to use her name, don't you worry about that."

When the tirade was over, I reminded Karp: "Bridey Murphy died over a hundred years ago. Even if she did float back from some Dublin cemetery, how could she prove damages?" I said.

Carrying the torch into Melbourne Stadium during the Australian Olympics, 1956. Some cigar lighter.

*Unless otherwise indicated, all photographs are reproduced courtesy of Stan Freberg/Freberg, Ltd.*

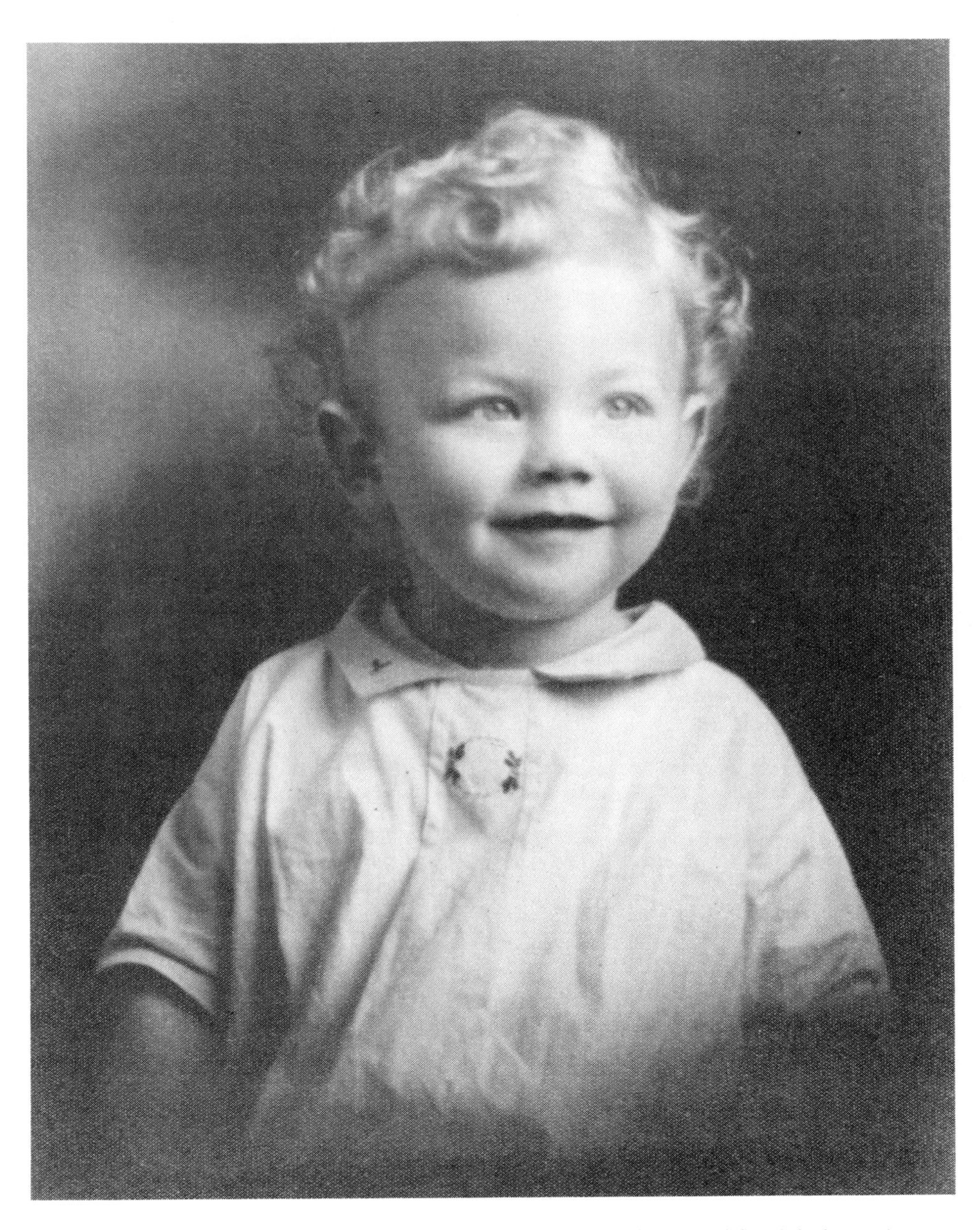

The young Stanley Freberg smiles out at the world with bunnies on his suit.

My father, the Reverend Victor Freberg, age twenty-one, at BIOLA Theological Seminary, L.A.—a lasting moral influence.

My grandfather, the Reverend W. W. Conner, in his Sunday preaching coat. With all these ministers, where did a satirist come from?

My mother, Evelyn Dorothy Twyla Conner, age sixteen, in her tennis dress. A beautiful lady and a great audience.

The fourteen-year-old Freberg, on the front lawn with sister Gwennie in Pasadena. After a few minutes of fresh air, I would rush inside to get back to the radio.

Uncle Raymond—Conray the Great!—with one of the many rabbits I raised for his act.

Hairy von Bell

# ASSEMBLIES

Alhambra High School assembly —in the midst of my one-man show. I heard those laughs and was hooked forever.

Pfc. Freberg performing at McCornack General Hospital. Later I was bumped all the way up to the rank of corporal.

Red Fox and His Musical Hounds. Truly a class act. Left to right: Rick Fay, clarinet; me, guitar and banjo; Jack Coons, trumpet; George Howard, piano. Seated: Red Fox, drums.

*Time for Beany!* Daws Butler (left) performing Uncle Captain and Beany, and me doing Cecil the Seasick Sea Serpent and Dishonest John, on the nightly TV show circa 1953. Looks like my head is in the shot again. *Photo by Alan Grant,* Life *magazine. (*Time for Beany *characters © 1950 by Bob Clampett.)*

The *Beany* show won three Emmys. Left to right: Daws Butler, me, Charlie Shows (writer), Bill Oberlin (art director). Creator/ producer Bob Clampett is not in this shot.

On the weekly CBS television show *Musical Chairs* in 1952. Left to right: songwriter/performer Bobby Troup, jazz vocalist Frances Faye, me, legendary songwriter Johnny Mercer, and moderator Bill Leyden. *Photo by Joe Mathews.*

With Fred MacMurray and Dorothy McGuire in the MGM picture *Callaway Went Thataway*.

Doing my version of Johnny Ray singing his big hit "Cry" in a frenzy of tears, in the Republic Picture *Geraldine*. I went through twenty-three shirts running the film over budget. My version of the song was "Try."

Conferring with Jack Webb on the set of *Dragnet* in 1953, before I recorded "St. George and the Dragonet." Between Webb and me is Alan Livingston, then president of Capitol Records.

At rehearsal on *The Ed Sullivan Show.* When "St. George" hit the top of the charts, Sullivan flew me and my cast to New York to perform it on his CBS show. Left to right: Ed Sullivan, me (as Webb), June Foray, and Daws Butler.

Recording in Studio A at the Capitol Tower in Hollywood. The small audience on my left, silently performing right along with Daddy, is my daughter, Donna Jr.

Karp gritted his teeth. "Change the name," he said.

"I have to use 'Bridey'!" I yelled. "Otherwise nobody will know what I'm kidding!"

Karp closed his eyes for a moment. I could see I'd worn him down a millimeter.

"I'll give you 'Bridey,' " he said. "But the last name better be a name I can't find in the central Los Angeles telephone directory."

Twenty-four hours later, I walked in with a single typed-out name and laid it on his desk.

"Hammerschlaugen?" he said. "Alright, let's just check that one." He reached under his desk, produced a central L.A. directory and started flipping through. I knew I was safe. I'd already peeked. After he couldn't find any Emily or Hubert Hammerschlaugen, I rose to go. But suddenly he buzzed his secretary.

"Would you please bring me the New York telephone book," he told her. The man was calling in an unexpected telephone book for a second opinion. His secretary walked in and set it down on Karp's desk with a great thud. I held my breath as he wet his finger and flipped through the *H*'s.

"Ah-*hah!*" he said suddenly, as my heart stopped.

"Ohh, Hammacher-Schlemmer, excuse me," he mumbled. Finally, he gave up and slammed the Manhattan telephone book shut. "Okay, I guess I can live with that name," he told me. And that's how "The Quest for Bridey Hammerschlaugen" came to be released.

I learned to get around the legal department most of the time, running rampant through the blaring excesses of rock 'n' roll. Some of the records that did escape were lampoons of hits like "Sh-Boom," "The Great Pretender," and Elvis Presley's "Heartbreak Hotel."

When Mitch Miller recorded a serious version of

"The Yellow Rose of Texas," featuring a huge chorale, with a snare drum driving the orchestra, it was played on the air day and night. I decided we were in danger of being snare-drummed to death. In my version I yelled at my out-of-control drummer, Alvin Singer, to no avail. "Excuse me . . . that's just a little too loud on the snare drum. . . . Can you hold it down? I 'preciate it!" I shouted in a Texas accent, over the sound of the Jud Conlan singers and the Billy May orchestra.

One of my most devastating records was a send-up of the Lawrence Welk TV show on my record, "Wunnerful, Wunnerful!" By the end of the record I cast Welk out to sea, as the old Aragon Ballroom broke loose from the Santa Monica Pier in a tidal wave of champagne bubbles. With the band bravely playing in the background, the floating ballroom was nearly saved by a passing ship but was finally passed by as an apparent mirage. At fade-out we heard the bandleader's plaintive cry for "Help-uh, turn off the bubble machine!" punctuated by a flock of disinterested seagulls, as the Welk ensemble drifted into the sunset.

One of the few times I ever saw Ken Nelson hesitate was when I wanted to satirize the Army-McCarthy hearings, which were being televised from the Senate Caucus Room, as the Watergate and Iran-Contra hearings were more recently. This was of course in the middle of what is now referred to as "the McCarthy era." As Senator Joseph McCarthy focused on the entertainment industry, people's careers in Hollywood and New York were crumbling left and right—much of the time from some vague insinuation that they might have had a milkman, say, whose brother-in-law's chiropractor once subscribed to a communist newspaper. I remember Nelson doodling on a pad furiously, his brow furrowed. "Look," he said, "you know it doesn't matter to me, but I'd hate to see Joe McCarthy decide to investigate *you.* He's not exactly somebody to fool around with."

I said, "I know that."

Then he asked sort of nervously, "Do you, ahhh, have any reason to think he might be able to pin something on you in case he isn't amused by this record?"

I said, "Actually I do, now that you bring it up."

He stopped doodling and stared at me.

I said, "I happen to be a card-carrying member of the Little Orphan Annie Fan Club of America."

Nelson laughed, and that was the end of the discussion. But the Capitol legal department was not so easily persuaded. They finally let me go in and record "Point of Order," but a much watered-down version. I played McCarthy with his many monotone interruptions: "Point of orderrrr Mr. Chairmannnnn." The record in its final version is not one of my favorites. But the fact that I was willing to lampoon McCarthy, while he was still a threat, made me a minor hero in many quarters, and the record took off immediately.

As the television show *Dragnet* became more and more popular, I began to wonder if there wasn't some way to kid the way Jack Webb talked in that interesting monotone voice.

In 1953 I was still doing the *Beany* show every day with Daws. I asked him to help me write the *Dragnet* spoof, since he had also helped write the Godfrey and Sullivan records. The Capitol lawyers were still as arbitrary and nervous as ever, and Karp insisted I get a written clearance from Jack Webb, who was not only the star but the creator of the *Dragnet* series. Alan Livingston, the president of Capitol Records, was enthusiastic about the script and accompanied me to the Disney Studios, where Webb rented space to shoot *Dragnet*. I had the script inside my sport coat. Alan, a very smart man and a fan of my records who wanted to see this released, advised me: "Don't read him the script unless we have to. Just try and get a blanket clearance." Livingston was a free spirit like myself and hated the idea of his lawyers making me go to Webb for a clearance, but I wanted to borrow his actual *Dragnet* music, so I was forced to do the record with his blessing. On the set we watched Webb shoot for a while, and finally he walked over to us on a break.

After quickly explaining that I wanted to parody *Dragnet* for my next record, Webb smiled at me. "Sounds like a great idea. You got a script for it?"

"He has some rough ideas sketched out," Livingston said quickly. "Nothing set in concrete."

Set in concrete? The script was burning a hole inside my Harris tweed jacket. "No problem," Webb said. "I know it'll be great." Then he squeezed my arm. "Hey!" he told me. "I'm a fan." He ended up not only saying I could use his musical theme, but let me hire the same orchestra who recorded the show each week. Walter Schumann, who wrote the theme, conducted for me. June Foray, Daws Butler, and I played all the parts. Here's how it went:

## *St. George and the Dragonet*

**MUSIC:** *DRAGNET* THEME

**ANNOUNCER:** The legend you are about to hear is true —only the needle should be changed to protect the record.

**MUSIC:** UNDER

**ST. GEORGE:** This is the countryside—my name is St.

George—I'm a knight—Saturday, July tenth, 8:05 P.M.—I was working out of the castle on the night watch when the call came in from the chief—a dragon had been devouring maidens—homicide—my job—*slay him!*

**MUSIC:** CUE

**ST. GEORGE:** You called me, chief?

**CHIEF:** Yes—it's the dragon again—devouring maidens —the King's daughter may be next.

**ST. GEORGE:** Uh, huh—you got a lead?

**CHIEF:** Nothing much to go on—say, did you take that .45 automatic into the lab to have 'em check on it?

**ST. GEORGE:** Yeah. You were right.

**CHIEF:** I was right?

**ST. GEORGE:** Yeah. It was a gun . . .

**MUSIC:** CUE

**ST. GEORGE:** 8:22 P.M.—I talked with one of the maidens who had almost been devoured.

**SOUND:** DOOR KNOCK AND OPEN

**ST. GEORGE:** Can I talk to you, ma'am?

**WOMAN:** Who are you?

**ST. GEORGE:** I'm St. George, ma'am—I want to ask you a few questions, ma'am—I understand you were almost devoured by the dragon—is that right, ma'am?

**WOMAN:** It was terrible, he breathed fire on me—he burned me already . . .

**ST. GEORGE:** How can I be sure of that, ma'am?

**WOMAN:** Believe me—I got it straight from the dragon's mouth!

**MUSIC:** CUE

**ST. GEORGE:** 11:45 P.M.—I rode over the King's highway—I saw a man . . . stopped to talk to him—Pardon me, sir—can I talk to you for just a few minutes, sir?

**MAN:** Sure—I don't mind.

**ST. GEORGE:** What do you do for a living?

**MAN:** I'm a knave.

**ST. GEORGE:** Didn't I pick you up on a 903 last year for stealing tarts?

**MAN:** Yeah, so what do you want, to make a federal case out of it?

**ST. GEORGE:** No, sir, we heard there was a dragon operating in this neighborhood—we just want to know if you've seen him.

**MAN:** Sure, I seen him.

**ST. GEORGE:** Ummm—could you describe him for me.

**MAN:** What's to describe—you see one dragon—you seen 'em all!

**ST. GEORGE:** Would you try to remember, sir—we just want to get the facts.

**MAN:** Well, he was—you know—he was big and green . . . with orange polka dots . . . purple feet . . . breathing fire and smoke . . . and one big bloodshot eye right in the middle of his forehead and like that—

**ST. GEORGE:** Notice anything unusual about him?

**MAN:** No, he was just a run-of-the-mill dragon—you know—

**ST. GEORGE:** Yessir—you can go now.

**MAN:** By the way, how are you going to catch him?

**ST. GEORGE:** I thought you'd never ask—a Dragon Net!

**MUSIC**

**ST. GEORGE:** 3:05 P.M.—I was riding back into the courtyard to take my report to the lab—and then it happened—

**SOUND:** DRAGON ROAR

**ST. GEORGE:** It was the dragon!

**DRAGON:** Hey! I'm the fire-eating dragon—you must be St. George—right?

**ST. GEORGE:** Yes, sir.

**DRAGON:** I see you've got one of them new .45 caliber swords!

**ST. GEORGE:** That's about the size of it.

**DRAGON:** (LAUGHS) You slay me!

**ST. GEORGE:** That's what I wanted to talk to you about.

**DRAGON:** What do you mean?

**ST. GEORGE:** I'm taking you in on a 502—you figure it out.

**DRAGON:** What's the charge?

**ST. GEORGE:** Devouring maidens out of season—

**DRAGON:** (SHOUTING) Out of season! You'll never pin that rap on me! Do you hear me—*Cop!*

**ST. GEORGE:** Yeah—I hear you—I've got you on a 412, too.

**DRAGON:** (SHRIEKING) A 412? What's a 412?

**ST. GEORGE:** Overacting! Let's go!

**MUSIC:** CUE

**ANNOUNCER:** On September fifth the dragon was tried and convicted. His fire was put out—and his maiden-devouring license revoked. Maiden devouring out of season is punishable by a term of not less than fifty or more than three hundred years.

**MUSIC:** UP AND OUT

On the flip side, using the *Dragnet* theme, I got one more lick in against Senator McCarthy's "red" baiting.

**ANNOUNCER:** The story of Little *Blue* Riding Hood is true. Only the color has been changed . . . to prevent an investigation.

***Stan Freberg*** ✍

Within two weeks the *Dragnet* spoof had sold 900,000 records. By the end of three weeks, it crossed the million mark. It was documented as the fastest-selling single in the history of the record business. I had sent an advance copy to Webb, who told me later that he had called "Quiet on the set!" so he could play the record for the cast and crew. Everywhere I went, people called out to me, "Just the facts." Incidentally, the line had been uttered by Webb maybe once or twice in all of the series. I had just picked it out of a random episode I had studied and decided to make a running gag out of it. Later, Webb told me, "I hardly ever said that. *You're* the guy who said it mostly. Now I'll have to write it into the show." He also reminded me that *Dragnet* had only been the number 2 show, but after my record it had gone to number 1. It was nice of him to give me the credit.

Webb was a perfectionist but had a picture on his wall that he said helped keep him humble. It was a large black and white blowup of his star on Hollywood's Walk of Fame. JACK WEBB, it proclaimed, but a dog had left his regards in the middle of the star. Years later, when I got my own star, I remembered that picture.

By 1958, after a string of hit records, a call came in to my agent from Australia: "Could Stan do a concert tour for thousands of Freberg fans down under?"

Why not? Flying over on Quantas, I read in the Sydney *Morning Herald* that the Olympics had at last come to Australia! My show would precede the Olympics by a couple of weeks. *Hmmmmmm,* I thought, as I flew over Fiji, *there must be some way I could kid around with the Olympics. The Australians have invited me here because of the outrageous way I've lampooned all the top American record artists. They'll expect me to do something equally outrageous to them.*

The Olympics seemed a perfect vehicle. The Aussies had waited many years for the games to finally be held in their country. What if I made my entrance carrying a duplicate of the Olympic torch . . . and then lit someone's cigar with it? Would that be outrageous enough? Probably.

Aboard the plane were several American record artists, including Don Cornell and Buddy Rich, the great jazz drummer, who would perform with me, backed by a huge Australian orchestra. As the jumbo Qantas plane wheeled up to the gate in Sydney I saw several hundred people waving and jumping up and down. A few years earlier, I had come off a TWA flight from Los Angeles to New York and seen a similar crowd down below waving wildly. As I descended the steps at La Guardia, I had heard what I perceived to be my name cutting through the cheering: "Freberg! Freberg! Freberg!" I remember smiling and throwing my shoulders back, striking a jaunty pose as I came down the steps.

The first man coming toward me was holding a CBS News camera on his shoulder.

"How's it going? Great to be in New York!" I yelled into the camera, which seemed to be aiming . . . over my *shoulder?*

He moved swiftly past me, followed by NBC, ABC, and assorted cameramen from the Associated Press and the New York *Daily News,* bumping me out of the way.

*Well, that's pretty rude,* I thought to myself. *What could they—?* A cheer burst from the crowd, and I looked behind me.

There, posed demurely at the top of the steps, was the attractive girl with the close-cropped hair who had been sitting behind me on the flight. She was Jean Seberg, the fresh new discovery of Otto Preminger's, arriving in New York to promote her first starring role in *Saint Joan.*

What the newsmen and crowd had been yelling was, of course, "Seberg! Seberg! Seberg!"

Talk about an embarrassing moment! I remember disappearing quickly into the crowd.

Now, in Sydney, when the stewardess finally opened the door, a beaming little lady in a flowered hat bounded up the steps and pumped my hand. "Pearla Honeyman!" she cried, introducing herself. "Welcome to Australia, Mr. Freberg. I'm with Lee Gordon, the man who brought you here."

I blinked into the sunlight, peering over her head at the crowd below, which was waving and cheering. "Who are all those people cheering for?" I asked her, cautiously.

"Why, Mr. Freberg!" Pearla Honeyman exclaimed, smiling and gently squeezing my arm. "Don't you know? They're cheering for *you!*"

THE CHEERING AT THE AIRPORT WAS NOTHING COMpared to what awaited me later on as I jogged toward the stage with my flaming Olympic torch. But then . . . I already told you about all that back in the first chapter of this book.

As I descended into a sea of cameras and microphones, I had no idea that when I would board this same flight weeks later, it would carry me back not only to America, but to a whole new career in the world of advertising.

# 12

# *Lifting Its Long Neck Like the Lock Ness Monster, the Advertising Business Suddenly Raises Its Head Out of the Water —A Challenge I Can't Refuse*

AFTER I RETURNED FROM AUSTRALIA IN 1956, I WAS resting up at the new home I had bought my parents in Pasadena when I received a call, totally out of the blue, from the creative director of a San Francisco advertising agency. The caller's name was Howard Gossage, and he was a fan, he said, of my records and television appearances. He said he had a client who was in trouble, and he had a hunch that humor might help. Gossage was a copywriter who created mostly print ads. He said he thought he could talk the agency and client into a radio campaign, but he didn't want the ordinary type of "straight" radio spots. He said that was why he was coming to a professional comedy writer who had also been successful creating humor for the "ear."

Gossage had an endearing stammer.

"Have you ever done any aaaa-aaadvertising?" he asked.

"No," I answered.

"Good." he said. "Juuu . . . just the man I want."

Feeling the way I did about advertising, hating the hard sell I was assaulted with from my car radio each day, I felt I suddenly had been given the opportunity as a consumer to, in effect, answer back, to create some commercials that didn't take themselves so damn seriously. I decided to try it as a lark.

Gossage flew down to Los Angeles, and we had lunch at the Brown Derby. Within minutes I realized I had met a rare bird indeed. As a radio and television performer, I had been exposed to many agency people in the sponsor's booth. To a man, they all acted like every word of their commercials was straight from the Bill of Rights. The hard and boring sell they were responsible for were holy words. Worse, they took themselves as seriously as if they were delegates to the United Nations. The cliché supposedly attributed to advertising men, "Let's run it up the flagpole and see if anybody salutes," was no joke. I personally experienced similar ad-speak many times in the past, working as a voice-over actor in commercials. Once while doing the voice-over for an animated Snickers candy bar television spot, I had been directed from the booth by an advertising executive from the Leo Burnett agency who kept overriding the animation director John Hubbley. Apparently, I had been giving a "soft-sell" reading to the sponsor's name. He demanded that I harden it up. Finally, he demanded that I pronounce the final *s* on Snickers with more emphasis. "Sock it in there, kiddo!" he told me. "Let's hear that final *s!* SnickerZ," he overemphasized. I decided to toy with him on the next take. "SnickerZZZZZZZ," I said. He was not amused. He was on his feet in the booth, yelling into the intercom: "Look. I was purposely bending the tree too far in the opposite direction," he informed me, "in the hopes that some of the branches would fall into place."

I could detect no qualities of the Leo Burnett man, or any other ad man I had met, in Howard Gossage. In fact, here was an advertising man whose contempt for the content of most commercials and ads easily equaled my own. Gossage, a brilliant copywriter, had his own unique sense of humor as well as a terrific sense of style. He showed me a copy of a recent *New Yorker* magazine containing a full-page ad he had written for his client Quantas, the Australian airline. The headline was surely a first for an airline: BE THE FIRST ONE ON YOUR BLOCK TO WIN A KANGAROO.*

I realized I had met what for me was a first: an ad man who refused to take himself or advertising too seriously. At that time he was employed by Brisacker-Wheeler & Staff in San Francisco. It was to become such an interesting and profitable company—thanks largely to the things Gossage, and later I, were responsible for—that it was eventually bought by Cunningham & Walsh.

After a few years Gossage started his own agency and came to be recognized as a genius whose beautiful and humorous ads for Eagle Shirtmakers, Irish Whiskey, and Rainier Ale, for whom he invented the Beethoven sweatshirt, influenced a whole generation of art directors and copywriters. He also became my best friend. But that

* Quantas *did* give a real live kangaroo away, of course, but not before a subsequent ad ran that I helped Howard produce, featuring a strange cast of judges indeed: the actress Anna May Wong, Olympic Decathlon Gold Medal winner Reverend Bob Richards, satirist Stan Freberg, and a live kangaroo. There we all sat in evening clothes, the Reverend Mr. Richards holding his vaulting pole and a tux tie on the kangaroo. The Quantas people thought Howard was really bonkers, until the mail poured in and their Australian airline became visible in America for the first time.

day at lunch I only knew that I was talking to a fellow iconoclast.

Gossage had an immediate problem with one of his clients, Contadina Foods. After being successful for years, this little tomato-paste packer was suddenly in danger of being buried by the giant Hunts company. He wondered if I could create and produce some radio commercials and later, TV. "Only if I can do them as unorthodoxly as possible," I said. He assured me that he would be disappointed with anything less.

The radio commercials I created were immediately questioned by everyone at his agency. The first thing they heard was a song I had written, which never mentioned the sponsor's name. Upon learning from Howard that there was the equivalent of eight tomatoes smashed down into each can of Contadina tomato paste, I came up with a jingle: "Who Puts Eight Great Tomatoes in That Little Bitty Can?" I sang it myself with the Buddy Cole Jazz Quartet, and after repeating the question three times, I ended the song not with the sponsor's name, but with the line, "You know who, you know who, you know who!" After an embarrassing pause, an announcer cleared his throat and straightened it out: "Ahem. . . . In case you don't, it's Contadina tomato paste."

Although I was not present when the agency heard my commercials, Gossage gave me a blow-by-blow report.

When they first heard them, he said, they were more or less stunned. "Where are the recipes the client wanted demonstrating how to use tomato paste?" they asked Gossage. "How come he didn't tell how much thicker Contadina is than Hunts?"

Howard just smiled and played the next Freberg spot. Would they get those recipes now? Not likely. The scene was a quiet conversation taking place on the windswept top of the Empire State Building.

**FREBERG:** Now look, you got it straight what we want you to do?

**MAN:** I think so, uhh, you want me to take down the tower from on top of the Empire State Building here and put up a three-hundred-foot can of Contadina tomato paste.

**FREBERG:** That's right.

**MAN:** (NERVOUSLY) Look, have you checked with the Empire State Building people? I mean . . . is it all right with *them?*

**FREBERG:** Wellll, there's always somebody working on the building. . . . They won't know the difference.

**MAN:** Yeah, but that tower was put there to moor zeppelins to.

**FREBERG:** Let's face it—how many zeppelins have moored there in the last week?

**MAN:** Well . . . not many, but I'm not sure I want to get involved.

**FREBERG:** You want us to get another contractor? Is that it?

**MAN:** No, but we could be arrested!

**FREBERG:** Suppose you let me worry about that, okay? Now, don't forget to have the can blink day and night the words "There are many delicious uses for Contadina Tomato Paste."

**MAN:** Wait a minute! I thought you wanted it to blink "Eight Great Tomatoes in That Little Bitty Can"?

**FREBERG:** Hmmmmmmmmm.

**MAN:** Which do you want?

**FREBERG:** Well, let me sleep on it. Okay?

**MAN:** Okay.

After a long silence, the head of the agency, Robert Brisacher, spoke: "That's it? That's the end of the commercial?"

Gossage pointed out that Contadina's main competitor, Hunts, was using normal advertising. Maybe the way to get people's attention was to use *ab*normal advertising.

"It's not *any* kind of advertising, as far as I can see. What the hell *is* it, anyhow?" muttered one old-line account executive. "It's just two guys talking on top of a building! How can we play *that* for the client?"

How indeed. They just got on a plane for San Jose the next day at Howard's insistence and played it for the Marrici brothers, who owned Contadina, and their staff.

Everyone hated the commercials. Everyone except the president, Marty Marrici, who happened to be the only one who laughed. "Let's see what the brokers say," Marrici shrugged. They were played for his food brokers and salesmen. To a man, they hated them too. In spite of this avalanche of negative opinion, and over the protesting of his staff, Marrici okayed the campaign, and the first Stan Freberg commercials hit the air. They were an immediate smash hit with disc jockeys, who went on talking about them on the air long after the commercials had ended, and after a few weeks sales were up dramatically.

Within three months Hunts had cut its price twice, and six months later it was giving away to the grocers one free case with every ten in an effort to catch up. Contadina recovered from the staggering blow Hunts had dealt it originally and raced way ahead of its competitor. *Advertising Age* magazine late that year picked the two most outstanding marketing successes of the year. One of them was my Contadina campaign.

In today's broadcasting environment we seem to be up to our ears in "funny" radio commercials, most of which miss the mark by poor writing and pitiful production. But when the original prototype that I created hit the air over three decades ago for Contadina, advertising people didn't know what had hit them. It was like a Frank Lloyd Wright building thrown up overnight in a sea of Victorian architecture.

Suddenly I was established as some new kind of problem solver in advertising. I continued to create all of Contadina's radio and television commercials for the next seven years, until their national success and the image I had helped create for them made the company so appealing that the giant food company, Carnation, snapped them up. Little did I know that this would become a pattern for me: help pull a little company up by its bootstraps by interesting new advertising, until its sales curve is reversed and heads upward; watch them be acquired by some giant conglomerate whose new advertising agency quickly kisses me off, without even a gold watch. Ah, well.

Marty Marrici, president of Contadina, in a speech to the Los Angeles Advertising Club just before he sold out to Carnation, recalled how everyone at the beginning had urged him not to run my commercials. Undaunted, he had put them on the air because of a gut feeling that they would work. "They didn't sound like *regular* advertising," he said. "that's what I liked most about them."

I remember the first time I met Marrici. After two or three years of successful Contadina campaigns, the Marrici brothers invited me to San Jose for lunch. They had gone to a lot of trouble planning the most elaborate Italian feast I had ever encountered. Every type of pasta and Italian specialty known to man was laid out in the elegant restaurant they had taken over for the afternoon. It made Dino DeLaurentis's lavish delis look like McDonald's.

I met them at their executive offices at the Contadina plant. They were very gracious. Marty Marrici smiled benevolently and introduced me all around. They all wore dark suits, some pinstriped, some not. Marrici's second in command was named Marty Scarpace, a name right out of a George Raft movie. "Well, well, well," Marrici was saying from the back of his darkened executive suite, while his men stood around in the mahogany-paneled shadows. "So this is the young genius. Come on, let's go eat."

On the way out the front door, I noticed several massive Contadina semi-trucks parked across the driveway. In huge letters on the sides they proclaimed my line, EIGHT GREAT TOMATOES IN THAT LITTLE BITTY CAN. Then I looked down. A tarnished brass plate set into the brick factory wall did not read CONTADINA; it read HERSCHEL PACKING CO. I thought that a little strange. Suddenly, Marrici opened the rear door of a long black Cadillac limousine. "Get in," he said.

I found myself crushed between Marty Marrici and Al Marrici. Marty Scarpace drove. I tried not to think about things like being taken for a ride. After all, what had I done to displease them? In fact I had created advertising that had rescued them from marketing quicksand. Still, I felt a certain anxiety. The cigar smoke was becoming memorable, and my arms were literally pinned to my sides by the Marricis' bulk.

I made a stab at small talk. "Tell me something," I smiled. "How did you happen to get into tomato paste?"

Marty slowly turned to me. After a long stare, as though I were some smartass investigative reporter, he told me. "Back in the Prohibition days, our daddy was in the sacramental wine business. A distributor."

"Back in Chicago?" I ventured.

His eyebrows shot up. "How'd ja guess? Anyhow, our daddy used to do a kind of cute thing. He started watering the wine down. You know, got five barrels out of three." They all laughed heartily at this ecclesiastical prank. "One day, he had problems."

"The priests started complaining about the wine?" I ventured.

"Naw, they never even noticed. But our daddy discovered that the guy *he* got the wine from was watering it down before it even got to *him!*"

"Some people have no conscience," I said.

"Anyhow, one thing led to another, and our family decided to leave the Chicago area. It was very sudden. We came out west and bought into the packing business."

As he droned on, my mind reeled off a fantasy scenario on the Marricis' rapid departure from the sacramental wine business. They're in a Dusenburg with the pedal to the metal, heading for the Chicago city limits. They've knocked out the rear window, and the Thompson submachine gun is singing. Finally, they lose the pursuit car. The driver yells, "Where to, boss?"

"Head for California!" says Daddy Marrici.

"What business we goin' into now, boss?"

The elder Marrici flips a coin: "Heads unions, tails tomato paste." He peeks under his fingers at the flipped coin. "Well, boys," he smiles, "we're in the tomato-paste business."

Suddenly, I snapped back as the limo pulled up at the Italian restaurant. Relief swept over me. Still, I couldn't resist one last nosy question. (Would I never learn?)

"Tell me something, Marty. Your name is Marrici, and you own Contadina Tomato Paste. But there's an old brass plate by the door that says HERSCHEL PACKING CO. Who is Herschel?" Marrici studied his diamond ring. "What happened to him?" I asked.

Marty Scarpace turned around from the driver's seat and cleared it up. "We got rid of *him,*" he said, smiling. Then we went in to lunch.

IN THE MEANTIME, GOSSAGE CONTINUED TO HIRE ME for other accounts at Cunningham & Walsh. I created campaigns for Pictsweet frozen foods and others. A commercial I wrote and produced for Crown Zellerbach's Zee paper products had a man placing a roll of Zee paper towels in a player piano to see if it would play "Japanese Sandman." This was the first time anybody had ever started a commercial in the middle of a conversation, a device I occasionally use to this day:

**MAN:** She what?

**GUY:** This lady says she put a roll of Zee paper towels in her player piano and it played the song "Japanese Sandman."

**MAN:** Wait a minute. Zee towels are very versatile, but I doubt they'll play "Japanese Sandman."

**GUY:** Uh-huh.

**MAN:** All the same, slip a roll of Zee into the office player piano there, and we'll see. You pump.

**GUY:** All righty.

**SOUND:** PEDALS PUMPING PIANO MUSIC; SINGERS AND ORCHESTRA PLAY ZEE JINGLE. AS IT CONCLUDES,

WE HEAR THE FLAP! FLAP! FLAP! FLAP! OF PIANO ROLL WINDING DOWN.

**MAN:** See, I told you it wouldn't play "Japanese Sandman."

Without realizing it, I had more or less created a new form: the radio commercial that not only didn't take itself too seriously, but was actually something you would *wish* to hear as opposed to turning it off. The Zee campaign was very successful for Crown Zellerbach, as the Contadina campaign had been. Even so, the people at the agency themselves still couldn't grasp the idea of humor being a tool that could be used to sell products. How could it be *real* advertising? It seemed too much like entertainment! And yet, it had worked.

It must have been a fluke.

Fluke after fluke.

# 13

# *Sailing onto the CBS Radio Network in a Banana Boat*

WITH MY NEWFOUND SIDELINE IN ADVERTISING, and the roar of the Australian audiences still ringing in my ears, I continued pursuing my two careers. By the spring of 1957 I had a new hit record on Capitol: "Banana Boat," a takeoff on Harry Belafonte's hit recording of "Day-O." It had seemed to me that Belafonte SHOUTED much of his song, in a more piercing manner than absolutely necessary. I leapt to my typewriter within a few days of hearing this earsplitting folksong on the air. I created a folksinger who sounded a lot like Harry and a jazz bongo player with sensitive ears, who unfortunately stood next to my folksinger:

**MUSIC:** BONGO DRUM ROLL
**SINGER:** *DAYYYYYYY-OH! DAY-A-A-OH!*
*Daylight come and me want go ho-ome.*
*DAYYYY—*

**BONGO MAN:** (INTERRUPTING) Wow, man, I'll have to ask you not to shout like that . . .

**SINGER:** Well . . .

**BONGO MAN:** No, it's too piercing, man. Too piercing! Could you move away from me a little bit?

The record continued with me as the singer moving a little further away every few bars. Finally, the bongo man asked me to leave the room entirely. You heard my footsteps walking away, then a door opened and closed, as my voice shouted from wayyyyy *outside* the door. It went like this.

**BONGO MAN:** No, it's still too piercing, man. Would you mind leaving the room?

**SINGER:** Okay.

**SOUND:** FOOTSTEPS GOING OFF. FROM A DISTANCE, A DOOR OPENS AND CLOSES.

**SINGER:** (MUFFLED) *Dayyyy-oh! Day-a-a-oh!*

**SOUND:** DOOR OPENS AND FOOTSTEPS RUSH BACK UP TO MIKE.

**SINGER:** *Daylight come and me want go home.*

**SOUND:** FOOTSTEPS GO OFF AGAIN. DOOR CLOSES.

**SINGER:** (MUFFLED) *Day-oh! Day-a-a-oh!*

**SOUND:** DOOR OPENS AND FOOTSTEPS RUSH UP TO MIKE AGAIN.

**SINGER:** *Daylight come and me want go home* . . . (etc.)

After the pattern was repeated throughout the song, the singer was heard rattling the knob and beating on the door.

**SINGER:** (MUFFLED VOICE FROM WAY OFF) Heyy!

**BONGO MAN:** (ON MIKE) Yeah, man.

**SINGER:** I locked myself out.

**BONGO MAN:** Craaaaazy!

**SOUND:** FOOTSTEPS RUNNING FOLLOWED BY A CRASH OF GLASS!

**SINGER:** I come through the window!

**CHORUS:** *Daylight come and me want go home!*

Peter Leeds, my friend from radio and a gifted comic actor, played the hip bongo man.

The studio musicians I used on the record were marvelous, including classical guitarist Laurendo Almeda, and a young twelve-string-guitar player named Glen Campbell. As I was laboriously working out the sound patterns with my sound man Gene Twombly (Jack Benny's sound-effects wizard), the band looking on with great amusement, I glanced up at the Capitol control booth in Studio A. A fascinated face was glued to the window. It was Andy Griffith, who also had made some records for Capitol. He stood there for hours until the whole thing came together at last. I remember his affectionate comment to me after the session. "I just wanted to see how it was done," he drawled.

Sales of "Banana Boat" soared, and Leeds and I performed it live on both American and Canadian television. Suddenly, out of left field came a call from the CBS radio network. It catapulted me into a childhood dream come true: my own radio show! Jack Benny, one of my idols, was about to leave the network to devote more time to his television show. A friend of mine, Bill Froug, was West Coast vice president of CBS radio. Bill was a fan who had repeatedly, I discovered later, submitted my name to the New York vice president of programming, a tense man named Howard Barnes. According to Froug, I almost didn't get on CBS at all.

Every time, his suggestions of Freberg had been squashed by Barnes. Finally, Froug flew to New York to attend a final meeting to decide who CBS would pick to replace Jack Benny. The president of CBS, Arthur Hull Hayes, presided over the meeting. Barnes was a wiry, opinionated, and humorless man. Before the meeting he instructed Froug: "Whatever you do, don't bring up Stan Freberg."

Froug stared at him as the door burst open and Arthur Hull Hayes swept into the executive conference room. After hearing suggestions from the various brass, including Howard Barnes, as to what kind of show should replace the great Jack Benny, the president cleared his throat.

"Well, now, we haven't heard from Bill Froug. What kind of show do you think we should put on, Bill?" All eyes swung to Froug. Froug told me that he was perspiring lightly in the shaft of light trained on his face from a ceiling baby spot.

"Well, Mr. Hayes," Froug began, "I think it's important that CBS maintain some continuity with the audience. I think we shouldn't put any kind of show in that time slot but a comedy show."

"That makes sense to me," Hayes nodded. "You have anybody in mind?"

Froug forged straight ahead. "Yes I do, sir. I think we should put somebody on like Stan Freberg."

Nobody breathed for a moment. "Freberg? Isn't he the guy who did that record spoof on *Dragnet?*" Hayes asked.

"Right!" Froug said. "I think he's an original young comedian who can build an audience. If CBS doesn't help develop network talent, where are the new stars going to come from?"

"Well, I think that's a very interesting idea, Bill," the president said. Then he swung around to Barnes. "Howard, what do you think about that?"

Without missing a beat, Barnes smiled at the president. "I couldn't agree more, Mr. Hayes. Freberg is exactly right."

The president slapped the table and beamed at Froug. "Freberg it is then, as long as we all agree. Draw up a contract, and let's get moving!"

After the meeting, Froug told me, he was standing at the urinal in the executive men's room when Howard Barnes walked in and stood at the next urinal. Froug waited for the acid comment that was sure to come. Silence. After a few moments they both washed up and left without a word.

BARNES DIDN'T MENTION MY NAME AGAIN UNTIL A FEW weeks later. He almost killed my first show before it got on after accidentally hearing the tape.

The master tape of Show #1 was supposed to have gone out on a live-feed to New York from the West Coast at the appropriate time, Sunday evening at seven P.M. EDT, the old Jack Benny time. The show had been prerecorded Thursday night before a live audience, and they laughed and cheered. I had a great stock company of actors: Daws Butler, June Foray, Peter Leeds, vocalist Peggy Taylor, Jud Conlon's Rhythmaires, and the Billy May orchestra. Plus Bill James and Gene Twombly, the great sound-effects men I had inherited from Jack Benny and *Gunsmoke*. My producer Pete Barnum and I had sweated over the first show. That's the one the critics would review, and Jane Morse, a reporter from *Time* magazine, was in the audience covering it firsthand.

Afterwards, an engineer on the West Coast had what was to him a brilliant idea. Instead of having to come in to CBS Sunday afternoon at four o'clock to feed the Freberg show to New York so they could take it off the line and broadcast it live, why not feed it ahead of time? Say Friday. That way he could take the weekend off to go sailing in Balboa. New York could just take it off Friday and hold it for broadcast on Sunday, and he wouldn't have to work quite so hard.

That engineer never knew the anguish he would cause me. Unfortunately, when my show came in on the line Friday, word got around CBS New York fast. "*The Freberg Show* just came in!" Instead of waiting to hear it live on Sunday, their curiosity got the best of them. Within a couple of hours the brass was piling into a conference room to check out the new mild-mannered, harmless comedian they thought they had bought. Everything went great for the first five minutes of the show while I interviewed a man who had tied bells around the necks of his herd of sheep. The bells were arranged chromatically so that the sheep herder could play his herd of "tuned sheep." He would tap various sheep with his crook, and they shook their bells. The number he had selected to play was "Lullabye of Birdland." Although I'm sure this was a great deal more "off the wall" than they had expected, they tolerated this piece of Frebergian wildness. Then the bottom dropped out of the conference room, and the brass went ashen. I had devoted the rest of the show to a "Freberg Fable," set sometime in the future. The fable drove a savage satiric sword into the heart of Las Vegas, Nevada. A few weeks before, I had visited Las Vegas with Froug, and after two days the oppressive atmosphere began to get to me. I would go to bed having walked past an old lady pumping her life savings into a slot machine and the next morning would pass the same lady standing in the same room at a different slot machine, a stricken look on her face. My Baptist roots began to rebel against the place. (Over the years I have repeatedly turned down offers to play Las Vegas. I don't particularly care if other people perform there. I may even go and applaud them. I just don't care to be the cause of some family accidentally dropping their house payment at the tables because they came to see me perform.) I thought it was prophetic that the atomic testing grounds were a stone's throw from Las Vegas. *Someday,* I thought to myself, *a strange rain may fall on this town*. The beginnings of the satire I put into my first CBS show took root on that trip to Vegas.

I named it "Incident at Los Voraces" ("the greedy ones"). As I, the narrator, looked back on the years leading up to "the incident," listeners got the idea that the city had been devastated. It all started with a rivalry between the two biggest hotels, the El Sodom and the Rancho Gomorrah. When one hotel built the world's largest pool and hired long-distance swimmer Florence Chadwick to swim the length of it, complete with a Coast Guard cutter following behind—she didn't make it, incidentally, and had to be pulled exhausted from the water—the other hotel, the El Sodom, retaliated by cutting the Gaza Strip into sections. Then they numbered the sections the way William Randolph Hearst used to move great treasures of art to San Simeon and transported the pieces to Los Voraces, to be reassembled in the new Suez Room. The customers were treated to three wars a night with live ammunition. Fatalities ran high with hundreds of gamblers and croupiers biting the felt, and the war got a bad press. To compete with this, the Rancho Gomorrah briefly considered booking "peace," by arranging to have the world's leaders appear three times a night in a summit conference, until someone pointed out that they had booked one into Geneva and it laid an egg. So since peace was considered a risky venture at best, the Rancho Gomorrah decided to go for the ultimate; they would arrange to book—for one night only—*the hydrogen bomb!* And of course they did, and that was the end of the city.

When I got to the hydrogen-bomb line, word had it that Arthur Hull Hayes nearly had apoplexy. Looking back now, it all seems so tame. But in the summer of 1957 joking about the Gaza Strip and the H-bomb was off limits at the network. Even satirizing Las Vegas was considered, well . . . not nice. After I had the city destroy itself, we heard nothing but a plaintive voice singing through the wind:

*Los Voraces was a golden city*
*As the history writers all have penned*
*But her days were numbered*
*In that heavenly book*
*And she pushed her own button,*
*In the end.*

**SOUND:** WIND AND ONE LONELY COYOTE

CBS went into shock. What kind of comedian was *this?* They seemed to forget that they had hired a satirist, if indeed they had ever known it. It was like they were expecting maybe Henny Youngman and got Jonathan Swift.

If only the show had gone out from the West Coast on Sunday as planned; then CBS would have heard it for the first time as it was going out live on the air. This way they felt there was time to censor me, which they promptly did. The script had already passed through continuity acceptance, and the program-practices people. What I was facing here was censorship by nervous network executives at the corporate level, on the top floor of the CBS Building.

***Stan Freberg*** ✍

The first long-distance phone call CBS placed to my agent Lester Linsk insisted that I cut the entire Las Vegas fable. I was to write, produce, and record before a different studio audience a brand-new twenty-minute sketch. Something a little less satiric, please! This was on a Friday, mind you, and the show went out over the air Sunday. Of course, I refused and almost walked off the air. But my friend and producer Pete Barnum cooled me down. Finally, I arrived at a kind of compromise with CBS radio. They would allow the Las Vegas satire to stay in the show providing I made a few changes. First, they told me, kidding around with the Gaza Strip was anti-Semitic. I fought hard. I told Howard Barnes, "Look, I'm not satirizing the Middle East! I'm trying to attack the grossness of Las Vegas. If those guys thought they could jam people into a showroom to watch a live war fought on a transported hunk of the Gaza Strip and do big business with it, then they'd do it! I'm trying to point out that nothing is sacred to Las Vegas."

CBS was adamant. They made me say that "an international incident" had been cut into sections and moved to Nevada, forbidding me to use the words Gaza Strip in any way. "*Oh,* and one more thing: Cut the hydrogen bomb. *No hydrogen bomb, Freberg. Period!*" This meant that I would have to dream up a whole new nonnuclear ending to my fable. A different kind of excess to be booked into Los Voraces, which would ultimately destroy them.

It was Friday night. The next night, Saturday, would be my last chance to retape the last twenty-two minutes of my show before it went out over the air Sunday. This meant CBS had given me twenty-four hours to rewrite the script, then rehearse with the cast, sound men, and orchestra, who had to be called back in all over again to perform in front of a new audience.

Postponing the show for a week was out. CBS was unyielding. The press had been alerted for the debut of Freberg, and they couldn't run an old Jack Benny tape or a thirty-minute news update. So I just rolled the blank yellow paper into the typewriter and tried to channel the anger into satire and humor. Even today much of my writing springs to life under such adverse conditions. I have a hate/love association with this "black cloud over my mind" condition at the typewriter. The satirist in me loves the rage hanging there above the Olivetti, but the humorist pleads for a little funnier atmosphere, thank you.

At any rate, Pete Barnum stayed with me for moral support until about midnight, then left to get some sleep. Barnum had been an NBC television producer under Pat Weaver and was driven by a lot of the same outrage that I was. So then it was just me, all alone at the typewriter, as it has been for most of my life. I worked through the night in my small CBS writer's cubicle and into the next day, finishing about noon. My show secretary, Lee Willway, rushed my new script to mimeo. CBS pages were already handing out newly printed tickets for the new *new Stan Freberg Show.* I raced home to Pasadena to shower and change.

"But why do you have to do your show all over again?" my mother asked. "What did you do wrong?"

"I mentioned the hydrogen bomb, among other things," I said, leaving her staring at the bathroom door.

At two o'clock the cast was assembled, marking their new scripts, and we started to rehearse. At four o'clock the band came in. Billy May had to rewrite some of the music cues on the spot, and the copyists wrote out new parts right in the studio. The pressure was really on, but at seven o'clock we were all standing at our mikes when Barnum in the booth raised his huge arm to cue the downbeat.

**ANNOUNCER:** From Hollywood! *The Stan Freberg Show!*

The new ending that the audience heard was this: The Rancho Gomorrah Hotel had assembled a *semi*ultimate big attraction. A simulated earthquake, which would rock the showroom floor and knock patrons to the ground as ceiling plaster rained down on them in the new San Francisco Room!

But on opening night an interesting coincidence occurred in Los Voraces. Before the special-effects technician could push the button in his booth high above the giant showroom, the one that would activate the computerized series of tremors and realistic effects, the city started to tremble as a *real* earthquake, 9.2 on the old Richter, destroyed the San Francisco Room, the El Sodom, Rancho Gomorrah, and the entire city of Los Voraces.

Not quite as good as the hydrogen-bomb ending (this way I had God intervene directly, whereas I felt the Lord would have allowed Las Vegas to push her *own* button in the end), but not such a bad rewrite under duress. Once again, I worked into the night with Barnum, editing the various parts of the two shows together. The next day, Sunday, I was on the air.

Depressed that my original script had been watered down, it was very encouraging when the show was critically well received in all the right places.

Jack Gould, radio/TV critic of *The New York Times,* wrote: "The impudent gentleman of the recording world unveiled a new half hour that showed there is still life in the sound medium. . . . He has a quick and active imagination, and is a man who reads the papers. His humor has the virtue of a point of view, and he is not reluctant to poke fun at the world's foibles."

Kay Gardella of the New York *Daily News* headlined RADIO'S TIRED BLOOD REVITALIZED BY DR. FREBERG! "He is the man responsible for bringing radio back to life."

Syndicated columnist John Crosby, writing for the *New York Herald Tribune,* said, "Stan Freberg, the man of many voices who can reduce me to helpless laughter with his better satiric flights, now has his own radio show. . . . Freberg is not only a satirist, but a man with a great gift for fantasy which is something delightful and sometimes gets him into trouble. The show's opening was a wonderful demonstration of the man's versatility and imaginative range."

Bill Froug, my champion at the radio network, had meanwhile moved on to CBS TV. He called to congratulate me on the opening show and to tell me how vindicated he felt after reading my marvelous reviews. Meanwhile . . . not a word of praise or support from the big boys at CBS radio in New York.

*Time* magazine had fortunately not only covered my original show, but returned to witness the second version. Naturally, they leapt upon the censorship of Freberg in the story that hit two days later. *Time* quoted me grumbling that "network nervousness hangs between a satirist and his public like a tapioca curtain."

*Time* concluded: "He served up 30 minutes of his exaggerated wildly allusive humor. If the network censors will just stay out of his hair, he promises to deliver a fresh bright new sound that may wrench people away from their TV sets."

A few days later, I flew to New York for a quick

trip, and I will never forget the sight of Howard Barnes striding up Madison Avenue alongside me, his hands deep in the pockets of his dark suit and a scowl etched into his unsmiling face. "CBS doesn't appreciate being referred to as a tapioca curtain!" he snarled. Once again, I was refusing to play ball with the boys. Except that I *had* played ball. I had rewritten my show at their request. My sin was, of course, that I had told *Time* magazine what CBS had put me through.

My show gathered a lot of other critical praise along the way and eventually built a loyal following of about six million listeners. *Variety* said: "If Freberg doesn't watch out he may become the Chaplin of the kilocycles. He also operates as co-director and writer in a splendiferous satire that brings forth an inventiveness, imagination and vigor of which television, in or out of summertime, is so sadly bereft."

Cecil Smith, TV critic of the *Los Angeles Times,* added: "He is the funniest man currently riding the airwaves. Since his new radio show took to the air six weeks ago, it has built up an enormous nationwide following of articulate listeners who storm Stan with mail thanking him for bringing 'literate comedy back to the air.' "

Finally, *Newsweek* magazine announced that I had "gazinkus," whatever that was. On their Newsmakers page they proclaimed: "Freberg: he has gazinkus—a kind of magnetism. FDR had it. Billy Graham has it. Another who seems to have it is the star of CBS's new Stan Freberg Show, a man who does great business with such arcane sound effects as 'the eyebrows of John L. Lewis getting a crewcut for the summer.' "

About halfway through the series some fairly obvious feelings about the advertising business surfaced in a sketch called "Gray Flannel Hat Full of Teen-Age Werewolves," a hybrid of several movies currently in release. It was the story of a werewolf who looked like a normal werewolf to the *other* werewolves but who kept a terrible secret to himself. As the werewolf himself put it: "They are unaware of that nameless terror of which I dare not speak! For when the sun comes up, a strange metamorphosis takes place, over which I have no control!"

**MUSIC:** HARP GLISSANDO

**WEREWOLF:** My fangs become blunt . . . my head becomes crew cut . . . and I feel my fur slowly turning into dark gray flannel!

**MUSIC:** HORROR MUSIC BUILDS.

**WEREWOLF:** And . . . all of a sudden I realize that I am turning into . . . *an advertising man!!*

This not too subtle outpouring should have somehow forewarned me that I might end up squaring off with Madison Avenue. And sooner than I thought.

Around CBS the word was that I had done it again. How does Freberg hope to attract advertising men to buy his show if he makes them out to be werewolves? He has bitten the hand (neck?) of the very person we had hoped would feed us by buying his show.

I guess I hadn't made it all that easy for the network sales department. First, I hadn't let them sell "spots" in the show, holding out for one or two sponsors to buy the whole show, as Benny had been sponsored by Jell-O, State Farm Insurance, and American Tobacco. Speaking of tobacco, I also had written into my contract that they couldn't sell the show to sponsors that I felt were undesirable, like underarm deodorants and cigarettes, among others. As a result, CBS had to turn down two different cigarette companies that wanted to sponsor me. That did not put them in the best frame of mind, considering that in 1957 radio was fading fast on the network level, and most sponsors were putting the big bucks into television. And so, after about fifteen weeks, in spite of a very healthy audience for radio, and much critical acclaim, CBS pulled my connection to six million listeners out of the wall.

My radio series would have been distinctive if for no other reason than this: It inadvertently made me the last network radio comedian in America. After *The Stan Freberg Show* finally went off the air on October 20, 1957, there were no more commercial network radio comedy shows. As television eclipsed radio, they became extinct, and apparently I was the last of the species: the snail-darter of network radio comedians.

I ran a full-page ad in *Variety* and the *Hollywood Reporter* in which I appeared as a doctor in a white coat with a stethoscope administering to a sick radio.

Under this was the New York *Daily News* headline that had proclaimed: RADIO'S TIRED BLOOD REVITALIZED BY DR. FREBERG. Except that a large executioner's ax had severed my head from my body. In political cartoon style the ax read C.B.S.

Satirists have the last word. Sometimes.

# 14

## *Not on CBS Television, You Don't!*

WHEN *THE STAN FREBERG SHOW* WENT OFF THE air, my agent Lester Linsk immediately entered into talks with CBS to make a deal for me to do the same kind of thing on television. Finally Lester, or "The Killer," as he was affectionately known around the broadcasting and literary world, made a deal with CBS television to shoot a pilot for a weekly comedy-variety show based roughly on the satiric humor and point of view of my recently departed CBS radio series. The Writers Guild of America had voted my opening show the best written comedy radio script of 1957. After a few weeks, I sent the pilot TV script that I had written to CBS, and now I stood somewhat nervously on the top floor of CBS Television City in Hollywood, outside the office of Hubbell Robinson, the CBS network vice president for programming.

"Remember, these guys are on the hook for the pilot at least, so try and keep everything nice and low key,"

Lester was confiding, leaning into my ear. "Even if they want to make changes in your script, be a good boy, okay? Let's just play the game. After you get on the air, you can be as wild as you want, but . . ."

"You can go in now, Mr. Linsk." A cool, upswept-blonde secretary was ushering us into an elegantly designed suite typical of most CBS-TV interiors, heavy on the Charles Eames and Eero Saarinen.

"Killer!" Robinson rose from behind his desk, shaking my agent's hand.

"And . . . Stan the Man!"

My peripheral vision noted two other executives sprawled in black leather Barcelona chairs. "I think you know Bill Dozier, Hunt Stromberg, Jr." He waved us into chairs. "Well now," Robinson smiled. "I thought maybe we should discuss what kind of show Stan Freberg sees himself doing."

Was this some kind of joke? Had my mind wandered and missed a stroke somewhere? Off to one side of his desk I noted my thirty-minute pilot script, which I had messengered to CBS the previous week. This script was exactly what I wanted to do. It was a funny show, I thought, with the same tone as my irreverent CBS radio show, but purely visual, pointing my satiric guns on the medium of television itself, politics, and advertising. Little did I know that these three subjects were at the top of the list of areas to avoid kidding around with on network television, ahead of motherhood and the flag. But the main sin I had committed, apparently, was that I had created a show that was much too strange. Too far from the "normal" criteria of TV. Disneyland had opened a few years earlier, and I had titled my script "Freberg-land." Apt, I thought, since the show would be a weekly ride through the tunnels, nooks, and recesses of my mind: the world as seen through Freberg's glasses. But the title was only a temporary one. They wanted to change it? No sweat. But could my troubles run deeper than just the title? The first problem was that he hadn't mentioned my script at all and now was asking what would I like to do? Perhaps he was toying with me. Okay, I would rise to the bait.

"Well, actually, I thought I might just do that script on your desk there."

Robinson's eyes flicked ever so casually toward my pilot script.

"Mmmmmmm, nooo, actually we found that script a little too . . . strange for CBS. The title of course is no good. 'Frebergland' is a little too presumptuous."

My agent leaned forward in his chair. "Hey, you don't like the title, Hub? Easy fix. Stan is open to other titles."

Nobody spoke for a moment. Robinson shrugged. "I think it runs a little deeper than the title, Lester. Some of these areas Stan has gotten into are a little iffy, but overall the show comes off a little weird."

"Can you give me an example?" I asked.

Dozier shifted in his chair. "The gag where you get into the elevator, for one thing," he said. He was referring to a spot in the show where I wander up to a pair of elevator doors standing in limbo. The doors open and I get in. We cut to the indicator over the doors and see the arrow rapidly go from the tenth floor down to the first floor. Cut back to the doors, which quickly open. Out of the elevator bursts a band of Mexican mariachi musicians singing and playing guitars. Three of the twelve people are carrying me aloft with a rose in my teeth. A Spanish dancer, with her castanets clicking, leads the group as we rush toward the camera.

"I don't understand this joke," Dozier said. "One guy gets into an elevator, which doesn't stop at any other floors on the way down, and thirteen people get out."

"If you don't understand it," I told him, "there's no way I can explain it. My feeling is that television comedy is much too predictable. What is needed are occasional flights of the unexpected. TV should be *un*predictable once in a while."

"Nobody would swallow that," Dozier kept on, like a dog with a bone. "They'll wonder how such a thing was possible." Once again, the dark suits were sitting around dissecting my humor.

"I think you're making too much out of the thing," I said. "It's just a wild joke. Kind of a cartoon gag. You can't question it too much. You just accept it or you don't."

Perhaps the opening title had put them off. I had faded up on the CBS "eye" logo in animation. It appeared to be sitting on some railroad tracks. An animated man rushes out and attempts to shove it off the tracks. Now we hear a diesel train horn not too far off. The man looks off in panic. He shoves some more at the eye. No good. He races off screen and then back with a large crowbar. The train is practically upon us now. With a superhuman wrench, he nudges the huge CBS eye off the tracks just as the train tears through the scene. The train is a series of letters spelling out the show's title: FREBERGLAND.

I decided to bring it up. "How did you like the animated opening with the CBS eye?" I asked.

Robinson shook his head slowly back and forth as he might have to a small child who had asked to play with something very valuable. "No playing around with the corporate logo. That's a no-no."

Lester again: "Hey, no problem, Hub. Stan wasn't locked into that opening anyhow. Besides, who needs the added expense of animation, right?" Agreement all around the room.

I made one more stab. "I think if a network has the guts to kid themselves a little bit, people respect that. It shows that this big corporation doesn't think they're so sacred that they can't have a little fun with the CBS eye."

Lester shooting me looks now. Robinson wanting to dump it and move on. He cleared his throat. "Hey, I like the idea myself, Stan, but I'd never get it past New York. Legal would kill it anyhow. You don't fool with the eye."

"How about 'feeding the monster'?" I asked. "How did you feel about that?"

At one point in the script I had written a savage commentary on the voracious appetite of television. I had a man in overalls standing next to me suddenly announce in a loud voice, "Feeding time!" Then he runs off and reenters, pushing a wheelbarrow full of scripts. He wheels it over to a huge mock-up TV set on a giant stand and shoves his shovel into the pile of scripts. Suddenly, I reverse the angle so that it is the point of view of the TV set looking down at the old man with the wheelbarrow. "Heeere we go!" he cries, shoveling scripts into the camera lens. The roar of a hungry monster is heard. "ROOOWWWWRRR!!"

"A few more unbelievable situation comedies!" Another shovelful, more roars.

"A little more sex and gratuitous violence!!" More scripts devoured, loud roars, and contented chomping.

"And last but not least . . . a little public television!" The old man holds up a very small script . . . no more than a pamphlet, actually. The television set roars with anger and disapproval. The feeding man looks over at me. "He doesn't like educational TV shows very much."

Finally, he tosses it in and after a pause, a loud *gulp* is heard. The old man explains to me, "He finds these hard to swallow."

I waited for Robinson's comment on this satiric excursion. "Too esoteric. Wayyyy over the audience's head. You're talking about inside gags here. We may find that funny in our business, the idea of how much material TV consumes week after week, but . . . hey! Do they care about that in Peoria?"

My agent was waving the whole thing away with his perfectly manicured hand. "These are just suggestions, Hub. Stan was giving you some rough ideas that might or might not be developed."

What was Lester talking about? Suggestions? Rough ideas? This was material exactly as I had planned to do it. Camera ready. Final draft!

Dozier spoke up again. "I'll tell you what I see. I see you doing more like *An Evening with Bea Lilly.*"

Bea Lilly? Bea Lilly, the English music-hall comedienne? He must have meant that he'd like to see me doing more of a harmless little outing with music. Gentle, funny, but with no teeth. Nothing relevant to the medium I would be appearing in. I stared at him for a moment. Now Robinson again saying something about commercials.

"Pardon me?" I asked.

"I said I noticed that you wrote the commercials in the show. Why?"

"Well, I thought it might be nice if the commercials were as entertaining as the show," I told him.

"Why would you worry about something like that?" Robinson frowned. "We have advertising agencies to do that."

"Yes, I've seen their work," I told him. "Look," I said, warming to the subject, "You know how just before a commercial your set goes to black? I think that serves as a warning device to millions of viewers that they have a split second to get out of the room." The room was silent except for my agent fidgeting in his chair. "What if the commercials were as funny as the show they were interrupting?" I continued. "What if people actually stayed in the room to watch the commercials on purpose?"

Robinson was uneasy with the kind of fantasy I was describing. "Why did you pick a product like Jell-O to do the commercials about?

I shrugged. "I had to pick some product just as an example. Besides, Jell-O is basically funny."

"Why is it funny?" he said.

"Because it wobbles," I explained. Silence. More explanation was probably called for. "Actually, Jell-O used to sponsor one of my idols, Jack Benny," I went on. "Probably I was influenced by that. I realize Jell-O may not sponsor my show. But General Foods might. Whatever. The big challenge to me would be to create funny commercials for a product that isn't basically a funny product," I said. "Like tomato paste."

Hunt Stromberg's eyebrows arched. "Tomato paste??"

"Yes," I told him proudly. "I created a very successful campaign for the Contadina company. You probably heard the commercials."

They all shook their heads.

"Did they buy a schedule on CBS?" Stromberg asked.

"No, no," I explained. "It was on radio. A radio campaign."

"Oh, well, *radio!*" he smiled, dismissing the medium

and my campaign with a wave of his thin wrist. I suddenly realized I was dealing with a roomful of total television people. Still, I pushed onward: "You know, eight great tomatoes in that little bitty can?"

A vague flicker of recognition from Dozier. Had he heard it on his car radio? Hard to tell. He nodded politely to make me feel better. Otherwise, there was no comment.

"The principle is the same on radio or television," I said. "My theory is, Why should people be bored out of their skulls by advertising? *If* we have to live with it, why not make the commercials at *least,* if not *more,* entertaining than the show itself? What if people were afraid to leave the room for fear that they might have missed one of the entertaining commercials? Wouldn't that be the best of all possible worlds for the sponsor?"

The room became as quiet as a morgue.

Robinson leaned forward on his elbows. Apparently, they weren't dealing with any normal, ordinary comedian here. They were dealing with a lunatic.

"Look!" Robinson said, a cold edge to his voice now. "You want me to level? You're a little too intellectual for the masses as it is. That means you're already uncommercial enough from a programming standpoint. God forbid we allow you to get into the commercials themselves." He mumbled something about my humor not being adaptable to the moving of consumer goods.

I was flabbergasted. I had sold millions of records to the very people who would watch my show. I attempted to point this out:

"Excuse me, but I've already sold millions of Capitol records to *somebody* out there."

"Oh, well . . ." Stromberg explained, "those were record buyers, not consumers."

Transfixed by the clarity and power of that rationale, I made a decision. I would prove my point if it was the last thing I did.

Meanwhile, Robinson was leafing through my pages. "You couldn't get away with this shooting gallery thing in a million years!" he admonished me.

He was referring to a part in the show where I walk up to a shooting gallery in limbo. (The whole show takes place in a kind of white limbo.) This is right after the animated titles and the first time the audience sees me. I peer into the shooting gallery, and we now see that instead of rows of ducks, television sets are moving along as targets, one after the other. Out of each set comes a hard-sell commercial. The man in sleeve garters behind the counter hands me a rifle. As I take aim, we cut in close to see each commercial moving along before I shoot out the picture tubes one after another.

**ANNOUNCER (FIRST TV SET):** When headache strikes you need *fast fast fast relief!*

BANG! CRASH!

**ANNOUNCER (SECOND TV SET):** Stomach acid burned a hole right through this handkerchief. See?

BANG! CRASH!

**WOMAN (THIRD TV SET):** I tried everything for my constipation . . .

BANG! CRASH!

**ANNOUNCER (FOURTH TV SET):** Proof! Clinical proof that a fluoride toothpaste like this, when applied in a conscientious program of dental hygiene . . .

BANG! CRASH!

**ANNOUNCER (FIFTH TV SET):** (TALKING OVER A SHOT OF A DIGESTIVE TRACT) . . . Sluggishy, upset. In your digestive tract, your golden liver bile . . .

BANG! CRASH!

**FREBERG:** (TURNING AND SPEAKING INTO THE CAMERA) Good evening, I'm Stan Freberg.

I had figured that if I was right and most Americans hated those kinds of hard-sell spots as much as I did, the audience at home would have been cheering before I'd shot out the second picture tube.

But CBS wasn't buying that joke. Especially not in the nervous atmosphere of 1958, where they were very careful not to offend the giant drug companies, and their agencies, which produced those bodily function gems. But what did I know? My true feelings about most advertising and the hard-sell era I was living in had found their way into my pilot script, but CBS wasn't putting *that* on the air! Was I kidding, or what?

Robinson suddenly lifted my script off his desk and tossed it onto a side table piled with magazines. It hit a slippery stack of *Hollywood Reporters*, ricocheted off, and sailed onto the carpet. I could hardly believe this was happening. A vice president of CBS had more or less thrown my script onto the floor, where it now lay, unloved by anyone in the room but me and unrescued from its final resting place on the old Antron III.

Robinson leaned back in his black executive desk chair, lacing his fingers behind his head.

"Now . . . " he smiled at my agent, "what kind of show does Stan Freberg see himself doing?"

# 15

## *Decisions in a Parking Lot*

AN HOUR LATER, I STOOD IN THE CBS PARKING LOT in Television City in Hollywood. As I stood blinking into the sun, the black CBS Building at my back, I noticed that my agent was immaculate. After the bashing my script and my spirits had received, I felt wrinkled and wrung out. But Lester looked like he had stepped out of the pages of *Gentleman's Quarterly*. He squinted up at me in the hot California sun.

"You realize we're walking away from a commitment to shot a pilot here, right?"

"I know that," I said. "But if CBS doesn't like that script, they won't like anything I do."

Lester moved me out of the path of an approaching Ferrari. "Not necessarily. Hub's a fan. He's just not too crazy about that script."

"Not too crazy about it?" I shouted. "He treated it as though it had leprosy!" My high volume echoed through the executive parking lot. Lester took a step or two away in case whoever stepped out of the Ferrari was someone he knew.

"Hold it down, kiddo. Let's not wash our dirty linen in public, okay?" Lester was whispering out of the corner of his mouth while acting like he didn't know me.

"I don't care if he didn't understand my script," I said. "A lot of times over the last eight years, Capitol Records didn't exactly understand why I wanted to record a certain satire, and there may have been blood on the walls, but in the end they trusted my instincts."

My agent stared at his Gucci loafers for a moment, saying "Maybe something a little less . . ." (a slight shrug) ". . . offbeat. After you get on, you can be as revolutionary as you want, like I keep telling you, but for now . . ."

"That's not the answer," I told him. "What Robinson has in mind for me is some nice safe sitcom like *The Donna Reed Show* or *Ozzie and Harriet*. I just want to do what the people who bought my records would expect me to do on television. In the meantime these guys don't believe I'm 'commercial.' I've sold all those records and sold all that tomato paste using my same sense of humor . . ."

"You pointed that out to them," Lester reminded me.

"Yeah, but they don't seem to be able to accept it," I said. Standing there in the CBS parking lot that day, I made a major decision that would affect the course of my life. I decided that I would walk away from what I knew would end up being a watered-down, emasculated show with all its satiric teeth removed. I figured that the only way I could prove to CBS that my humor was capable of selling things would be to put my pilot script on hold while I proved my point. I would enter the advertising world in all seriousness. But from inside a Trojan horse.

Whenever Lester wanted to humor me, he called me by an affectionate name that didn't make any sense; he called me Meyer. After hearing me explain the Trojan horse battle plan, he stared up at me for a minute. Then he squeezed my arm, as he would that of a son who was loved but hard to discipline.

"Let's sleep on it, Meyer. Okay? Hmmmm?"

I slept on it for about three weeks. Then I incorporated myself in California, doing business as "Freberg, Ltd. (but not very)." My friend Saul Bass, the great graphic designer, designed my logo. I decided my motto should be the Latin words *"Ars gratia pecuniae"* ("Art for money's sake") and that I should have as my corporate seal a real seal with whiskers. Saul put it all together as The Great Seal of Freberg, Ltd., on what would become for him an award-winning letterhead. Later, I observed that the seal was wearing a tiny medal on its chest with a picture of a tiny fish. I supposed that was what a great seal would have on its medal. I asked Saul, "What kind of fish is that?"

He said, "A bass. I had to get a little credit, didn't I?"

At the last minute I noticed that Saul had added something else. Since my offices were in Southern California, he had drawn a pair of sunglasses on the great seal. Perfect. When I opened the doors of Freberg, Ltd., I was determined not to operate out of your normal steel and glass high rise. I felt that my surroundings should reflect my offbeat, atypical approach to advertising. I would be a businessman, all right, but did that mean I had to *look* like a businessman? I settled on an old vine-covered house straight out of the work of my friend Charles Addams, the macabre *New Yorker* cartoonist who provided the inspiration for the television series *The Addams Family.*

Little did I dream as I stood out there looking out of my leaded English windows . . . that within five years one of my clients would be the CBS television network! They would come to *me*—the guy who was supposed to have been so uncommercial—and ask me to create and produce all the commercials to promote their new fall television shows.

It was with the greatest personal satisfaction that I accepted the job. The guy who hired me was Lou Dorfsman, CBS VP of design, who also got into CBS's corporate advertising. He was the brilliant designer responsible for the clean graphic look of everything associated with CBS. I never got around to telling Dorfsman what a great moment of triumph it was having CBS hire me as an advertising consultant.

One of the shows I was hired to promote was *Hogan's Heroes,* a situation comedy set—I still can't believe it—in a Nazi prisoner of war camp. As a satirist, I couldn't help lampooning the whole idea of the thing. Here's how one commercial ended up, with me interviewing Bob Crane, the star of the show.

**FREBERG:** Where does the show take place?

**CRANE:** In a Nazi prisoner of war camp in Germany.

**FREBERG:** Always a good situation comedy locale. What are some of the amusing ingredients?

**CRANE:** Oh, German police dogs . . . machine guns . . . the Gestapo . . .

**FREBERG:** Just a few of the laugh-provoking elements to be seen this fall on *Hogan's Heroes,* Friday nights on CBS. Shall we say, "If you liked World War II, you'll love *Hogan's Heroes?*

**CRANE:** No, let's not say that, no.

George Bristol, VP of advertising under Dorfsman, thought that script and a few others a little controversial but he and Lou okayed them. It was deemed, however, that the new president of CBS television, John Schneider, should personally approve them.

I flew to New York and once again found myself on the top floor of a CBS television building, this time the tall black impressive rectangle designed by Eero Saarinen and referred to in the industry as Black Rock. As I walked into the new president's office on the thirty-fourth floor, a photographer from *Newsweek* was shooting his picture, a secretary was taking dictation, and an interior decorator was flying about the office like a butterfly trying to get Schneider to approve fabrics for his new office. I had come on the first official day of his new job.

"Go ahead, Stan," he called to me. "I'm listening!"

I read all fourteen commercials while the photographer was walking around with strobe lights going off, and the decorator interrupted periodically: "Shall we *definitely* go with the white wool herringbone on the sofa then?"

Schneider tried his best to concentrate on my scripts, but just as I would get to a punch line, the photographer would say to him, "Don't look at Stan, look at *me!*" It was a circus. As I got almost to the end of the *Hogan's Heroes* commercial, the decorator waving fabrics at him cried out, "Ah! *Voilà!* The black peau de soie *silk* on the sofa, and the white herringbone wool for the *drapes!!* All right??"

As I recall, Schneider okayed most of the scripts, and the decorator approved the last three. In a reciprocal arrangement, I okayed a kind of charcoal gray linen for the accent pillows.

# 16

## *The Long Pause*

As FATE WOULD HAVE IT, I DIDN'T HAVE TO WAIT long for new business in my quaint little headquarters. A coffee company from Omaha, Nebraska, called and wanted to fly out. Its name was Butter-Nut, and although not well known in Los Angeles, it had like 60 percent of the coffee business in the Midwest. Its marketing people had heard of my success in pulling the Contadina company out of the doldrums with my offbeat approach, and now *they* needed help.

They trudged up my creaking stairs, loaded down with sales graphs and cans of their regular coffee. One man, Charles Harding II, a pleasant Freberg fan, was the account director with the company's advertising agency in Omaha. The other man was the VP of marketing at Butter-Nut, Donald Keough. Later, after the Coca-Cola Company gobbled up Butter-Nut Coffee, Keough eventually became president of Coke. But that day he simply held a jar of his new Butter-Nut coffee in his hand with a slightly chagrined look on his face.

"We're the last coffee in America to come out with instant coffee," he admitted. "It's been five years since instant hit the market. Everybody but Butter-Nut has an instant coffee by now. But we just kept on making regular ground coffee. *Now* we're finally coming out with an instant, five years too late. It's kind of embarrassing, frankly. Anyhow, we just thought you could help get people's attention with some funny commercials." After okaying my fee, they flew back to Omaha, leaving me staring at their belated jar of instant coffee. In a couple of weeks I called them on a conference call, read their commercials to them, and sang the song I'd written. I told them that their whole campaign was keyed to the line, "Five years isn't exactly instant."

What happened then at the other end of the phone was a phenomenon I would come to recognize hundreds of times. It is what I call The Long Pause.

After a respectable silence, I picked up the conversation. I told them they should come clean and admit that they were late with their instant coffee, but that's the breaks. I had written a jingle as well, which started off "Five years isn't exactly instant, but that's how long it took," etc.

Finally, as the shock wore off, they laughed at the funny spots I had written, and Keough decided to give me the go-ahead. "You've taken a negative and turned it into a positive," I remember him telling me.

The radio commercials hit the air in the Midwest, and within three weeks Butter-Nut had sold over a million jars of their new coffee. And that was just in the four states where it was distributed. They had so many orders, their packing machinery couldn't keep up. They ended up taking carloads of their instant coffee over to Hills Brothers, who graciously packed it for them.

Next, they let me do a television commercial kidding subliminal advertising. A small, animated man walked onto the screen:

**MAN:** Ladies and gentlemen. this commercial is going to use sublim . . . sub . . .

ONTO THE SCREEN FLASHES THE WORD SUBLIMINAL, BUT ONLY FOR HALF A SECOND—JUST LONG ENOUGH TO REGISTER.

**MAN:** (CONTINUING) Subliminal advertising! That means you will *not* be able to see it on the screen. Oh, it'll be there all right, but the naked eye cannot detect it. In the meantime, just sit back and relax . . . while I tell you this rather amusing, heh heh, story. It seems that these two men decided to take a trip.

FROM THE BACK OF A SCREEN BEHIND HIM, A SKYROCKET BURSTS, OBLITERATING THE MAN'S DIALOGUE. THE ROCKET BURST BECOMES THE WORDS INSTANT BUTTER-NUT COFFEE, WHICH FILL THE SCREEN. THE BAND IS PLAYING LOUDLY AND THE MAN HAS SHRUNK TO A SMALL SILHOUETTE IN THE CORNER OF THE SCREEN. WE SEE HIM TALKING, BUT WE CAN'T HEAR HIM. THE GIANT MESSAGES ON-SCREEN ARE HUGE, IMPOSING, ANYTHING BUT SUBLIMINAL. A STRING OF DANCING GIRLS DRAGS IN THE WORDS IT TOOK FIVE YEARS TO MAKE, BUT IT WAS WORTH IT. SUDDENLY THE MAN POPS ON FULL SCREEN, AND WE HEAR HIM AS THE MUSIC CUTS OFF.

**MAN:** So the second man goes *back* to the dry cleaners, and . . .

A BURST OF FIREWORKS BLOTS OUT THE MAN

IN MID-SENTENCE. THE WORDS TRY SOME APPEAR FULL SCREEN, FOLLOWED BY AN ELEPHANT STOMPING THROUGH WITH THE WORD TODAY!! FINALLY, THE WORDS INSTANT BUTTER-NUT COFFEE PULSATE A FEW TIMES, FILLING THE SCREEN, AND WE SEE THE MAN AGAIN, BY NOW AT THE END OF HIS STORY.

**MAN:** So the third guy says . . . "Okay. But you'd better bring back the hangers." Ahh heh-heh.

THERE IS A SLIGHT PAUSE AS THE MAN REALIZES HIS STORY HAS NOT GONE OVER WELL. HE EXITS SHEEPISHLY. FADE TO BLACK.

The animation for the commercial was done by John Wilson's Fine Arts Animation company. It won many awards for us, including the New York Art Director's Gold Medal. But the only prizes that mean anything to an advertiser are improved sales and an increase in awareness for the company's product. The campaign had done both for them. *Now* they were ready to come out to Los Angeles and take on the tough Southern California market dominated by Yuban, Maxwell House, Hills Brothers, and Folger's.

They wanted just to put on the instant coffee commercials that had been so successful in the Midwest. But I told him, "Wait a minute. People here don't know you from Adam. In Omaha you'd been in business for seventy years. People are very blasé in Los Angeles. Before they can care about your *instant* coffee, they'd better know you make *regular* coffee. We need to cut through people's indifference and get their attention first."

About that time, a beautiful blonde walked into my life who got *my* immediate attention.

My small company was getting into more and more

commercial production, and I was also appearing on NBC television. I was in Burbank three days a week, doing a comedy spot on the *Chevy Show*. I needed someone with real production experience to assist me in both studios. I had met Donna Andresen when I was a guest on the Frank Sinatra television show on NBC. She was assistant to the producer/director, Jack Donohue. She had worked with him for many years on *The Red Skelton Show, Martin & Lewis, The Lucy Show, The Colgate Comedy Hour,* and many others. I had been impressed by Donna's fantastic ability to do about five things at once in the booth while these shows were on the air live—grace and cool under tremendous pressure. Then I had lost track of her. When she walked into my office, a couple years later, I already knew what a terrific help she could be to me in production, but I had forgotten how beautiful she was.

*No way!* I said to myself. *How could I possibly keep my mind on the work with* her *around?* Of course, I didn't tell *her* this. I mumbled something about getting back to her, as I tried to avoid looking into her great big blue eyes. At the time, she had just finished a season with Peter Lawford. She had gone to work for him when he started filming *The Thin Man* television series at MGM. They were not in production at the moment. Since Lawford was married to Pat Kennedy, sister of the soon-to-be-president John F. Kennedy, they were very busy with Kennedy's campaign. Donna found herself reporting for work in Lawford's Santa Monica beach house. Dealing with the social world of the Lawfords was not exactly working in production.

I realized suddenly that fate had transpired to make this talented woman temporarily bored enough to actually consider coming to work for *me!* I came to my senses and overcame my sexist attitude. Not only was it theoretically possible for a woman to be beautiful, sexy, and extremely efficient at the same time, I thought to myself—she was sitting there staring at me. I hired her on the spot.

I decided to create a five-minute radio commercial for Butter-Nut Coffee. It would be a mini-musical comedy with an original score, which I would write. I had wondered about the sound of "original-cast" Broadway record albums, like Rogers and Hammerstein's *Oklahoma!* Everybody seemed to *shout* the lines that led into the musical numbers. There was a good reason for this. They were recorded in an empty theater when it was "dark," but the actors projected their lines with great voice as though the audience were there. In the empty theater their voices echoed and bounced around the theater, with no human bodies to absorb the sound. This is what gave the recording its "original-Broadway-cast" sound. To me, it sounded ridiculous.

I decided to spoof this aspect as well. After I finished writing the three songs for my little musical commercial, Billy May did the arrangements and also created an "overture" to kick it off. Since I was parodying *Oklahoma!*-type musicals, I decided to call it "Omaha!" after the town where the coffee was made. Since I reasoned that I'd never be able to buy time for a five-minute commercial on the air, I decided to write it so that the coffee would not be mentioned until literally the last minute. *Maybe* we could get away with *that*. I sang the part of the hero Biff, and a hilarious comedienne, Frances Osborne, played the ingenue Julie. We both sang the songs in our "Broadway" baritone and soprano voices, using more vibrato than even the Metropolitan Opera could have stomached. The Jud Conlon chorus of sixteen singers supported us, Billy's orchestrations employed about twenty musicians, and other actors made an original cast of forty people. We recorded the commercial extravaganza at Capitol Records in Hollywood. While writing, I had called the Omaha Chamber of Commerce, to check on any unusual things about the city, and received an extremely thin brochure. They seemed to be hard-pressed to find many things to brag about. I finally settled on a couple of obscure facts, to open the musical:

**MUSIC:** TIMPANI ROLL

**BIFF:** (SHOUTING) Say! What city makes over three hundred collections of daily mail from over six hundred street collection boxes?

**CHORUS:** (SHOUTING) Omaha!

**BIFF:** And if you wanted to hit America smack in the bread basket . . . where would you hit her?

**CHORUS:** Omaha!

**BIFF:** And what is Omaha spelled backwards?

**CHORUS:** Ahamo!

**MUSIC:** OVERTURE HITS.

The exuberant musical played out with dialogue and song. Every time someone asked what was so special about Omaha and someone else would attempt to tell them it was where a certain coffee was made, the singers would burst into song without mentioning the product. The most ridiculous song was "Omaha Moon."

**MAN:** Would you try not to burst into song every time I ask you a question?

**BIFF:** Sorry.

**MAN:** Why are you singing about Omaha anyhow? What's so hot about Omaha?

**BIFF:** Because Omaha is the home of delicious . . .

**JULIE:** Biff! Oh, Biff! Isn't it a lovely moon tonight?
**BIFF:** Yes, Julie. Back here we call that an Omaha moon!
**MAN:** (ANTICIPATING A SONG) Ohhhh, no!
**MUSIC:** LOUD BELL NOTE
**BIFF:** *O-maha moon,*
*Keep shining*
*On, Omaha keep shining down.*
*We'd like it if you*
*Wouldn't shine on Council Bluffs,*
*Or for that matter*
*Any other town.*
*Omaha moon, we*
*Heard that*
*You shined on Cedar*
*Rapids last June.*
*We'll thank you*
*To remember*
*That you are a*
*One-town moon.*
*Don't forget,*
*Your name is*
*Omaha Moooon!*

Don Keough, the advertising manager, okayed the script and score without ever telling his boss, the man who owned Butter-Nut Coffee, what Freberg was up to. He just went back and played him the finished tape of "Omaha!"

The man was Paul Gallagher, chairman of Paxton & Gallagher, who owned and packed Butter-Nut. As the long commercial started, the old man seemed enthralled with the glorious musical sound. Then his brow became deeply creased as time went on with no mention of his coffee. A small tic started in his cheek as he began to calculate what this must have cost, and *still* no Butter-Nut coffee. Finally, in the last minute, as the coffee was not only mentioned but sung about by the large chorus, he actually cried. When Keough asked him at the end why he was crying, Gallagher said, "I'm just so grateful that they mentioned my coffee! My God, for a minute there I thought they weren't going to mention it at *all!*"

In writing "Omaha!" I became carried away. What had started out as a five-minute Rogers and Hammerstein spoof now clocked in at six minutes and thirty-five seconds, from overture to final curtain. It was either the world's longest commercial, or shortest musical comedy, depending on whether you were judging it from Madison Avenue or Shubert Alley. The media department of the Omaha ad agency, Buchanan Thomas, who handled Butter-Nut Coffee, technically speaking, didn't have a clue as to how they could buy time for such an unwieldy commercial. They were dumbstruck at the prospect of getting it on the air in Los Angeles, the market for which I had tailored it. Charles Harding, the account director, loved it, but reported to me the disgruntled comments of his media people: "They say, 'No way we're going to get this on the air. No way. Can't you get Freberg to cut it down to a minute like a regular commercial?' "

I thanked him for his comments and hung up the phone in Hollywood. I decided I'd just have to buy the time myself. Obviously, since there was nothing in a station's rate book about a six-and-a-half-minute commercial cost, I'd have to let them first hear how entertaining it was and then take it from there.

I went to KNX, the big CBS station that had carried my recent radio show, and the head of sales loved it. But he couldn't accept the commercial, of course. Was I kidding, or what? A six-and-a-half-minute radio commercial? The station was geared to sell sixty-second spots. Period.

It took it to KFWB and KABC with the same results. I was starting to sweat now. I went back to my office and sat there for a while with a cup of Butter-Nut coffee. Donna came in and told me that Harding was calling from the agency in Omaha. "How's it going with the time buys?" he asked me. "Fair," I said, overstating the actual situation. "I'll call you when we have a definite schedule."

There were dozens of other stations, of course, spread over Southern California. But even if I spread Butter-Nut's dollars out over all these little stations—that's assuming they would even *take* the commercial—I wouldn't particularly get anyone's attention. I felt they needed to go *bang* and wake up Los Angeles to the fact that there was a new coffee out here. To do that, I needed a highly rated radio station with a huge share of audience. There was only one station left that could do that: KMPC, a big fifty-thousand-watt Los Angeles institution. Their morning disc jockey, Dick Whittinghill, had the highest-rated audience in drive time. They also had the exclusive rights to carry the Dodger baseball games, starting every day at five P.M. But how could I get them to take my oddball commercial? Should I have gone to some place like the Harvard Business School so I would know better than to write myself into corners like this? The thought crossed my mind and was out my left ear in about three seconds. I've rarely doubted my instincts.

I had saved the best radio station for last. It was also the *only* radio station left that could help me pull it off. I called for an appointment with the head of sales and drove down Sunset Boulevard with the reel-to-reel tape on the seat. It was very clear to me: If the man said no,

I'd see if I could get booked back to Australia. And stay there.

The VP of sales for KMPC was a big, gregarious salesman named Stan Spiro. He ushered me into his office with a wide smile, darting a glance at the tape under my arm. I had met him a few times when I had been a guest on *The Dick Whittinghill Show*. He waved me to a comfortable chair, and I sat down, wondering if I was starting to develop an ulcer. "Stan the Man!" he said. "Whattya got? New record?"

"Something like that," I told him. "Why don't you just play this first, and then we'll talk."

He put it on his expensive tape machine, and the overture hit, playing through giant fifteen-inch speakers. He sat back, awed by the music. As it continued, Spiro was laughing and I was perspiring lightly in his air-conditioned suite. When it finally got to the coffee part in the last minute, his eyes widened. As it ended, he leaned forward at his desk: "You mean this was a *commercial?*"

I nodded, smiling.

"How long is it, for God's sake?"

"A little over five minutes," I said truthfully. "Now, here's the good news. Because you're the top station in L.A., I'm pretty sure I can get Butter-Nut to give you an *exclusive*."

*"Exclusive?"* he said. "You mean you wouldn't run it on any other stations?"

"Well, not any other *big* stations. I think I can guarantee that," I said.

"No good," he shook his head. "An exclusive is an exclusive!"

I studied my Bass Weejuns for a minute. Then I got up and paced a couple of times, my hands in my pockets. Finally, I put out my hand. "Okay," I said. "You win,

Stanley. I think we can live with that." He was on his feet now, shaking my hand. All of a sudden, reality struck as he started to speak, and his face froze. This was the moment I had dreaded. Once again . . . the long pause.

"Wait a minute!" he said. "Where am I going to put a five-minute commercial?"

Without missing a beat, I said, "Sit down, and I'll lay it out for you." He sat, and I started to improvise. "I realize it's tough to drop into normal scheduling, but how about in the middle of the Dodgers baseball game every day?"

"No, I can't do that," he said. "The fans would never stand still for interrupting the game for that long a commercial."

"Okay, at the end then. How about immediately following the Dodgers every day? I'll record some little one-minute spots that you can play in the morning drive time and all day long. They'll be sort of like promos for a little Broadway show, telling people to listen for 'Omaha!' right after the game." I was striding up and down now, making it up as I went. "People will stick through the Dodger game," I told him, non-sports fan that I am—"just to hear 'Omaha!' right after the game."

"They don't need an excuse to listen to the Dodgers baseball game," he told me.

"Whatever," I continued. "Then just when they're sorry the game is over, here comes a great little musical they hadn't counted on, all right? And here's the best part: Butter-Nut will take little ads in the paper, advertising 'Omaha!' "

He was nodding, trying to keep up with me.

"What kind of ads?"

"On the theater pages of the *Los Angeles Times,*" I ad-libbed. "I'll make 'em look just like ads for a Broadway show called 'Omaha!' but we'll say, 'Tune in immediately following the Dodgers game on KMPC.' We'll also buy them right by the TV listings. We won't mention the coffee at all."

Spiro stared at me, swept along by it all. "You won't mention the coffee at all?"

"Not in the theatrical ads. They'll look mostly like ads for your station."

"Do I have to pay for the newspaper ads?" he asked.

"Not a chance," I told him. "That's our gift to you. Do we have a deal?"

He blinked for a minute. "You're sure I'm not going to hear 'Omaha!' on CBS or KABC?"

I looked him right in the eye. "You have my personal guarantee," I said. "They can beg me for it, but they can't have it. You have the exclusive in this town. Okay?" I held out my hand. "Deal?"

He grabbed my hand. "Deal!" he said, smiling smugly at the fantastic exclusive he had wrangled from Stan Freberg.

Back from the brink in my office, I recounted the entire episode, lying down from the strain. Donna stood staring down at me. "Do you like living on the edge like this?" she asked me.

"It keeps me on my toes," I said. "I knew it would all work out." She shook her head and walked away. In a minute she was back with a cold towel for my brow.

I suddenly realized that being at the end of the Dodgers game put me on at about 5:15 P.M., in the heart of drive time, the best time of all each day. Butter-Nut Coffee thought it was a bit strange that we would only be on the one station, but they backed me up. "It's more audacious this way," I told them.

And indeed it was. The ads hit in the *Times* and the

*Herald,* and the promo spots started on KMPC. After the first few playings of "Omaha!" the whole town started talking about it. I got calls from everybody, including Spiro. "Say," he informed me, "do you realize that thing runs six and a half minutes?"

"What's the difference?" I told him. "If they just sat through a four-hour baseball game, a six-and-a-half-minute commercial is a drop in the bucket."

The *Los Angeles Times* did a feature story about the whole thing, and people began looking for this upstart coffee in the supermarkets. The sports announcer for the Dodgers started telling people as the game wound down every day, "Be sure and keep your radio set right here for 'Omaha!' following the game. *Exclusively* on KMPC."

The Los Angeles market is a very fractionated one. The leading coffee at that time, Hills Brothers, was only able to get 18 percent of the Southern California market. After a year of things like "Omaha!" and subsequent campaigns I produced for them, Butter-Nut ended up with 12 percent of the L.A. market, a quadruple increase in sales.

About this time I received a letter from the managing director of the Omaha Symphony Orchestra. He had heard from someone that I had written a musical called "Omaha!" Could this be true? If so, would I consider coming to Omaha for one of their summer pops concerts and conducting the symphony myself? "There has been so little written about our fair city," he wrote. "Is there a chance for this new work to be conducted by the composer?"

I could hardly believe it. The man was serious. Did he know that it was actually a commercial? Hard to tell. I picked up the phone and accepted. Although I had indeed written the score, I knew nothing about conducting a symphony. A few weeks later, being a train buff, I was on the Union Pacific train headed for Omaha. Donna traveled with me, as did Billy May and his wife. As the train veered around the mountains, Billy gave me conducting lessons in the lounge car. He had brought me a white baton and rehearsed me by humming loudly as I followed the score to a small metronome. As I waved my arms wildly, I nearly put out several eyes, as passengers lurching through the car came abreast of my flashing baton.

We got off at the station in Omaha to be greeted by a small brass band, the Jaycees, and several American Indians from the Omaha tribe, who gave me a peace pipe. It was seven in the morning. The Union Pacific had somehow cut off the water to our sleeping car, so we had to get off without brushing our teeth, not putting me in the best of moods. Billy May had simply brushed his teeth with gin. (This was in Billy's drinking days.)

Chuck Harding drove us to our hotel and told us the concert the next night was a sellout. Billy had reorchestrated "Omaha!" for seventy-two musicians, and Jud had printed enough vocal parts for a thirty-two-voice chorale. Since the "work" was a bit short, I had written an additional song for the occasion. "I Look in Your Face . . . and I See Omaha!" The symphony committee still had no idea, however, that the thing ended up as a Butter-Nut coffee commercial. I brought this up to Harding and Keough, who just shrugged and said, "Too late now. They'll find out tomorrow night."

The rehearsal was a little rough, but Billy straightened out some of the notes, told me I was doing great, and gave me encouragement. When I first brought the baton down in front of the orchestra, the tremendous symphonic blast from all those instruments was something I had not been prepared for. "Don't let these guys inhibit you," Billy told me. "It's just like a studio band. There's just more of them. Give 'em a harder downbeat maybe, and look out for the tempo change to three-four time at bar 5, then back to four-four at bar 9."

I could hardly sleep that night from the stress. *More on-the-job training,* I thought to myself.

The next night in front of several thousand symphony lovers, newspaper and television coverage, and a reporter from *Time* magazine, I walked out in tails with my white baton to enthusiastic applause. The amphitheater used by the symphony for their summer pops series was called Peony Park. The names of the performers were straight out of something Bob and Ray might have written. The soloists were Lyle DeMoss and Mildred Slocum, backed up by the Loretta Sneed Singers. I'm not making this up. You can check the program.

With the smell of hyacinth and jasmine in the air, I took a bow and stepped up onto the podium in front of the Omaha Symphony Orchestra. Seventy-two sets of eyes peering over black ties and long black dresses watched me like a convention of hawks. The soloists were at their mikes, and Loretta Sneed smiled at me in front of her chorale. *Arms, don't fail me now!* I thought. As I raised my baton, horns and bows whipped into position. Then I plunged it down, and the sound almost knocked me over. I was off and running! The thrill was something I couldn't begin to explain. I was halfway through the overture now, and I hadn't screwed up. Watch the score . . . another tempo change coming up . . . cue the percussionist . . . a few more bars and . . . I cued the singers. Everything sounded great to me. Seven minutes later I still hadn't screwed up, but the cymbals player had. I threw him the cue, and he just stared at me, crash cymbals raised in the air. He later told me that he was so impressed with the way I was conducting, he had gotten busy watching me and forgot to count bars.

I held my arms out, building the singers and orchestra to a big crescendo, and cut them off. The audience cheered. I had come through it unscathed. I turned and gestured for the symphony to stand up as strobe lights went off all around and the applause went on. Billy May rushed up and shook my hand. "Leonard Bernstein's job is safe," he told me, "but you did great!" I walked backstage, and Donna stood smiling proudly in the wings. Were those tears in her eyes? I had fallen in love with this beautiful and talented woman.

The *Time* magazine story ran in the Showbiz section and was highly complimentary. It covered my debut not only as a conductor but as a highly unorthodox advertising man. The first line read, "The owl-eyed odd-ball had never set foot in Omaha before." Owl eyed? Capitol later pressed "Omaha!" as a record.

The following January, Donna and I were married. We are still married, which is something of a record for people in show business. She is my best critic, my editor, and my producer, among other things. She is also the smartest person I know. She has given me two beautiful children: a daughter, Donna Jr., and a son, Donavan, who both inherited her beauty and brains.

My father performed the wedding ceremony in Pasadena. The organist played two of my songs: "This Is Forever," the love song I cowrote with Victor Young, and at the last minute I slipped in the sheet music to "Omaha Moon." The first part of our honeymoon was spent in Carmel, California, and the last part in Australia, where I returned as a guest star with Frank Sinatra and the Red Norvo Quintet.

"G'day again, Stan!"

I was glad Donna could see firsthand the great reaction from the thousands of Australian fans who were as enthusiastic as they had been three years earlier. Sinatra was marvelous, as he always is, and the audience loved him. Frank has always been very nice to me and a fan of my work, which is why he invited me, along with the Red Norvo Quintet. But as usual, he had problems with certain members of the press, who seemed to goad him deliberately.

One night in Melbourne, as I finished my act and was introducing Sinatra, I heard a terrible clatter in the wings. I heard men shouting, followed by what sounded like glass breaking. I kept on introducing Sinatra, hoping the audience couldn't hear the commotion. I concluded with, "Ladies and gentlemen . . . Mr. Frank Sinatra!" and the usually immaculate Sinatra seemed slightly disheveled as he walked onstage to a mighty cheer.

"Stanley baby!" Frank called out to me as we passed each other. The man was the height of cool, casually straightening his tie and launching into "Chicago" with Red Norvo's group behind him onstage and the big band down below.

As I came backstage, I saw bedlam, and the events were recounted to me by Lee Gordon, the entrepreneur who had brought Frank and me to Australia. Security guards were now jostling with a photographer, and a reporter had his head tipped way back trying to stanch his nosebleed. Apparently, the photographer and reporter from the morning newspaper had approached Frank as he was about to walk out on stage. "No pictures now, please, okay? I'm getting ready to go on," he had told them. But the photographer had shoved his camera in Frank's face and fired a flashbulb in his eyes, partially blinding him. Who wouldn't be irritated by this? Then the other Australian newspaperman had said something like, "What about Ayyyy-va, Frankie? You ever gonna get back together with Ayyyy-va?" That did it. Frank shoved him and smashed the photographer's Speed Graphic against a brick wall.

Donna was trying to steer me away toward my dressing room. "Don't *you* get into it now!" she told me sternly. The next morning, the press retaliated for actions they clearly had started. Instead of giving Frank a bad review, they did worse. They ignored him. They reviewed "THE STAN FREBERG SHOW . . . with the Red Norvo Quintet!"

The review praised everything I had done. They praised the great American jazz group headed by Red Norvo, listing the numbers he had played. The review ended with this line: "Norvo's group had about the same personnel as the last time he visited Australia, except that he has added a boy singer." Frank never mentioned the review, and *I* certainly wasn't about to bring it up.

Toward the end of the Melbourne engagement, Lee Gordon came up to me as I came offstage. "Stan, uhh" —he was whispering out of the corner of his mouth— "Frank wants to know if he could use your dressing room for a few minutes after the show." I said fine. Sinatra never used a dressing room backstage, choosing to walk in the stage door immaculately groomed and ready to perform at precisely the right moment. He hated standing around backstage. Now the man wanted a little privacy in my dressing room for some reason. Fine. Whatever. No problem. I watched Frank sing at the top of his form that night as I cooled down in the wings before heading into the cold night air. Donna gave me my scarf and topcoat, and we smiled goodnight as Frank came off. Then I saw a striking brunette back in the shadows also smiling at him. She was beautiful and suddenly very familiar. It was Ava Gardner, of course, in Australia to film *On the Beach* for Stanley Kramer. Frank took her arm. Then they walked into my dressing room and closed the door. Donna steered me toward the stage door.

"Close your mouth, dear," she said.

# 17

## *You Could Have Foiled Me*

As MY REPUTATION AS A PROBLEM SOLVER IN ADVERTISING became known, more and more big agencies began calling me in as a consultant.

Although an agency may have a great creative department, solving a marketing problem through the use of humor was and is very tricky. If an agency feels they want to attempt this, they are usually better off going outside the agency to a specialist. Since I was practically the only one doing this work in 1959, that is what increasingly began happening.

By the time the searching party from the huge advertising agency Young & Rubicam found me, they already knew they shouldn't expect a normal ad campaign if they hired me. What they didn't expect was that they would find the entire company having a picnic on the grass beside my office. After getting no response from the doorbell on my un-Tishmanesque building, they wandered through a flower garden, peered around a giant hydrangea bush, and there we were under a tree, in mid-picnic. I remember staring up at a collection of dark suits as it suddenly threw a shadow across my deviled egg. They had arrived early, but they declined to join us. (One does not picnic in a three-piece Brooks Brothers suit.) Finally, they seemed so uncomfortable that we all moved upstairs into my office. They had flown down from the San Francisco office of Y&R to see if I'd like to create some commercials for Kaiser foil, a product of Kaiser Aluminum, one of many divisions of Kaiser Industries, the huge conglomerate owned by Henry J. Kaiser. (Kaiser Steel, Jeep Automobiles, etc., etc.) They had also brought along a tremendous marketing problem, which they didn't reveal to me at first. Clients or agencies rarely do. They like to pretend that everything is just fine and all they really want are some funny commercials. Sometimes that *is* the case.

But more often than not their products face some dilemma, running from minor to excruciating. *Much* of the time, the situation can be helped by facing up to it in the advertising. *Most* of the time, companies opt to ignore it, and their advertising agency, seeking to preserve the status quo and its 15 percent commission, rarely wants to open those cans of peas. In fairness, marketing problems are tough to solve, and the easiest thing to do is just tippy-toe around the dilemma.

Of course, all these business subtleties were lost on the young Freberg of 1959. Not having spent one day working in an advertising agency, and oblivious to the sensitive area I was walking into, I asked what seemed to be a perfectly legitimate question: "Does Kaiser have any particular problems with foil that I should know about before I start writing these commercials?"

A moon-faced Y&R creative director named Hanno Fuchs smiled at me. "Just give us your usual funny Freberg commercials," he said, ducking the issue temporarily.

A small bell went off in my head. These guys were not telling me everything. My experience with Butter-Nut Coffee and other clients had taught me how it was possible to solve some marketing problems by facing them head on in the commercials. My audacity knew no bounds. "Why don't you pretend that I'm a doctor," I persisted. "A foil specialist. How can I help you if you don't tell me where it hurts?"

A couple of executives began to readjust themselves in their chairs. "No problems, particularly," one of them said. There was a moment of silence. Then, a line I will never forget from Hanno Fuchs.

"Why don't we level with him?" he said.

I couldn't imagine what would come next. I remember one of the longest pauses I had ever heard. Then another Y&R voice was heard. Bill Riley, a stiff-necked account director, with a faint southern accent. "Well, actually, ahhhh, Kaisuh foil has a little distribution problem."

*"Little!"* Hanno smiled. "They hardly have any distribution at all."

*Whoops*! The foil was out of the box. It turned out Reynolds Wrap, the leading brand, had something like 80 percent of the foil market. Alcoa had the next 10 percent, and out of the dregs, a pitiful 5 percent to Kaiser foil, roughly. Amazing. The reason they were selling so little foil was that it was barely on the shelf. In most stores people couldn't have found it with a Geiger counter. The impact of this hit me full on.

"You mean even if I give you the greatest commercials in the world, it won't do any good because people won't be able to locate Kaiser foil?"

"Wellll," Hanno started.

"Heah, you don't concern yourself with that!" Riley admonished me. "You just give us some nice, funny TV spots, and let the agency worry about the distribution. Okay?"

I backed off temporarily. It turned out that the main airtime for these spots would be once a week in the ABC television show *Maverick*, starring James Garner. I remember wondering why a company would buy time on an expensive network show if its foil wasn't in most stores. Years later, I found out that Henry Kaiser played golf with his friend David Reynolds, CEO of Reynolds Wrap, who sponsored some big network show, and it was embarrassing to Kaiser that *he* didn't have a network show *too*. So he ordered the agency to buy some nice highly rated show. They bought *Maverick*. That way, even if nobody could buy his aluminum foil in most stores, he could at least say, "Ahem! I have a TV show too, you know!" when he played golf with David Reynolds. It was "The Emperor's New Foil." He wasn't selling a lot, but at least he had a TV show like the big boys.

Of course, this insight wasn't available to me at the time. But no matter. I decided to take on Mr. Kaiser's distribution problems in the advertising itself, but I sensed it would scare them witless if I brought it up at that point. So I didn't. We settled on a fee to me above and beyond all production costs, to create a TV and radio campaign. Everybody overruled Riley, who thought my fee was high.

"Highway robbery!" he grumbled. "Wheah's youah gun and mask?"

I began working in my head, before they had even filed out of my office.

"Clark Smathers, Kaiser Aluminum Foil Salesman, Faces Life!"

That would be the name of the one-minute soap-opera episodes I'd create for radio, supporting the TV spots. It would be the heartrending story of a poor Kaiser foil salesman who couldn't feed or clothe his family, because the mean old grocers wouldn't stock Mr. Kaiser's foil. Each radio spot, an episode per week, would play in all the major markets across America, many times per day. Each radio commercial would mention the *Maverick* TV show—cross-plugging it—and hopefully pull additional viewers into the TV show. The TV spots would be the animated adventures of the same struggling foil salesman.

The first radio drama started with a throbbing soap-opera theme as the voice of the great radio announcer Jim Ameche (Don Ameche's brother) came in over the music.

**MUSIC:** SOAP OPERA THEME

**ANNOUNCER:** Clark Smathers, Kaiser aluminum foil salesman, faces life. As we join Clark Smathers, veteran, daddy, organizer of Little League teams, it's been another in a series of not-too-successful days with the grocers in his territory.

**SOUND:** DOOR OPENING

**CLARK:** I'm home!

**WIFE:** Hello, Clark! How did it go with the grocers in your territory?

**CLARK:** (SIGH) It was another in a series of not-too-successful days.

**WIFE:** You mean they still haven't agreed to stock Kaiser foil?

**CLARK:** No . . . not to any appreciable extent.

**WIFE:** (SOB) Then this means I won't be able to have my operation!

**CLARK:** Please, let's not discuss it in front of the child.

**CHILD:** (IN A SMALL WISTFUL VOICE) Did you bring me some new shoesies, Daddy?

**CLARK:** Ummm . . . Daddy doesn't have any *money* for shoesies *these* days . . . because the mean old grocers won't stock Daddy's foil.

**CHILD:** But haven't the animated commercials on *Maverick* forced distribution to any appreciable extent?

**CLARK:** Not yet, honey. These things take time.

**CHILD:** But my feet . . . they're so cold!

**CLARK:** Wait! Watch this.

**SOUND:** FOIL CRINKLING

**CLARK:** There you go. You'll have the shiniest feet on the block.

**CHILD:** Whoever heard of making shoesies out of Kaiser foil?

**MUSIC:** UNDER

**ANNOUNCER:** There are *many* uses for Kaiser aluminum foil.

In the next episode, the wife has made curtains in their threadbare house out of Kaiser foil. When the gas company calls to tell her they have to shut off the gas, she delivers this final line on the phone:

**WIFE:** Well . . . if you have to shut it off, you have to shut it off. That's right. It's the house with the shiny curtains.

And so forth.

Meanwhile, on television an animated Clark Smathers walks up to an unsuspecting grocer. He carries a display case reading KAISER FOIL.

**CLARK:** Clark Smathers, Kaiser foil.

**GROCER:** What can I do for you?

**CLARK:** (REACHING INTO HIS CASE, HE WHIPS OUT A GIANT CARTOON MALLET AND SMACKS THE GROCER OVER THE HEAD. *WHAM!*) You can stock a little Kaiser foil for a change. That's what you can do for me!

**GROCER:** (RUBBING HIS HEAD) But I haven't got room on my shelf!

**CLARK:** What's that? No room on the shelf?? (HE WHIPS HIS BRIEFCASE OPEN AND IT EXPLODES INTO A PITCHMAN'S SIDEWALK STAND. A TINY MARCHING BAND WALKS RAPIDLY BACK AND FORTH PLAYING "THE STARS AND STRIPES FOREVER.")

**CLARK:** (OVER THE MUSIC) This is America! There is room for everyone . . . big man, little man, other foil . . . Kaiser foil. That's the American way!

A TINY ROCKET GOES UP AND EXPLODES, AS A MINIATURE AMERICAN FLAG IS RAISED UP A LITTLE FLAGPOLE. ALL THIS IS HAPPENING ABOUT A FOOT IN FRONT OF THE GROCER'S NOSE. WHEN HE SEES THE FLAG, HE SALUTES, AS DOES CLARK.

**CLARK:** You know what I'm going to do? I'm going to make some little one-minute animated commercials, put 'em on *Maverick*, and tell the American people the truth about you! (HE EXITS THE STORE, HITTING THE GROCER OVER THE HEAD ONE LAST TIME WITH A BOX OF KAISER FOIL: *BONK!!* IT FALLS INTO THE GROCER'S HANDS.)

**GROCER:** No! He's not . . . is he?

THE CAMERA ZOOMS IN ON THE KAISER FOIL BOX IN HIS HANDS. FADE OUT.

I flew to San Francisco—where the Kaiser account was handled—about a month later. I had tentatively lined up my friends at Playhouse Pictures to do the animation for Freberg, Ltd., in case Kaiser approved my campaign. They were Ade Woolery, who had founded Playhouse when he broke off from UPA, Bill Littlejohn, who would do the actual animation, and Bill Melendez, the animation director. (Melendez later produced and directed all the Charlie Brown* animation so brilliantly.) But for now, I was armed with only my radio scripts, some television animation storyboards, and my wits. When I walked into the conference room at Young & Rubicam, I was startled to see not only the original three or four men who had hired me, but about thirty other agency people. Art directors and creative men and women jammed the room to capacity. Hanno introduced me, and I began talking.

Even though most of them realized that Kaiser had practically no distribution, I recapped the dilemma so they would better understand the radical approach I was recommending. I put my storyboards up on an easel and began acting them out. Much laughter. Then I read the soap-opera radio scripts. *More* laughter. When I finished, the room exploded with applause and a standing ovation. No audience reaction I had ever received as an entertainer made me feel warmer. After these appreciative creative people filed out of the room, I was left with the original group. Hanno Fuchs was smiling ear to ear and pumping my hand. But Bill Riley looked like he had gone into shock. Finally, he found his voice.

"It's—it's unheard of, doing a thing like this. It's embarrassing to Kaiser, telling everybody they don't have any distribution."

"It's the truth, isn't it?" I asked.

* My son Donavan would later become one of the voices of Charlie Brown for Melendez.

"What's *that* got to do with anything? Look, all you were hired to do was write some funny commercials. I certainly wasn't prepared for anything like *this*."

"I just figured as long as you had a marketing problem . . ."

"You leave the marketing problems to the advertising agency," Riley grumbled, raining on my parade. "Besides . . . it's liable to offend the grocers. It's outrageous!"

Hanno stepped in. "Of course it's outrageous! That's the whole idea! I think it's brilliant. Everybody did. Come on, Bill . . ."

But Riley was on a roll. "It's dangerous!" he told me. Then he leveled his finger at me like a gun. "You didn't go to the Harvard Business School, did you?"

"No, I didn't," I said.

"Well, I was sure of *that*," he snorted. "If you *had*, they would have taught you one of the primary rules of marketing: Advertising cannot force distribution."

Everybody sat there for a moment. I thought about what he had said. Could the man be right? It was true that I had certainly never gone to Harvard or *any* business school. Therefore, I didn't know that advertising could not force distribution. Nobody had ever *told* me that, so I didn't know it.

Suddenly, I realized that Hanno was asking me a question. "I said, would you be willing to go over to the client in Oakland and do your presentation all over again. For Kaiser?"

"*Henry* Kaiser?" I asked.

Everybody laughed at my naïveté but Riley.

"Now, just a minute, Hanno . . ." he said. But Hanno rode over him.

"No, not *Henry* himself, but if we could get some top management people together. The marketing VP, advertising manager, you know." He looked at his watch. It was almost noon. This whole day is etched in my memory step by step. He suggested that I return to my hotel and that if he could arrange a meeting, a car would pick me up and drive us all to the Kaiser building in Oakland.

I returned to the Clift Hotel, in downtown San Francisco, and barely had time to have room service before the car showed up. It was a limousine containing just Hanno, Riley, and another faceless man from Y&R. I climbed in with my scripts and storyboards, and we took off across the Oakland Bay Bridge.

As we went up in the elevator of the huge Kaiser building in Oakland, Hanno reassured me. "These guys will be a pushover," he said. "Just do the same thing you did back at Y&R."

Suddenly, I was ushered into a huge boardroom. Around the table sat maybe nine noncommittal-looking men. A stocky executive rose up from the head of the table, smiling at me. He was Mort Werner, a former NBC television executive, hired away by Kaiser to become his television consultant. (He later returned to NBC to become VP of network programming.)

"Hi, Stan. Welcome to Oakland," Werner said, shaking my hand. "This is Stan Freberg, gentlemen. He's been hired by our agency to create some new commercials for Kaiser foil. God knows we need *something*. Right?" No comment from anybody as the Y&R trio sat down at the table.

I wondered who all these other men were. Could they *all* be concerned with the marketing of Kaiser foil? They could. One of them was Al DeGrassi, advertising manager for the foil. Once again, I launched into my proposed campaign. *This* time there was no appreciative laughter. A few appreciative *smiles* maybe, and a lot of deep-furrowed brows. As I launched into the radio commercials with the poor Kaiser salesman making shoes for his child out of Kaiser foil, Mort Werner started to laugh. It was not particularly contagious. But by the time I finished, they were over their initial shock and had given me what must have been, for them, hearty laughter. *Nervous* laughter, mind you, but hearty. There was no applause, however. I sat down.

Al DeGrassi liked it, with some reservations. A heated debate started up about whether the grocers, not now stocking the foil on their shelves, would be so insulted that they might *never* stock it. I told them it was a calculated risk that Kaiser should take, in my opinion, because the only direction they had to go was up.

"Interesting," somebody said. "You've made us the underdog."

"I didn't *have* to make you the underdog," I told him. "You *are* the underdog."

Riley's eyebrows were shooting up and down at me. *Cool it*! his eyebrow language was telling me. *Be quiet. No need reminding them how poor their position is in the marketplace.* What he really was thinking was probably, *No need reminding them how years of Y&R advertising hasn't made much of a dent.* I overrode the eyebrows.

"If this works right," I said, "We'll have consumers all over America going into grocery stores and demanding Kaiser foil. As a consumer, that would be *my* reaction. I'd go walking into Safeway and demand to know why the only foil I could find was Reynolds Wrap with a teeny space for Safeway's private-brand foil. 'Where's the Kaiser foil?' I'd yell at the store manager. 'You call that a choice? You call this a democracy?' "

In the stunned silence I remember seeing the light go on in eyes around the board table. It was like, "Eureka! Could this thing possibly work?" They had never thought of consumers as a force that might be harnessed on their behalf.

Werner said he thought the concept was brilliant and that in his opinion Kaiser should go ahead with it. There was a long pause. Riley and Hanno had been huddling at the other end of the table.

"Stan," Hanno said, to the loose cannon on the deck, "why don't you go on back to the Clift Hotel. We'll be in touch. Leave the storyboards and scripts. Okay?"

So it was back across the bridge to San Francisco, all by myself this time. I no sooner had walked into my hotel room when the phone rang. It was Hanno.

"Come back to Oakland," he said.

Down in the elevator, into the limo, back across the bridge. The commuter traffic was heavy by this time, which delayed me, and an annoyed Riley was pacing in the Kaiser boardroom, checking his watch. Hanno and the faceless man from Y&R rose as I came in. All the other men were gone now.

Hanno put his hand on my shoulder. "It looks good," he told me. "Werner was able to convince most of them, but you have to do it all over again one more time."

"All over again? Now?" I asked.

"*Right* now. You have to read it for Dusty Rhodes, president of Kaiser Aluminum.

"I thought Henry Kaiser was the president," I said as they all hustled me out of the door toward the elevator.

"Mr. Kaiser is chairman of the board. He lives over in Hawaii," Hanno said. We rode up in the elevator toward the top floor of the Kaiser building.

It's too bad Mr. Rhodes couldn't have been in the meeting too," I remarked.

"Doesn't work that way!" Riley said to the elevator buttons. "You go a level at a time in this business."

Hanno was talking out of the corner of his mouth as though the elevator had ears.

"If Dusty Rhodes approves this, we're in. He reports only to Henry Kaiser." The doors opened into a plushly carpeted foyer, with an executive receptionist who waved us on.

Now we were walking down a very long, dimly lit hall, heading toward a pair of giant mahogany doors, Hanno carrying my storyboards and scripts under his arm. Just before we reached the president's office, the faceless man—without warning—reached out and literally slammed me up against the wall. Everybody stopped in their tracks. He leaned into my face:

"Let's get one thing absolutely straight," he muttered like a Mafia enforcer. "You work for us. Okay?"

The meaning was very clear. He meant that as far as Rhodes was concerned, I was not an outside consultant, but someone from the ranks of Young & Rubicam. It was my first real experience with the long knives of advertising agencies. I felt a chill run through me. Just what I needed to brace me for my third performance of the day.

We walked into a huge executive office, and a portly pleasant-faced man with glasses walked around his desk to greet us. Dusty Rhodes, president of Kaiser Aluminum, was next in command to the great industrialist and founder Henry J. Kaiser, then in Honolulu building his huge Hawaiian Village Hotel. Introductions were made all around, including the implication that I was in the creative department of Y&R.

Once again, I launched into the Clark Smathers campaign after a quick justification for why I had taken this unorthodox approach. Only Rhodes, the three people from Y&R, and I were in the room. We were casually seated around a huge coffee table at one end of his office. As I enacted all the characters in my little drama for the third time that day, nobody was laughing. But out of the corner of my eye, I could see Rhodes smiling broadly. Some progress at least.

When I finished, there was a brief pause. Dusty Rhodes was peering at me with his jaw slightly slack. "You're with Y&R, is that right?" he said.

"Yes, sir," I said.

Then he slowly reached out to shake my hand.

"Congratulations!" he smiled. "That's the first thing they ever showed me that I liked."

After an embarrassed silence, Riley spoke.

"You . . . have no questions about this campaign, sir?"

"Only one," Rhodes said. "How fast can you produce the commercials and get them on the air?"

I told him I thought we could get the animation produced in about eight weeks, and the radio would be ready to ship to the stations at the same time.

"Sooner the better," said Rhodes rising to his feet. We all stood up. Feeling exhilarated, I couldn't help asking one last question. "Are you going to tell Mr. Kaiser about the campaign?" I asked, treading on thin ice. Nobody breathed. Then Dusty Rhodes turned and walked to his huge picture window looking out across the bay toward Hawaii. He took off his glasses and stared into the sun starting to sink into the Pacific. After a very long pause he turned to us and put on his glasses.

"Nnnoooo," he said, "I don't think so."

As we all filed out, he shook my hand once more. "Congratulations again," he smiled.

TWO MONTHS LATER, THE CAMPAIGN STARTED. THE radio spots started nationally, and the TV commercials were dropped into the *Maverick* show, Sunday nights on the ABC network. Y&R and I were able to talk the Kaiser people into letting us buy additional airtime around America so that if viewers didn't happen to see the *Maverick* show, they saw the Kaiser commercials on other shows. Then I made an important last-minute modification to my campaign strategy. I decided that if the grocers themselves were the true stumbling block, and the idea was to get them to come around and give us a break, we might win many of them over if we leveled with them: told them what we were going to do *before* the campaign started.

Bill Riley and the account group at Y&R had mixed emotions about my suggestion.

"It's a very dangerous thing to do," Riley informed me on the phone. "What if the grocers that *do* stock the foil are so offended by the way you've made the grocer the villain, they throw us out of the store?"

"I don't think that'll happen, but what if they do?" I told him. "Hopefully, they'll be offset by the hundreds of new placements of Kaiser foil!"

"Hundreds!" he snorted. "We'll be lucky to get a couple of dozen new placements." Then he reminded me again that advertising couldn't force distribution. I bit my tongue. Then I told him that tipping the grocers off ahead of time was not only the fair and honest thing to do, it would make them feel like they were a part of the whole thing. It was like inviting the enemy in for tea before the battle started. After I hung up in Hollywood, I made the same speech on the phone to several other people at Y&R. I told them I'd make a special little tape just for the grocers, making a joke out of the fact that Kaiser was such an underdog that we'd been forced to do this—all in a self-deprecating humorous way. I told them that the salesmen should gain an audience with the buyers at the grocery chains, then play them the special little message I'd create, followed by playing them the radio and TV spots. They would have to drag along their own portable audio-video equipment.

Finally, Y&R and Kaiser agreed to do it this way. I also talked them into sending little "Grocer Survival Kits." Each grocer would receive in the mail a package containing a cardboard mallet so they could fight back against overzealous Kaiser foil salesmen. It also contained a small first-aid kit to repair bumps on the head. Within a day or two, after the grocer wondered what the heck the point of the survival kit was, the Kaiser salesman would show up and run him the campaign. Then he would tell him if he stocked a little Kaiser foil, we would give him a supply of medals for his clerks to wear on their coats. The medal would glitter, being laminated to quilted Kaiser foil. The medal would read DON'T HIT ME, I'VE GOT IT. When a customer would ask, "You've got *what*?" the clerk could say, "Kaiser foil. Aisle 3."

Freberg, Ltd., produced the finished art for the kit and the medal and shipped it to Y&R. When I got a sample of the final produced kit, it looked great. But there was something wrong with the medal. It didn't have any pizzazz. Then I realized they had eliminated the foil. Instead of glittering on the clerks' coats, the cardboard medal would just . . . be there. Okay, but not nearly as good. Furious, I called Y&R. Everybody passed the buck to Riley.

"We had to cut somewhere," he growled. "This thing was getting out of hand, cost-wise. Foil is expensive!"

I was flabbergasted. I felt like Alice, who had fallen down the rabbit hole where nothing made sense. You would think if there were *anything* Kaiser had an overabundance of, it was foil. All the foil you might want to laminate to cardboard medals if it would help them sell more of the stuff. Right? They had foil stacked in warehouses, up to the wazoo! But it was too late. The medals were printed, Riley told me, and that was that. I was frustrated about the medals but soon cheered up beyond my wildest hopes.

As it turned out, the campaign worked from the very beginning. Although a couple of humorless grocers *did* get mad and took the foil out of their stores, the majority of them around the country laughed at the audacity of the whole thing and gave the salesmen order after order. The new placements of foil across America rejuvenated the sales department at Kaiser Aluminum. One of the greatest benefits to a company when its advertising starts to work after years of struggling to no avail is the tremendous boost to the morale of its employees. When the campaign had forced eleven thousand new outlets for the foil, *Newsweek* did a feature story in its business section, complete with a picture of Clark Smathers slamming the grocer with the mallet. Other national press followed.

Finally a few months later, Y&R admitted to *forty-three thousand* new outlets for Kaiser aluminum foil in stores across America.

In a later phone conversation with Bill Riley, I

couldn't resist a final comment. "I thought you said advertising couldn't force distribution," I said.

"It *can't*," he answered. "Something must have gone wrong."

Just to show you how things work on Madison Avenue: Bill Riley, who should have been demoted for almost torpedoing the Kaiser campaign time after time (in government I believe it's referred to as obstruction of justice), instead was later promoted to a better job in the New York office of Young & Rubicam. Eventually, he became vice chairman of Y&R, until he took his retirement. If I seem unduly harsh on rigid ad executives like Riley (I have met his counterpart a hundred times), it is because I am angered and depressed that people like that in advertising, or any business, stand in the way of progress with horse blinders on their heads. In their rigidity they attempt to thwart anything new that they don't understand. They have held innovative advertising back, whenever they could. Worse, they have impeded the attempts by their creative people to communicate in a more effective way with consumers, on behalf of the products they have been entrusted to sell.

People a lot higher up than Bill Riley were guilty of trying to kill revolutionary approaches to advertising they couldn't understand.

After Kaiser gained all that distribution and I became more or less a hero around the Kaiser building, I was told by a marketing VP how Henry Kaiser finally learned of the radical campaign his company had launched: in front of his TV set. Stretched out with a cool drink in Honolulu one lazy Sunday evening, he proudly watched his *Maverick* show come on. When the set went to black, he sat up in anticipation. This meant his commercial for Kaiser foil was about to come on. He knew what it would be. Since only Kaiser made foil that was "quilted" (a patented process that supposedly made the foil easier to crimp around things—the knowledge of which had meant *zilch* to the grocers, who up to now wouldn't have stocked it if it had been quilted, crocheted, and hand embroidered around the edges, because Reynolds Wrap had gotten in there early and grabbed all the shelf space), his ad agency had created an animated boy: the Kaiser Kid, who galloped around on a horse named Quilty. Henry Kaiser waited now for Quilty the horse to ride onto his TV set.

What he saw instead almost gave him a coronary. A Kaiser foil salesman had walked into a grocery store, pulled out a huge mallet, and slammed the grocer over the head. Kaiser leapt to his feet. What the hell was going on here? When the show resumed, he snatched up the phone and dialed Dusty Rhodes at home. He said he didn't know whose supposedly brilliant idea *this* was, but he wanted it pulled off the air. Rhodes reportedly told him he was sorry, but they couldn't do that. Too much of Kaiser Aluminum's money had been invested in the campaign, and the ship had sailed. He also told him he thought it was going to help gain some much needed distribution. Kaiser reluctantly went along against his better judgment. After he hung up, he probably mixed himself the Mai Tai of the Year.

Later, when the foil had achieved the forty-three thousand new placements in stores, Edgar Kaiser supposedly said to his father, "Well, Dad, what do you think now? Do you still dislike Freberg?"

Henry Kaiser said, "It's not that I dislike Freberg. It's just that I dislike hitting grocers over the head!"

That Christmas I received a Christmas present from Oakland. I opened the two-foot-high box with great anticipation. *These people are going to show their gratitude in some small way,* I thought to myself. How right I was! Inside was a small cardboard replica of the Kaiser building in Oakland. The top of the building read OPEN HERE. Inside were three rolls of Kaiser aluminum foil: the small size, the medium size, and the large economy size. The card read, HAPPY HOLIDAYS FROM KAISER ALUMINUM.

# 18 ✍

## *"If You Can Sell Canned Chow Mein, You Can Sell Anything"* *

SHORTLY AFTER THE SUCCESS OF THE KAISER CAMpaign I was working out of my den at home in Benedict Canyon, when Donna walked in and said she had a man on hold calling from the Canadian woods. She said it was Bud Stefan. He sounded desperate. Bud was a former television producer and an old friend.

I picked up the phone, and the static was terrible. He was calling via shortwave radio from some Canadian lake. I suddenly remembered that Stefan had gone to work for an ad agency, BBD&O. He was sitting at some place called Nakomis Lodge, he said, owned by one of the agency's clients, the president of Chun King Chow Mein. He said he was there with all the agency creative people, and now he wanted me to talk to the client himself. It was hard to hear, and every time he wanted me to

* Bill Andresen.

talk he had to say "Over." But it sounded like he had said that the man's name was Jeno Paulucci. *A strange name,* I thought, *for a man who owns a Chinese food company.*

"Hello, this is Jeno!" someone was yelling into the phone then. "We were wondering if you'd be interested in creating some new radio and television commercials for me, and how much would that be? Over."

I told him it sounded interesting, but that the cost would depend on how big a problem he had, how much time was involved trying to solve it, and how many commercials I created. Over. "I got one hell of a problem," he was shouting. "These guys can't seem to sell my damn chow mein! But I hear you're the best. Look, you're in Hollywood, my company is in Duluth, Minnesota. How about we meet halfway . . . say in Chicago? Over!"

Halfway? Was this guy kidding? Chicago was just down the street from Duluth, so to speak. Beverly Hills was twenty-four hundred miles away. But he agreed to pay all my travel expenses plus a five-thousand-dollar consultant fee for the day in Chicago; so I agreed to go. About that time I felt the need for a really good business-affairs person to handle the business end of my operation. I had been through a couple of people already. Suddenly, I thought of Donna's brother, William Andresen, whose entire background was in the financial world. I managed to talk Bill into coming to work for me for a while to see how he liked it. He flew up from New Orleans and met me in Chicago, just prior to my Chun King meeting. Then the two of us walked into the boardroom of BBD&O's Chicago office. "Just sit back and observe this time out," I had told him. "We'll see how much of a problem they have and take it from there."

I remember that the room was filled with plenty of BBD&O account men and creative people but only one man from Chun King, the president and founder, Mr. Jeno F. Paulucci. After Young & Rubicam and other agencies had led me to believe that one must go through many levels of command before getting to the top man, this was a complete reversal.

Jeno was a totally new kind of client. There was no game playing. No levels. You dealt with the man himself, who cut through red tape like an Italian bullet train. Over the years, as I came to be associated with him—not only with Chun King, but with Jeno's Pizza and other companies he owned—I learned that this was how he always operated. But that day in Chicago Jeno was a revelation: a client who not only hadn't been within a thousand miles of the Harvard Business School, but appeared to be as much of a maverick as I, and like me, he operated mostly on gut instincts.

I recall the exact mood of the agency that day. Was it one of cordiality? Warm best wishes to Freberg there? Adolf Eichmann walking into a B'nai B'rith meeting would have been better received.

Suddenly, they were rolling a series of television commercials for Chun King. They had all been created by the agency BBD&O. As the spots played, I sunk down into my chair in the dark. Each one, it turned out, was worse than the one before. Hard sell, followed by stupid sell. In an embarrassing attempt at humor, an animated announcer leaned over an animated baby in a baby carriage. He asked him what he thought of Chun King. The baby raised up and gave him a loud raspberry, spraying animated saliva all over the announcer's face. The lights came up. I sat there in the silence wondering why all these people were so hostile to me. I hadn't said *anything*. Yet.

I was to find out years later from Bud Stefan that

just before he had called me from the Canadian lodge, Jeno had been ready to fire the agency. They had put various campaign ideas on large cardboard presentation cards they'd lugged all the way to Canada. When they had finished their pitch, Stefan said Jeno ran around the room knocking them off their easels. "I'm going for a quick walk around my lake," he announced. "If you haven't figured out something better than this by the time I get back, you're fired." After he had stormed out, Stefan had said to his agency, "Look, why don't we call in Stan Freberg? We have nothing to lose, and he might save us the account." The agency's creative people reluctantly went along with him, and when a somewhat cooled Jeno came back, Stefan suggested that they call me in.

"Congratulations," Paulucci said. "I never thought you guys were that smart. Get him on the phone!" That's when Stefan had called me.

Now, in Chicago, Jeno leaned forward as the lights came up. "Well?" he asked. "What do you think? That's what the agency has been running."

"You want the truth?" I asked him.

"Damn right I want the truth!" he said. "What do you think I'm paying you for?"

I paused for just a second, then I told him the truth. "Those are without a doubt some of the worst commercials I've ever seen."

Jeno slapped the table. "What did I tell you?" he yelled, endearing me to his agency.

I told him why they didn't work. Especially the feeble attempts at humor. "First of all," I told him, "the baby joke doesn't work because canned chow mein is not something you feed to babies. Humor has to be based somewhat in reality. An announcer just wouldn't ask a baby how he liked your product, so you've lost the audience immediately. And having the baby spit at the announcer was an instant turnoff. Do you guys think that spot is funny?" I asked the agency.

One of them said to me, "Well, no, I don't personally think it's all that funny but"—a shrug—"they might think it's funny."

"No good!" I told him. That's the attitude that's responsible for all the advertising that doesn't work. You can't act like your tastes are one thing and the audience's tastes are another. If you don't like an ad, why should anybody else? And who are 'they'? We're all consumers. We are them, and they are us! That's why I always create commercials for myself first of all. I am the consumer I know best. If I think it's a great commercial, I figure the rest of the people might think so too. I haven't been wrong so far."

When I finished my speech, I looked at Jeno. He was thunderstruck. I got the impression that none of his many advertising agencies had ever said these things to him before. At the end of the meeting I gave him a price for a series of radio commercials, followed by three television spots. He said he'd call me later at my hotel.

As we walked up Michigan Avenue, Bill Andresen said to me, "Well, I don't know if you sold Jeno, but you sold me. If you want me to work for you, I'd be proud to. Today I became a disciple." Bill did come to work for me and stayed for the next twenty-five years.

Meanwhile, that afternoon, Jeno called to say we had a deal. Bill returned to New Orleans to tell his wife Sue and his son Bill, Jr., to get ready to move to California.

The first radio commercial scripts were okayed on the phone by Jeno a couple weeks later, but even that

*Stan Freberg with the Original Cast.* When people ask me to autograph this album for them, I sign it very small, on my cast.

The one and only Billy May (far left)—my arranger/conductor for over thirty years—conducting one of my sessions at Capitol with a typical Billy May band.

A rare shot at a roast honoring Glen Wallichs, founder of Capitol Records, at the Friars Club. Left to right: (standing) Frank Sinatra, Danny Kaye, Gordon MacRae, Nat King Cole; (seated) Glenn Wallichs, Dean Martin, me.

In the studio, going over a script with Donna Freberg, my producer and wife (although not necessarily in that order).

Capitol put out a two-hour album of the best moments from my CBS radio network series, and it won a Grammy.

In front of my offices, Freberg, Ltd., on Sunset Boulevard. It wasn't raining, but you never can tell.

The Great Seal of Freberg, Ltd. (but not very). Saul Bass designed this award-winning letterhead for my company in 1958, and it's still on my stationery today. The Latin translates as: "Art for money's sake."

Bill Andresen, my VP of business affairs for over twenty-five years. For a money man he had a great dry sense of humor.

Sheet music of "Omaha Moon," one of the songs I wrote for "Omaha!," the world's longest radio commercial (six and a half minutes). Capitol put out the commercial as an actual record, and I later conducted the Omaha Symphony performing it.

I was made an honorary chief by the Omaha Indian Tribe, who presented me with this actual peace pipe. It looks like I'm reading the inscription: "Warning: Smoking this actual peace pipe could be dangerous for your health."

At work in my suite at the Algonquin Hotel in 1968, my home away from home to this day. I was born too late to sit with the wits at the Round Table, but I've done a lot of sitting upstairs at the typewriter. *Photo by Burton Berinsky.*

An animation frame from the Kaiser aluminum foil campaign. It won the Venice Film Festival Grand Prix.

CAPITOL FULL DIMENSIONAL STEREO

A SATIRICAL REVUE ESPECIALLY CREATED FOR RECORDS

The daughters of the American Revolution weren't crazy about this album, but a few million others were. It *will* be produced on Broadway. Please stand by.

Jeno Paulucci, founder of Chun King and Jeno's Pizza, and a self-made multi-millionaire, pays off a bet by pulling me in a ricksha down La Cienega Boulevard in Los Angeles.

"Nine out of ten doctors recommend Chun King chow mein."

This Great American Soups spectacular, which I wrote and directed for the H. J. Heinz Co., starred tap dancer Ann Miller and a set straight out of an MGM musical. It won two Clios and a pair of Silver Lions at Cannes. *Photo by Bill Bridges.*

# TODAY THE PITS... TOMORROW THE WRINKLES.

Man examining prune.

Well what do you do with a prune pit once it's in your mouth? Disgusting. There's no way you can get rid of a prune pit, gracefully. That's why Sunsweet has developed *The Pitted Prune.* How do we do that? We do it*. Let's lay our prunes on the table; until now, most people didn't like prunes very much. As a matter of fact there were those who wouldn't touch one with a twenty foot spoon. Apparently they didn't find anything all that appealing about a piece of wrinkled fruit that could knock out a $75.00 inlay. But that's all behind us now. Shake hands with the Pitted Prune; sweet, moist, although still rather badly wrinkled. One thing at a time please. Today the pits... tomorrow the wrinkles. SUNSWEET MARCHES ON!!!

* Does International Olive tell United States Cherry?

This is the print ad based on the Clio-winning Sunsweet Prune TV commercial. ("Tales of the Prune People" will be discussed in my next book.)

Sid Caesar, in one of the commercials I produced for Stanley Kramer's *It's a Mad Mad Mad Mad World*. I had the stars fighting in my TV spot, just like they did in the movie. *Photo by Bill Bridges.*

My children, Donavan Stanley (left) and Donna Jean Freberg (right), sit still for a more or less formal portrait with their dad in 1988. They both inherited my satiric sense of humor, I'm proud to say. *Photo by Harry Langdon.*

hadn't been quick enough for him. As I sat at the typewriter early one morning, lost in thought, my housekeeper, Frances, rushed into my den.

"Mr. Freberg! Some crazy man!"

"What?" I asked, standing up quickly.

"Some crazy man is buzzing the house in an airplane!"

It was true that I had noticed, in the back of my consciousness, the sound of a small airplane getting louder, then drifting away. But when I'm writing, a Sherman tank could drive through the living room, and I would be oblivious.

I rushed outside with Frances.

Over my house a small plane was coming around for another pass. As it came right over the top of my palm trees, I saw a long banner streaming out the back of the plane. STAN! JENO IS WAITING! it read.

Donna and I drove to La Quinta, the Palm Springs resort, for a three-day weekend to get away from it all before we went in to record. But as I lay in the sun, I began to think to myself: Would those radio scripts really make anybody pay attention to a canned chow mein? I began to give my own speech back to myself. *The commercials are okay, but . . . since when is just* OKAY *good enough*? Jeno had approved these commercials based on the running gag that a man named Jeno Paulucci owned a Chinese food company. But would people find the humor in that sufficient reason to go out and buy a can? Would I? Maybe. But why not do something that would be a blockbuster? *Really* get people's attention, for this invisible little product? I considered the environment into which my commercials would be dropped. At that time there was so little truth in American advertising as to be hardly noticeable.

Fraudulent claims and occasionally outright lies ran rampant. The Federal Trade Commission was nailing people left and right. Even Campbell's Soup was cited by the FTC—for hiding clear glass marbles in the bottom of their soup bowls in magazine ads so that the few scant vegetables would be forced nearer the surface, creating a false "chock full of vegetables" look.

Libby Owens Glass and its agency, in rehearsing a demonstration of their new "glare proof" windshield, determined that the TV lights created too much of a glare; so they *removed* the windshield altogether.

ANNOUNCER: Now! From Libby Owens . . . a glare-proof windshield! See? No glare!

The commercial ran for a long time before the FTC cracked down, making Libby Owens the creator of the world's first "open-air windshield." At any rate, I reasoned, any advertiser who did something really *honest* in a commercial would shine like a beacon.

What I decided to do for Jeno, instead of the scripts that had been approved, would utilize a favorite ploy of mine called "More honesty than the client had in mind."

His marketing people had showed me research saying that only 5 percent of the people in the USA had ever eaten Chun King chow mein. I figured that left 95 percent who *hadn't* eaten the product. Right? The thing to do seemed obvious to me.

CHORUS: (SINGING WITH ORCHESTRA)
*Ninety-five percent of the people in the USA*
*Are buying Chun King chow mein . . .*

FREBERG: (BLOWS A POLICE WHISTLE TO STOP THEM) Hold it please—that's not exactly true! Only *five* percent of the people are buying it. Ninety-five percent have never bought a single can.

**MAN:** Uhhh, you want us to *say* that?

**FREBERG:** Why not? Lay it on the line. Let's have a little "truth in advertising" for a change.

**MAN:** Okay.

**CHORUS:** *Correction,*
*Ninety-five percent of the people in the USA*
*Are* not *buying Chun King chow mein.*

**FREBERG:** That's better.

**CHORUS:** *It could be that they don't like the label,*
*Or simply think, it isn't gonna be very good,*
*But should that*
*Ninety-five percent of the people ever try Chun King,*
*They're gonna eat Chun King chow mein*
*For the rest of their life.*

**MUSIC:** OUT

**FREBERG:** Wouldn't that get a little monotonous?

**MAN:** Okay.

**CHORUS:** *For the rest of the week.*

**FREBERG:** How about . . . "occasionally"?

**MAN:** (SIGHING) Do you want to add anything else?

**FREBERG:** Well . . . just a little soy sauce maybe.

**MUSIC:** TAG

I called Bud Stefan at BBD&O in Hollywood and told him I had a better commercial. "Listen to this!" I said.

"A little controversial, maybe, but pure Freberg," he told me. "I'll have Jeno call you so you can read it to him."

I waited for his call. Finally, Stefan rang me back. He sounded sick. "Jeno's gone moose hunting in Canada and can't be reached. Meanwhile, our airdate is in two weeks! You'd better record the scripts he okayed."

"Not a chance," I told him. "I'm sold on this commercial now. That's what I want you to put on the air."

To Bud Stefan's credit, he put his neck on the line and backed me up on behalf of BBD&O, and approved the increased budget. A few days later, we recorded it with Billy May's orchestra, naturally, and Jud Conlon's singers. I played the guy who kept insisting on honesty, and the shocked man was played by Byron Kane. The advertising manager for Chun King flew out and walked up and down all night looking sick. His name was Tom Scanlon, and working for Jeno must have been a challenge. He knew Jeno was moose hunting and had not heard this new outrageous commercial, which was why he looked kind of green. "Are you okay?" Donna kept asking him. "There's a couch in the booth if you want to lie down."

Three days later, Jeno came back from Canada. He put the commercial on his machine and played it. Then he started yelling. He fired BBD&O, fired Tom Scanlon, and then called me on the phone. He told me he hated the new commercial. He told me he wanted me to create a new commercial. If I didn't like the one he approved originally, fine, but he was not going on the air with the 95-percent commercial! Period. Create a new one, he demanded.

"No, I'm not going to do that," I told him.

"Why?" he said.

"Because," I said, "if you don't like this, you won't like anything I do. This is my best shot."

"Hold on a minute," he said. Then I heard him put the phone down, go across the room, and play the commercial again. In a minute he came back to the phone.

"Telling everybody that 95 percent of the people are not buying my product is so—*embarrassing*!" he said. "Let me ask you this: Would you buy 90 percent?" I told him, "No. Ninety percent is no good. It has to be *95* percent."

"Why?" he demanded.

I said, "Because it's the truth."

He finally reconsidered and agreed to put the commercial on the air. I also insisted that he rehire Tom Scanlon and his agency. Before he hung up, he made me a bet. He said that if *that* commercial worked, he'd pull me in a Chinese ricksha up La Cienega Boulevard in Hollywood. Two days later, the commercial went on the air all over America.

Within three months sales were up nationally 25 percent. Jeno came out to Hollywood, rented a ricksha, and said, "Get in." He padded along block after block as motorists honked at him, and I sat back watching this multimillionaire pay off his debt. Finally, I said, "Enough already. Pull over, before you have a heart attack."

Jeno Paulucci became such a convert that he came to loathe normal advertising almost more than I did. He has been my friend and client for nearly three decades. One of my favorite Chun King TV spots involved a pseudo-hard-sell spot kidding "medical" endorsements. "Nine out of ten doctors," said the announcer, "recommend Chun King chow mein." The camera pulled back to reveal ten doctors in white coats. Nine were Chinese, and one was Caucasian.

# 19

## *Green Chri$tma$: "Deck the Halls with Advertising"*

ALTHOUGH ADVERTISING WAS TAKING UP A GREAT deal of my time by now, I still continued to work as a recording artist and performer. I appeared on television as often as I had time to do so, guesting on *The Tonight Show, Ed Sullivan, The Colgate Comedy Hour, The Frank Sinatra Show,* and the *NBC Comedy Hour,* to name a few. Frequently a hand puppet I had created worked with me. He was a small green alien who always regarded me suspiciously from a spaceship next to me. His name was Orville, and he made a great many caustic comments about the earth, from the point of view of a resident of the moon. It also allowed me to keep my "hand in" as a puppeteer. Orville still pops down from the moon from time to time and visits me on television.

Periodically, I would go into the Capitol Tower and record. One release in particular raised serious hackles up and down Madison Avenue. Many people in advertising couldn't understand why I would run the risk of offending some of the very advertisers who might hire me to create commercials in order to make my point as a satirist. If they wondered that, they didn't know anything about how the true satirist's mind works. We don't worry about things like that. You take your shots, and let the chips fall where they may. Even if it's on your head. Besides, almost everything I had done in advertising was a satire of sorts on the medium. The new humorous form I had created flew in the face of the traditional way to reach consumers. Nevertheless, with this record some people thought I had stepped over some kind of line in the world of business. As my friend the author and Associated Press columnist Bob Thomas put it: "You struck a nerve, Doctor!"

I certainly did.

"Green Chri$tma$" was probably the most controversial recording I ever made. All my life I had been disturbed by advertising's increasingly blatant intrusion into Christmas. True, my having been raised as a Christian, in a minister's home, was mostly responsible for my feelings about it, but once I began working as a professional advertising person around people in agencies and clients, I suddenly realized that the overcommercialization simply didn't have to be. It was a terrific revelation to me. These people had an *option*. If a company wanted to tie some product into Christmas that just didn't fit or that was grossly out of place, it was the job of its advertising agency to talk them out of it. If the *agency* was the one who had dreamed up ways of lashing some extraneous product into the holiday—say, dog food or underarm deodorant (any moment now we'll hear, "Christmas is a stressful time: Never let 'em see you sweat")—why then, it's the client's job to talk the *agency* out of it. Client and agency should save each other from themselves. Why? Because it is the ethical thing to do.

Never mind that Christmas started out as a remembrance of the birth of Jesus and the gifts brought to the Christ child in Bethlehem. Or that the essence of Christmas at its root level is simply to love and to do unto others as you would have them do unto you. The issue goes far beyond the religious aspects of the thing. What we are talking about here is "taste." Simple good taste, from a purely secular standpoint. I have no quarrel with companies advertising children's toys under Christmas trees, or facial cosmetics, or books, or cassette tapes, or luggage, or clothes to wear—things one might normally give as presents to one's family or friends—even food products, if they seem to be appropriate for Christmas. Guidelines should be apparent to any thinking human being. But unfortunately, as we are all only too painfully aware, blatant Christmas advertising has become as out of control as the proliferation of nuclear weapons.

As Christmas drew near in the last days of the fifties, I was appalled once again by the unfathomable taste of giant companies devising still new ways of tying their products into the holiday.

On millions of billboards and in full-page magazine ads, Santa Claus was seen climbing into a chimney with a full bag of . . . toys? Not a chance. Cartons of Lucky Strike cigarettes were peeking out of the top of his sack and overflowing it. American Tobacco's idea of Christmas giving. Another company, Coca-Cola, had decided years before to claim the icon of Santa for themselves and have Santa drinking a bottle of Coke after his hard Christmas work. THE PAUSE THAT REFRESHES, it said in a banner headline just under his beard, followed by their logo. Were they declaring that not only Coke, but Santa himself, were trademarks of the Coca-Cola Company, Atlanta, Georgia? Hard to tell.

At any rate everybody had talked for years about the overcommercialization of Christmas, but I hadn't noticed anybody doing anything about it. I started thinking about doing something about it, and what finally sent me into action was a magazine ad run in places like *Newsweek* and *Time,* showing a family coming down in their pajamas and robes on Christmas morning. As the mother, children, and dog look on in wonder, the father hovers back a bit on the stairs, a proud look on his face. There, under the tree, is a brand new set of five tubeless tires. Tires? The boy was expecting a bicycle, but no matter. These tires are a much niftier gift. Maybe Dad will let him help jack up the family car and put them on! Good tires on a car are very important. But talk to me about that during the other eleven months of the year, okay?

That tire company may think I'm just being flip here, and I am. But give me a break. When was the last time you came down on Christmas morning and discovered a set of tires under your tree? Did the tire tycoons think that anybody could possibly relate to that ad? What was being smoked by the people who came up with the concept, to say nothing of the ad manager at the tire company who approved it? The answer to these and other questions may never be answered. But one thing is for sure—those tires ended up on my record of "Green Chri$tma$."

Another ad that gave me pause at that time was a Jell-O Christmas layout from General Foods in all the magazines. A pear tree was laden with Jell-O, and *nothing else*. It was decorated with a different box of Jell-O on every branch. They apparently had decided it was a bit much and added a lone partridge on top. But under the tree was, you guessed it, nothing but different-colored Jell-O molds. Down below, the copy read, as close as I can recall:

> *On the first day of Christmas,*
> *My true love gave to me:*
> *Two lemon Jell-Os,*
> *Three grapes a singing,*
> *Four raspberries cooling . . .* (etc.)

I wonder if the wife of the marketing VP of General Foods' Jell-O Division ever tied boxes of Jell-O to her Christmas tree branches: "Yes . . . we're having a different kind of tree this year. Do you love it?"

Of course, when I sat down to write "Green Chri$tma$," I had to try to drain off enough of my outrage in order to be entertaining enough to make my point. As I have said, outrage in its natural state is not too salable. The hard part comes in covering the social message with the candy coating of humor. Otherwise, you end up as just another crackpot preaching on a soapbox, and I'm getting dangerously close to doing that right now. I'd better just tell you how "Green Chri$tma$" went.

I was assisted by the great Billy May, who arranged my original music. We had a huge studio orchestra, a fine cast of actors, and my friend Jud Conlon arranged the songs for twenty-four voices. After you read the script—which is not as good as hearing it, but you'll get the idea—I'll tell you of the problems I had with Capitol Records before it was released. I played the part of Scrooge.

**SCROOGE:** (SINGING) *Bah, humbug, everybody.*
**CHORUS:** *Good morning, Mr. Scrooge!*

**SCROOGE:** *Well, the meeting will come to order, if you please. Are all the advertising people represented here?*

**CHORUS:** *Everyone except Amalgamated Cheese!*

**MUSIC:** OUT

**SCROOGE:** Well, if they're not here for the Christmas pitch, I can't help them find new ways of tying their product in to Christmas. That's why I'm chairman of this board! Let's hear it for me!

**CHORUS:** Hear, hear!

**SCROOGE:** All right, Abercrombie, what are your people up to?

**ABERCROMBIE:** Ahhh, same thing as every year. Fifty thousand billboards showing Santa Claus pausing to refresh himself with our product.

**SCROOGE:** Mmmmm, hmmm, well, I think the public has come to expect that and . . .

**ABERCROMBIE:** That's right. It's become tradition!

**SCROOGE:** You there, Crass, uhh, I suppose your company's running the usual magazine ads showing cartons of your cigarettes peeking out of the top of Santa's sack?

**CRASS:** Better than that! *This* year we have him *smoking* one.

**SCROOGE:** Um-hmmm . . .

**CRASS:** Yes. We've got Santa a little more rugged, too. Both sleeves rolled up and a tattoo on each arm. One of 'em says "Merry Christmas."

**SCROOGE:** What does the other one say?

**CRASS:** "Less tar!"

**SCROOGE:** Great stuff!

**CRATCHET:** But Mr. Scrooge . . .

**SCROOGE:** What? Who are you?

**CRATCHET:** Bob Cratchet, sir. I've got a little spice

company over in East Orange, New Jersey. Do I *have* to tie my product in to Christmas?

**SCROOGE:** What do you mean?

**CRATCHET:** Well, I was just going to send cards out showing the three wise men following the Star of Bethlehem . . .

**SCROOGE:** I get it! And they're bearing your spices. Now that's perfect.

**CRATCHET:** No, no . . . no product *in* it. I was just going to say, "Peace on Earth . . . Good Will Toward Men."

**VOICES:** MUMBLING IN BACKGROUND

**MAN:** Well, that's a peculiar slogan!

**SCROOGE:** Old hat, Cratchet! That went out with button shoes! You're a businessman . . . Christmas is something to take advantage of!

**MUSIC:** PUNCTUATES

**SCROOGE:** A red and green bandwagon to jump on!

**MUSIC:** PUNCTUATES

**SCROOGE:** A sentimental shot in the arm for sales! Listen!

**MUSIC:** CYMBAL CRASH

**CHORUS:** *Deck the halls with advertising,*
*Fa la la la la la la la la.*
*While you can be enterprising,*
*Fa la la la la la la la la.*
*On the fourth day of Christmas,*
*My true love gave to me*
*Four bars of soap,*
*Three cans of peas,*
*Two breakfast foods,*
*And some toothpaste on a pear tree!*
*On the fifth day of Christmas,*
*My true love gave to me . . .*

**SCROOGE:** *Five tube-less tires!*

**CHORUS:** *Fo-ur quarts of gin,*
*Three ci-gars,*
*Two cig-ar-ettes,*
*And some hair tonic on a pear tree!*
(TEMPO CHANGES ROMANTICALLY)
*Chest-nuts roasting . . .*

**ANNOUNCER:** Sayyyy, Mother, as sure as there's an *X* in Christmas, you can be sure those are Tiny Tim Chestnuts roasting. Tin-y Tim Chestnuts are full-bodied . . . longer lasting! This visible shell . . .

**SOUND:** KNOCK-KNOCK

**ANNOUNCER:** . . . protects the nut! Now with X-K 29 added, for people who can't roast after every meal.

**GIRL TRIO:** *Tin-ee Tim! Tin-ee Tim!*
*Chest-nuts all the way!*

**ANNOUNCER:** Tin-y Tims roast hot . . . like a chestnut ought! And . . . they are (ECHO) mild, mild, mild, mild.

**ORCHESTRA:** PUNCTUATES

**CHORUS:** *Deck the halls with advertising,*
*Fa la la la la la la la la.*
*'Tis the time for merchandising,*
*Fa la la la la la la la la.*
*Profit never needs a reason,*
*Fa la la la la la la la la.*
*Get the money, it's the season,*
*Fa la la la la la la la la!*

**SCROOGE:** Words to live by, Cratchet!

**CRATCHET:** For *you,* maybe. Can't you just wish someone merry Christmas, for the pure joy of doing it?

**SCROOGE:** Why? What's the percentage in that? Let me show you how to make Christmas work for you!

**CHORUS:** *We wish you a merry Christmas,*

*We wish you a merry Christmas,*
*We wish you a merry Christmas,*
*And please buy our beer!*

**SCROOGE:** There you go, Cratchet! That's Christmas with a purpose.

**CRATCHET:** I know, but wait a minute. Don't you guys make enough profit the other eleven months? Christmas comes but once a year.

**SCROOGE:** *Humph!* Funny thing you should bring that up. That's exactly the point I was about to make. Hit it, boys!

**SCROOGE:** *Christmas comes but once a year,*
*So you better make hay while the snow is falling,*
*That's opportunity calling you!*

**CHORUS:** *Rub your hands, December's here,*
*What a wonderful time to be*
*Glad and merry!*

**SCROOGE:** *Just so you're mercenary too!*

**CHORUS:** *Buy an ad and show all the toys,*
*Show all the toys up on the shelf,*

**SCROOGE:** *Just make sure that you get a plug,*
*You get a plug,*
*In for yourself!*

**SCROOGE AND CHORUS:**
*Christmas comes but once a year,*
*So you better cash in,*
*While the spirit lingers,*
*It's slipping through your fingers,*
*Boy! Don't you realize*
*Christmas can be such a*
*Monetary joy!*

**CRATCHET:** Well, I guess you fellows will never change.

**SCROOGE:** Why should we? Christmas has two *s*'s in it, and they're both dollar signs.

**CRATCHET:** Yeah, but they weren't there to begin with.

**SCROOGE:** Eh?

**CRATCHET:** The people keep hoping you'll remember. But you never do.

**SCROOGE:** Remember what?

**CRATCHET:** Whose birthday we're celebrating.

**SCROOGE:** Well, ahem . . . don't get me wrong. The story of Christmas, in its simplicity, is a good thing —I'll buy that. It's just that we know a good thing when we see it.

**CRATCHET:** But don't you realize Christmas has a significance, a meaning.

**SCROOGE:** A sales curve! Wake up, Cratchet, it's later than you think.

**CRATCHET:** I know, Mr. Scrooge, I know.

**CHORUS:** *On the first day of Christmas,*
*The advertising's there, with*
*Newspaper ads,*
*Billboards too,*
*Business Christmas cards,*
*And commercials on a pear tree . . .*
*Jingles here, jingles there,*
*Jingles all the way.*
*Dashing through the snow,*
*In a fifty-foot coup-e*
*O'er the fields we go,*
*Selling all the way . . .*
*Deck the halls with advertising,*
*What's the use of compromising,*
*Fa la la la la la la la.*

**MUSIC:** AS TRADITIONAL HYMNS ATTEMPT TO BREAK THROUGH THE MUSICAL ENDING, IT BUILDS TO A CRESCENDO. WE HEAR "JINGLE BELLS" PUNCTUATED WITH THE SOUND OF A CASH REGISTER

RINGING UP SALES. ON THE LAST NOTE OF THE MUSIC, WE HEAR MONEY DROPPING IN AND THE CASH REGISTER SLAMMING SHUT!

I was in New York when a call came in from a man named Lloyd Dunn. He was the new president of Capitol. (Alan Livingston had recently left for the executive suites of NBC television.)

Dunn was a very square man from the world of marketing. If he had any sense of humor, he kept it well hidden under a rock. He also did not share my sense of moral outrage that Christmas had deteriorated into a sell-a-thon. He was calling now to tell me that on the advice of legal and many other people at Capitol he was pulling "Green Chri$tma$" off release.

I asked to speak to my A&R man, Ken Nelson.

"Ken has been overruled on this one," he barked. "This is a very offensive recording."

"Who is it offensive to?" I asked.

"Everybody in the world of business!" he said. "You'll offend everybody in advertising!"

"Not everybody," I said. "Just the ones who *should* be offended."

"One thing is for sure," he told me, "if we released 'Green Chri$tma$,' you'd never work again in the advertising business."

I said that was one of the hazards of being a satirist.

"Well, I'm *personally* offended by this record," he told me. "I came out of marketing, and I think this thing is in poor taste!"

"Haven't you got it all backwards?" I asked him. "It's the things I attacked that are in poor taste. The thought here is that the people who have used Christmas as merely a hook to sell products *will* be so shocked that they may rethink the whole thing."

"Capitol Records itself is guilty of the very things you attacked," he said.

"Go back and listen again," I told him. "You missed the point. I never said anything about toys, records . . ."

"Well, be that as it may," he told me, "we're killing the record."

"That being the case," I told him sadly, "I'd like to be released from my contract. This is the last straw. You people are keeping me from being able to make a living as a recording artist." He said he was sorry I felt that way, and we hung up.

I immediately called my friend Norman Granz, the jazz entrepreneur, and told him of my problems with Capitol. Granz had told me in the past that he wished I were recording for *his* record label, Verve Records.* He told me he would be happy to put out "Green Chri$tma$," without even hearing it. My name on it was enough for him, he said. I called Dunn back at Capitol and told him I wished to buy the master and take it to Verve Records, who would be honored to put it out.

Another long pause. Then Dunn said he'd call me back at my hotel room. Through all this, I had been unable to reach Glenn Wallichs, now Capitol's chairman. He was in Europe. Finally, a call came back from Dunn. Capitol had reconsidered and would put out my Christmas recording after all.

"We want you here on Capitol," Dunn told me, laying on the charm. "This is your home."

"And you *will* release 'Green Chri$tma$'?" I said.

"With just two very small changes," he told me.

"And they are . . . ?"

* Today, Norman Granz is, among other things, one of the world's foremost collectors of the works of Picasso. His jazz record label is now called, appropriately, Pablo Records.

"Take out any mention of whose birthday we're celebrating, and cut the cash-register sound effect off the end," he said. "Okay?"

I could hardly believe my ears.

"Noooooooooo way!" I told him.

I refused to become a victim of such censorship. I said to Dunn, "I've had it! I can release it as is with no cuts whatsoever on a different record label."

"Hold it," Dunn said. "I'll call you back."

He was stonewalling, but the next day he called and threw in the towel. He said they would release it as is against his better judgment.

Capitol sneaked "Green Chri$tma$" out under the door that first year, with no attendant publicity whatsoever. I finally bought an ad and paid for it out of my own pocket.

Here was a record that truly "escaped" from the Capitol Tower. The reaction from the advertising world was a small explosion, as was to be expected. I was attacked on the editorial pages of *Advertising Age* and *M.A.C.* magazine (before it was called *Adweek*). Even the *Los Angeles Times,* which subsists mostly on ads, blasted me in an editorial on Christmas Day. The editorial writer later sheepishly admitted he hadn't even heard my record, but he'd *read* about it. No wonder he missed the whole point.

If a few critics didn't understand it, most of the public did. The mail was 90 percent favorable. I got letters of praise and gratitude from bus drivers and senators, housewives and governors. The favorable responses from the religious community ranged from Protestants and Catholics to rabbis. Apparently, I had sent out a message that had cut across all boundaries.

A columnist with the *San Francisco Chronicle* reported that "Stan Freberg was in Gumps the other day spending some of his artist's royalties from 'Green Chri$tma$.' Freberg is a great one to talk about other people making money off of Christmas."

When I told the columnist that I had already donated my artist royalties from my record to the Hemophilia Foundation, he apologized with a retraction.

That first year the record was played on the air in New York City only twice—both times by the same disc jockey, Martin Block. He was promptly told by the sales department, "If you play that again, you're fired!"

In Los Angeles my friend at KMPC, Stanley Spiro, told me that they were playing it, but they had to be careful how they programmed it. Blatant Christmas advertisers who figured "the shoe fit" refused to pay for their commercials if they were positioned within fifteen minutes of my record. "The Freberg record negates our message," they told the station.

I had struck a nerve. I was set for an interview on the Los Angeles station, KCBS-TV, about "Green Chri$tma$," during which they planned to play excerpts from the recording. At the last minute I was "pulled" from the lineup by the station manager Robert Wood, who later became president of CBS. "Why was I removed from the show?" I asked him, point-blank.

Wood told me. "The record is sacrilegious. I'm a very staunch Catholic."

I was flabbergasted. "Sacrilegious?" I asked. "Have you heard this record?"

No," he said. "But I don't *need* to hear it. I heard all about it."

A few years later, *Time* came to me. They were doing an essay on the overcommercialization of Christmas. The writer, Barbara Wilkins, told me that "Green

Chri$tma$" was the focal point of the whole story. "You were just ahead of your time," she said. She interviewed me for a full day. The essay was to run in the Christmas issue. On Christmas Day I opened the magazine. There was no essay at all. Next day I called her at *Time* and asked what had happened. "The sales department of *Time* put pressure on the editors," she said. "At the last minute, they killed the essay."

Talk about striking a nerve.

Although I had been warned by many people that I had burned my bridges behind me in advertising, the irony is that within six months of the record's release, two of the companies I had harpooned on the record actually came to me and asked me to create campaigns for them. One—Marlboro Cigarettes—I turned down. (I was turning cigarette accounts down long before it became fashionable.) The other—Coca-Cola—I accepted. They had come to me because they had been stuck behind Pepsi-Cola in the Los Angeles market for a long time and Joe Murphy, president of Murphy Associates—the agency that handled the L.A. bottling company—thought I might help pull his client out of a slump. The television, radio, outdoor, and newspaper campaign I created to help them introduce king-size Coca-Cola was built around the line "Drink big!" And that's just what people did. The campaign moved them from one-fifth share of the Southern California market to one-third share, a position they hadn't enjoyed for ten years.

One spring day, resting up from the cola wars, Murphy told Donna and me that the chairman and owner of the Coca-Cola Bottling Company of Los Angeles had invited us for cocktails. He wanted to meet the man who had created the Coke campaign that had done "wonderful things for his bottling company." (For his *wallet* is what he meant, since he was the principal stockholder.) The gentleman's name was Stanley Barbee, and when we drove up to his home behind a huge white wall in Beverly Hills, we discovered that it was the same beautifully authentic Spanish house we had admired many times as we drove by. Amazing.

When his housekeeper ushered us in, we found Barbee smiling up from his beam-ceilinged Barcelona living room. He ambled up the tile stairs to the entry hall with his hand outstretched. "Well, well, so this is the young genius who sold all that Coke for me!" he said. Then he kissed Donna's hand. We told him how much we had admired his home from the outside, and he gave us a brief tour. Then we sat down and had a glass of wine with the eccentric tycoon, who looked a bit like W. C. Fields.

"Speaking of interesting architecture," I remember asking him, "how is it that your offices downtown are shaped just like a ship?" The unique Coke building was indeed constructed like a huge concrete sailing vessel, complete with portholes, masts, teakwood decks, railings, bulwarks, companionways, and a captain's cabin on the top deck where Barbee had his office. He cackled a kind of bad little boy laugh and told me the inside story. He said that for many years he had been in the habit of holding board-of-directors meetings aboard his yacht, a few miles off the coast of Malibu. Then the government ruled that directors meetings on the high seas were not valid. He was furious, he said. "Big brother telling me what I can and can't do!" So he commissioned architect Robert Derrah to design a new Coca-Cola building in downtown Los Angeles in the shape of a ship. This way he could still hold his directors meetings on a yacht of sorts. The block-long Coca-Cola schooner has floated there on Central Avenue since 1936, as if cast up by a giant tidal wave onto the asphalt shores of downtown Los Angeles. Her concrete prow buffeted by decades of carbon monoxide and the bewildered stares of passing motorists, the building has survived countless earthquakes and attempts to tear it down in the name of progress. It was finally declared a historical landmark by the state of California, and still houses Coca-Cola in L.A. But that day, Barbee told us that he was retiring to Hawaii and was thinking of selling his Spanish house. Donna and I sneaked a glance at each other. We had been house-hunting for months and once, when we had pointed the house out to a real estate woman, she had told us it was owned by an eccentric man who would *never* sell. She was halfway correct. Now it sounded like fate to me, and I offered to buy it on the spot. Barbee walked around thinking it over, while pointing out the fortress-like walls, some of which were four feet thick. After a bit of bartering, we agreed on a price and shook on it. A few days later we bought it. I am writing this from the library of that house, where I have lived and written ever since.

One of the first things I wrote in this room was an album I recorded that created not only additional controversy but an army of fans. This loyal following continues to this day and never ceases to astound me. But let me flash forward a bit.

# 20 ✍

## *"Stan Freberg Modestly Presents . . . the United States of America!"*

In 1985 the actor Martin Sheen introduced me, and I walked to center stage of the Opera House at the Kennedy Center, in Washington, D.C. With Lorne Greene playing straight man, I recreated a moment from a record album of mine called *Stan Freberg Presents the United States of America.* It was the scene just before the first Thanksgiving dinner, where a politician realized for the first time that a minority group—Indians for example—could be utilized as a political pawn. Then, in front of an audience of black-tied Washington society, I sang the song that climaxes the scene: "Take an Indian to Lunch This Week." My album—a satirical account of the history of America according to Freberg—has created a true cult following over the years since it was first released in 1961, at about the same time that my Chun King commercials were becoming a success.

One of the fans of this album and especially this

song happens to be an American Indian tribal leader named Peter MacDonald, chairman of the Navaho nation. He had asked me to take part and to sing at this very social event, "The Night of the First Americans." The evening was a tribute to American Indians, and nearly every tribe was represented. Among other things, the event helped raise money for Indian scholarships. The first chorus of the song goes like this:

> *Take an Indian to lunch this week*
> *Show him we're a regular bunch this week*
> *Show him we're as liberal as can be*
> *Let him know he's almost as good as we*
> *Make a feathered friend feel fed this week*
> *Overlook the fact he's red this week*
> *Let him share our Quaker Oats*
> *'Cause he's useful when he votes*
> *Take an Indian to lunch . . .*

And so on.

MacDonald told me he had worn out three albums. That the head Navaho, and indeed people from Indian tribes all over America, are fans of this album does not surprise me. But the fact that many teachers across the country from elementary to college level use it as a teaching aid to help make American history more interesting to their classes comes as a lovely surprise indeed. I must say that this use never occurred to me when I was writing it. The history teacher I was saddled with in high school simply managed to make United States history about as stimulating as a government brochure on the boll weevil, and I decided one day to see if I couldn't make history more interesting to *myself* at least. The result was this album about American history, which I created in a musical form, with original songs. Teachers tell me that they play my album on the first day of their new class each year, and all year long the kids feel like these historical characters, George Washington, Thomas Jefferson, and Betsy Ross, for example, are not only people they can relate to, but seem more like personal friends.

Since it was first released, fans have sprung up all over the world, from all walks of life, from all age groups, and demolishing all demographic boundaries: cab drivers to presidential cabinet memebers, waiters to university presidents, college kids to United States congressmen and senators. I have been approached in the airports of the world by fourteen-year-old boys, eighty-year-old women and yuppies, by CEOs of giant corporations, rock musicians, and nuclear physicists—all of whom proceed to quote verbatim from various parts of my album.

Upon the Beatles' first arrival in America, I was introduced to them at a press reception, only to discover that George Harrison knew most of my records by heart. And that John Lennon and Paul McCartney were also fans of this album. In a 1985 interview in *Playboy* magazine, Paul McCartney was asked from whence the Beatles got their wry sense of humor.

He answered that it probably came from listening to records by Lenny Bruce and Stan Freberg.

During the filming of the movie *Jaws,* the Universal Pictures crew endured long delays on Martha's Vineyard, waiting for the fog to lift so that shooting could resume. According to a *Time* magazine cover story on *Jaws,* Steven Spielberg, the director of the movie, and his star Richard Dreyfuss made the time pass "by singing Stan Freberg songs like 'Take an Indian to Lunch This Week.' "

I wrote the lyrics and music, but I had some great help on the album. My longtime friend Billy May did all the brilliant musical arrangements and conducted the orchestra, Jud Conlon wrote the vocal arrangements, and Ken Sullet helped write the sketches. Most of the creative work was done in my Beverly Hills home, a rather large, rambling Spanish house, where I have written most of my things over the years. The house is not actually all that huge, but Sullet, viewing it as at least a minicastle, promptly dubbed it Stan Simeon after the William Randolph Hearst abode.

One Christmas Ken gave me a sled on which the word ROSEBUD was painted. (Just like the sled in the movie *Citizen Kane,* a thinly disguised story of Hearst's life.) The sled sits in front of my fireplace as I write this.

Capitol Records was getting ready to do its usual press things to announce the release of this album, but I thought it might be fun to treat it as though it were a Broadway show and invite the New York theater critics to review the album. I was having lunch one day in New York with my friend Bob Bernstein, who was then president of Random House and is now chairman of the board. He loved my idea of inviting the critics to review it and suggested that maybe Bennett Cerf, the founder—and at that time chairman—of Random House, could host a party for me to which the press would be invited. Bennet graciously agreed to do it and suggested that we hold it at "21," the elegant and famous New York restaurant. I would send engraved invitations to the press and the handful of theater critics who hopefully would review the album afterwards, tongue in cheek, as though it were a new show that had opened. "Let me send the invitations out over my name!" Cerf said with his terrific enthusiasm. Capitol Records was also enthusiastic over my press party and not only installed a special playback system in "21" with giant fifteen-inch Altec Voice of the

Theater speakers so the people could get the full stereo impact, they also loaned me one of their top studio engineers in New York to run it. What follows now is what has become my favorite press-agent story:

Rogers & Cowan, the giant publicity firm, was handling the album. They were (and still are) considered the most efficient PR firm in show business. I was power-breakfasted at the Polo Lounge by the first team, Henry Rogers and Warren Cowan, as they pitched their worldwide offices and staff.

"L-leave everything to us, S-Stan," Rogers told me with his slight stammer.

Actually, there was hardly anything to *leave* to them. I, after all, had dreamed up the whole press-party stunt: sending engraved invitations to the theater critics, etc., with an assist from Bennett Cerf. The only thing left for Rogers & Cowan to do—other than keep taking a retainer from me—was to pick the date for the party. *The* night, when the critics could best make it. It would have to be a night when there were no other scheduled openings on Broadway, and we would work backwards from that. As everybody in show business knows only too well, once the top people at a talent or public-relations agency smilingly get you to sign with them, you are frequently shuttled down a notch, to be handled by someone entirely different. In this case I was handled on the West Coast by a tall, bespectacled man, who appeared in the doorway of my Charles Addams office one day. "Guy McIlwaine, Rogers & Cowan," he announced with a long serious face. "I'm your account executive." (Years later McIlwaine became upwardly mobile enough to rise to the job of chairman of the board of Columbia Pictures. He is now an independent producer. But that day he was merely the account executive assigned to the

Freberg account.) He opened his briefcase with great efficiency, I recall—*Thunk! Thunk!*—and began taking notes as I described the party. "All you guys really have to do is pick the right night," I told Guy.

"No problem," he said. "We've put this into the hands of our best man in New York."

"Warren Cowan? Henry Rogers?"

"Nnnooo, Henry and Warren are kind of tied up right now. But you're in good hands. Don't worry."

Later, in New York, Donna and I met this "best man." His actual name was Gene Aretzky. But we were never able to refer to him as anything but "The guy with the Band-aid on his nose," since he walked around with an enormous Band-aid for all the time I knew him. The invitation started off: "Bennett Cerf invites you to a 'sneak hearing' of a new musical created especially for the ear. *Stan Freberg Presents the United States of America.*" and so on. The last line read, "No floral horseshoes please."

Finally, the guy with the Band-aid called with the date.

I pinned him down: "You're absolutely sure there's nothing else to keep the drama critics away? No Broadway shows opening that night?"

"Nope. This is a good night. Trust me."

So the invitations went out from Bennett Cerf. On the afternoon of the event I was walking around the private room at "21" doing a sound check, and waiters were setting the tables with fresh flowers. "Good luck," the guy with the Band-aid told me. I never saw him again.

That night, as the guests poured into the room, a young lady from Rogers & Cowan, whom I had never seen before, stood by a table of press kits. "Where's the guy with the Band-aid on his nose?" I asked her. "Mr. Aretzky had a previous engagement," she told me.

As the evening wore on, everybody was having a great time. The wine was flowing, and the food was scrumptious. But Bennett Cerf was concerned. "I haven't seen one drama critic tonight," he told me. "Not Walter Kerr from *The Times,* not Taubman from the *Herald Tribune,* not Watts from the *Post,* nobody. What could have happened? I can't believe they would have ignored us."

I discreetly approached the girl by the press-kit table. She was having a glass of champagne.

"It's a wonderful party, Mr. Freberg!" she beamed.

"Yes, thanks. Listen, is there anybody here from Rogers & Cowan?" I asked her.

"Just me." A small giggle.

"What could be holding up the drama critics? There's nobody here yet!" I said.

"Ummm, I don't know." A girlish shrug. "I was just told to hand out the press kits."

Now Bennett Cerf was at my elbow. "We'd better play the album pretty quick now," he said, a worried look on his face. "People have been here two hours, and they're getting antsy! I don't know what happened to the theater critics, but we can't wait for them. Okay?"

I told him okay, and he stood up and got everyone's attention. Then he cued the engineer, and the overture boomed through the big speakers.

Everyone enjoyed it and laughed and applauded. Everyone but the missing critics.

Later that evening, about ten o'clock, I sat in the lobby of the Algonquin Hotel, where I was staying, having a nightcap. My friend Andrew Anspach, who managed the Algonquin, sat down. "You seem depressed," he said to me. "Not your usual effervescent self. What's wrong?" Before I could tell him, he glanced over at the elevator doors, just opening. "Excuse me for interrupting," he said sotto voce, "But you see all those men getting out of the elevator? They're all the New York theater critics. Look, there's Walter Kerr . . . Richard Watts . . ."

"What???" I practically shouted. "What are they all doing here?"

"Oh," Anspach said with a proud smile. "They've been holed up in a suite upstairs for hours. This is the night they pick the New York Drama Critics Awards."

·

AND PEOPLE WONDER WHY I AM SO PARANOID. THIS is also my favorite story about the delegation of responsibility. Rogers & Cowan themselves are totally professional men who had no doubt started off with the best of intentions, up there at the top. And they sure knew how to delegate responsibility. They turned me over to the next man in their corporate hierarchy, who in turn did the same, making me downwardly mobile a notch at a time, until I was finally torpedoed by some guy with a Band-aid on his nose. Perhaps the man hadn't been paying attention. Perhaps he thought I had asked him to pick the one *worst* night of the year.

In spite of this near sidetracking of my album, it finally began to take off and get airplay. A couple weeks later, I went on *The Tonight Show* and sang "Take an Indian to Lunch This Week."

After I sang it, I sat down next to Jack Paar. I have been a guest on the show many times with Johnny Carson, but Carson never throws you for a loop with some comment out of left field the way Paar could.

"Are you a hypocrite?" Paar asked me suddenly, narrowing his eyes at me. What could the man be driving at?

"No," I said. "Why do you ask?"

"How often do you yourself take Indians to lunch?"

"Actually," I answered, "I don't have all that much opportunity to lunch with a group of Cherokees or Mohawks. But I certainly . . ."

"Well, there you are," Paar said. I looked into the camera.

"All right, listen!" I said. "I invite any American Indians within the sound of my voice to come to my hotel at noon tomorrow, and I'll take you to lunch!"

The studio audience burst into applause. "At which hotel are you staying?" Paar asked me. "Appropriately," I announced, "the Algonquin."

The next morning, I had an appointment at ABC television with the network president, Tom Moore. When I left his office, I had sold him a TV special to be called *The Chun King Chow Mein Hour*. Bill Andresen and I were so elated riding back to the hotel that we had temporarily forgotten about the Indian invitation. *After all, chances are nobody would take me up on it, public apathy being what it is,* I had thought. About 12:30 we turned east on Forty-fourth Street and pulled up in front of the Algonquin. Andy Anspach was out in front, looking up and down the street desperately. As we jumped out of the cab, he said, "Stan! Thank God you're here! The lobby is full of Indians!"

And it was indeed. I peered over at what appeared to be wall-to-wall Indians in the small lobby. Indians of all ages, and sizes, most of them in native costume. As I walked over, they all stood up and applauded.

"See? Didn't I tell you he'd be here?" a pretty young woman in a buckskin dress shouted, beaming from ear to ear. I looked over at an enormous Indian gentleman, standing next to his wife, who was carrying a papoose on her back. He walked toward me. "I'm Chief Russell

Moore," he told me. "I play trombone with a Dixieland band in the Village. This is my wife and son. We don't normally walk around dressed like this, but after I saw you on the show last night, I called around, and we decided to come in costume."

I was deeply moved. Anspach was clearing his throat next to me. "Stan, ahhh, this is terrific, but what did you have in mind?"

"What indeed?" I said. "I'm going to take all these people to lunch! How many are you?"

"Twenty-six, including the baby," Russell told me.

"Plus Bill and me," I said. "Okay, let's go!" With me as the leader, we marched en masse toward the elegant Rose Room. An ancient and very crabby maître d' was in charge of the dining room then. He stood in his tuxedo, clutching his menus to his breast, and stared at the group moving slowly toward him. This was the sixties, remember.

*What the hell is* this *now?* his face said. *Some new militant group demonstrating? Some wacko protest march in off the street? Not in my dining room!* He backed up a step, getting a tighter grip on his menus.

"Table for TWENTY-EIGHT?" I shouted.

The man looked like he was on the verge of a stroke. "Ahh . . . just a moment!" he was choking. "Ummm, reservation?"

"No," I said, "They're not from a reservation. They live right here in New York City." Finally, Anspach stepped up and calmed the man. Then he told everybody to have a drink in the lobby while he got some tables pushed together. After we were finally seated and my guests had ordered, I went out to the lobby phone and called the guy with the Band-aid at Rogers & Cowan.

"Listen," I told him, "I'm having lunch with twenty-six American Indians at my hotel."

"Who set *that* up? I certainly didn't set that up," he said.

"Nobody set it up," I told him. "It just happened! That's the way it works in life sometimes. On *The Tonight Show* last night, on the spur of the moment, I just invited Indians to lunch. And here they are."

"Well . . . what do you want me to do?" the publicity whiz asked me.

Call all the papers, and ask for the city desk. Tell the editor what I said last night on the air and that twenty-six Indians took me up on it. Ask if he can send a photographer over to the Algonquin immediately."

"That's a good idea," he said.

"Then call your own photographer to come over right away and cover it."

"Why do we need a photographer if the newspapers are coming?" he asked me. I couldn't believe I was taking this public-relations man by the hand like this.

"What if none of the newspapers show up?" I explained. "This way we'll have our own backup photographer to record it for posterity."

"That's a good idea," he told me. As fate would have it, before we got to our dessert, the *Times* and *Daily News* burst into the Rose Room, plus the independent photographer. We made the next editions, and that night on *The Tonight Show* Jack Paar showed the pictures of Freberg making good his luncheon date. Years later, when I made my appearance at the Kennedy Center for "The Night of the First Americans," an Indian trombone player came up to me during rehearsal. He smiled at me and held out his hand. "Remember me, Mr. Freberg? I'm Chief Russell Moore. You once took me to lunch at the Algonquin." Then he took out a Polaroid picture of a handsome young Indian in an army uniform. "Remember my little boy? The papoose? Well, here's what he looks like now." A great moment. But I digress.

It was my original intention to record a *series* of history albums (and still is—more on that later) since the first one covered merely the early years, from Columbus through the Revolutionary War. On the Capitol album notes, I promised the subsequent volumes: "The Middle Years," going up through the Civil War, "The Late Years," and "The Late Late Years."

To this day, people come walking up to me, and I can tell in advance when they are going to smile and ask, "Sayyy, Mr. Freberg . . . what ever happened to the other volumes of your *United States of America* album?"

A good question.

The main thing that thwarted me at the time was in the form of a famous Broadway producer named David Merrick. If it hadn't been for Merrick, these albums would have been long since recorded so that I wouldn't have had to answer the question forever being posed to me. Of course, I can't blame it *all* on Merrick, although I'd like to. Just the first decade or so of the delay. After that we have to blame it on my own inertia, along with other extraneous roadblocks.

David Merrick first appeared in my life within a couple of years after the album's release. I met Merrick through a mutual friend, writer Bill Davidson, who had just written a story on me for the *Saturday Evening Post*. The meeting took place in Beverly Hills, by the pool at the Beverly Wilshire Hotel. Merrick, just in from New York, sat amidst a sea of bikinied bodies gleaming with suntan oil in a dark blue pinstriped suit, white dress shirt, navy polka-dot tie, and a carnation. Perched uncomfortably on the edge of a pink chaise lounge, he looked as though someone had accidentally beamed him down from a board-of-directors meeting in another galaxy. But one detail remains very clear: Although the sun was unbearably hot that day, Merrick through the long meeting never once sweated a single bead of perspiration. Very strange. But then, whoever said the man was from this world?

DAVIDSON HAD A PLAY MERRICK WAS INTERESTED IN and was thinking about turning into a musical. As they had earlier discussed who might write the score, Davidson brought up my name. Merrick had heard of me, but he wasn't familiar with me as a songwriter.

He was on the West Coast because his musical *Oliver!* was about to open in Los Angeles, on its way to Broadway. Davidson set up this meeting at the Beverly Wilshire Hotel, where Merrick was staying. Davidson, who knew Merrick loved attractive women, set the meeting by the pool. Little did he know that this was as casual as Merrick ever dressed. I never saw him dressed any other way.

"Haven't you heard Stan's album *The United States of America*?" Davidson asked Merrick. "Stan wrote all the words and music."

"Not only haven't I heard it . . ." Merrick said in his deep baritone voice, "I've never even heard *of* it. When may I hear it?"

A meeting was set up for the next day at my office on Sunset Boulevard.

At eleven o'clock the next morning Merrick climbed the stairs to my office with an associate and immediately called the theater box office to get the final tally on *Oliver!*

from the night before. Then he hung up the phone and said, "Let's hear it." I pushed the button on my tape deck, and a timpani roll came out of the stereo speakers. An Orson Wellesian voice announced: "Stan Freberg modestly presents . . . the United States of America!" An overture followed, composed of the various songs in the score. Then the opening scene between Christopher Columbus and Queen Isabella hit. The first line sets the tone of the whole outrageous premise:

COLUMBUS: All right, we'll go over it once again: First you hock the jewels, you give me the money, and I buy the ships. Then I discover the new world, you dump the King, and I'll send for you.

I watched Merrick closely. There was a slight twitch of his mustache. Could that have been a smile? The associate with him was a nice enough but somewhat nervous man named Alan Delynn. His usual facial attitude when in Merrick's presence, as I soon learned, was one of apparent deep concentration with a furrowed brow, as he studied his shoes. That way, if Merrick hated something, Delynn's face was already in a position to agree with him. On the other hand, if Merrick smiled, which was rare, but an occasional possibility, Delynn's face could easily reverse itself, to follow suit.

As Merrick listened to the music and dialogue pouring out of my speakers, his face was a mask. No visible reaction. Finally, during a scene on the deck of the Santa Maria, King Ferdinand, who came along because his doctor told him he should go to Florida for the winter, said to Columbus:

FERDINAND: We'd better sight some land soon, there's rumblings of mutiny!

**COLUMBUS:** Really?
**FERDINAND:** Come over here and listen.
**COLUMBUS:** All right.
**SOUND:** FOOTSTEPS ON DECK
**CREW:** (IN UNISON) Rumble, rumble, rumble . . . Mutiny, mutiny, mutiny!
**COLUMBUS:** Yeah, I see what you mean.

A silly joke, actually. But it drew a small smile out of David Merrick. Delynn's small smile followed a millisecond later, but he kept his furrowed brow just to be ready in case things should go the other way.

I was playing the part of Columbus and later Jesse White as Ferdinand joined me in singing an elaborate contrapuntal song called "Round Round World." As Merrick was bathed in the rich sounds of nineteen Hollywood studio musicians with Billy May conducting, sixteen singers, and two vocalists singing two sets of lyrics in counterpoint, he straightened up on my couch with rapt attention. Delynn straightened up only partially.

A few minutes later, I had the Manhattan Indians selling New York Island to a real-estate tycoon for twenty-seven dollars worth of junk jewelry. But at first, he was not sure anyone in his right mind would want to live in such a place.

To convince him, the Indians tried to show him how sophisticated Broadway would look some day. They burst into a song called "Put On Your Top Hat, White Feather and Tails." As the song built to a climax with a chorus of Indians tap-dancing, Merrick held up his hand.

"Hold it!" he said. Stop!"

The album had barely started. He hadn't even heard it up to the Revolutionary War era. I stopped the tape, not knowing what was coming. Delynn's face was a blank mask, just sort of hovering there until he knew which attitude to lock down. Merrick leaned forward and fixed me with his deeply hypnotic brown eyes.

"I demand the right to produce this as a Broadway musical," he said. Nobody spoke for a moment. Then Merrick said, "I think it's brilliant." Delynn's head was bobbing now: "Marvelous, marvelous!"

"Are you interested?" Merrick asked.

"I'll have to think this over," I told him. After about three seconds, I said, "I've thought it over. Why not?"

Merrick put out his hand solemnly, and I shook it. "Done!" he said. "Let's hear the rest of it."

So I played it up through the end of the Revolutionary War, which concludes the album. Merrick laughed loudly in several places, especially the part where Thomas Jefferson is trying to get Benjamin Franklin to sign a little document he has written called the Declaration of Independence. Franklin thinks it looks a little too radical and is hesitant. They launch into a song I called "A Man Can't Be Too Careful What He Signs These Days."

**JEFFERSON:** *Come on, and put your name*
*On the dotted line*
**FRANKLIN:** *I gotta be particular what*
*I sign*
**JEFFERSON:** *It's just a piece of paper*
**FRANKLIN:** *Just a piece of paper,*
*That's what you say*
**JEFFERSON:** *Come on and put your signature*
*On the list*
**FRANKLIN:** *It looks to have a very*
*Subversive twist*
**JEFFERSON:** *How silly to assume it*
*Won't you nom de plume it today*

*You're so skittish*
*Who possibly could care if you do?*

**FRANKLIN:** *The Un-British Activities*
*Committee, that's who!*

**JEFFERSON:** *Let's have a little drink-o*
*And fill the quill*

**FRANKLIN:** *It sounds a little pink-o*
*To me, but still . . .*

**JEFFERSON:** *Knock off the timid manner*
*If you want a banner to raise*

**FRANKLIN:** *Banner to raise!*

**JEFFERSON:** *You must take a stand*
*For this brave new land*
*For who wants to live*
*So conser–vative?*

**FRANKLIN:** *I don't disagree*
*But a man can't be*

**BOTH:** *Too careful what he signs these days.*

When the album ended, at the end of the Revolutionary War, Merrick said, "Why does it stop there? How long is that?"

I told him, "About forty-five minutes. I stopped there mainly because that's all you can put on a record. After that you start cutting into the label."

Merrick preened his mustache. "That's a problem we don't have in the theater. You could go as long as two and a half hours. Maybe bring it up to the present day. I'd want you to appear in it for the run of the play. Could you manage to get away from your other things in order to do that?" he asked.

"No problem," I told him. "I can create commercials in New York as well as Los Angeles. Besides, I don't socialize all that much. Most evenings I just hang around the house writing. I might as well go down to the Shubert Theater at eight o'clock every night and be a Broadway star."

Merrick smiled. "I like your arrogance," he said. "We'll get along just fine."

At that point there was little reason to believe otherwise. "One nice thing about having the performer the same person as the author and lyricist is that it guarantees you'll be on the premises," Merrick told me. "When things come up in the news worthy of satirizing in the show, I won't have to keep flying you in from Beverly Hills to add lines or rewrite a lyric."

"My thinking exactly," Delynn agreed.

I told Merrick that the next album—"The Middle Years"—up through the Civil War was already written and ready to record. "This new album should really set us up for the Broadway show," I said.

Merrick crossed his legs and fixed me with a cold look of steel that I hadn't see before.

"No more albums," he said.

I was stunned. "No more albums?"

"Not for now," Merrick said. "It will take the edge off the Broadway original-cast album we'll want to bring out."

It made sense at the time, I guess. But during my long on-again, off-again association with David Merrick, that adamant position by him held up the recording of all subsequent albums. But there I go, jumping too far ahead.

I managed to write the rest of the Broadway version of the "USA," along with somehow working around the clock creating, producing, and directing commercials for my many advertising clients.

Periodically, Merrick and the ever-present Delynn

flew out to Beverly Hills, to sit in my living room and be brought up to date as to where the material stood. I read the new scenes and sang the additional songs I had written, accompanied by my friend Paul T. Smith, the brilliant jazz pianist.

Raymond Massey, the actor, lived directly next door to me for many years. In addition to being known for the roles he had played in countless films and on television in the *Dr. Kildare* series with Richard Chamberlain, Massey was probably most famous for having portrayed Abraham Lincoln in the classic movie *Abe Lincoln in Illinois*. Merrick asked me to ask him if he'd be interested in recreating Lincoln in the Civil War section of our musical.

I discussed it with Massey one day over our mutual boxwood hedge. He told me that he loved being thought of as Lincoln and that he'd think it over, even though he wasn't really up for the grueling work involved in being in a Broadway show night after night. One Sunday Merrick was at my house to hear some new scenes, and he noticed that my wife was running back and forth serving a buffet spread with no assistance from Frances, our longtime black housekeeper, who usually brought coffee or drinks to Merrick when he came to visit. The truth was that we had just had another difference of opinion with Frances, for the umpteenth time. Frances was a terrific cook and housekeeper but somewhat temperamental. Even so, she was with us, off and on, for twenty years, but that Sunday she wasn't there.

Merrick noticed that she was missing. As Donna served him lunch, he asked, "What happened to Frances?"

After a pause I told him, "Mr. Massey came over and freed her."

For all Merrick's success as a producer, and he *was* a terrific Broadway producer, he seemed uneasy in certain areas. Donna finally put her finger on it. She said, "Most of his biggest hits he's brought over from England, where he had already seen the play performed in front of an audience. He hasn't done that many original shows. Even if they seemed original, they were adapted from something else." I thought it over. She was right, as usual. *Oliver!,* which was based on Dickens's *Oliver Twist,* had been brought over just as it was from London. The same was true of *The Entertainer, Look Back in Anger, Luther, A Taste of Honey,* and *Stop the World, I Want to Get Off,* to name just a few. *I Do! I Do!* the musical, was based on *The Fourposter,* a former play, and even *Hello, Dolly!,* his biggest hit, was based on Thornton Wilder's *The Matchmaker,* which Merrick had produced as a straight play a few years earlier. His longest-running production, *42nd Street,* is practically identical to the 1930s movie musical of the same name.

In other words, Merrick was most comfortable when he had already seen the work produced either in another country or another form. He hadn't *seen* my musical yet, but he had at least *heard* the first forty-five minutes of it on my album—the next best thing.

That was why he never questioned anything up through the Revolutionary War. He had already *heard* that produced with a big orchestra, singers, and actors. But the part that came after that, which *would* have been recorded the same way if he hadn't stopped me from making the album, he only saw on the paper and heard me reading. If he couldn't see something, in a previous form, it made him nervous. He had a hard time imagining it in his mind. Nevertheless, he continued to be enthusiastic, and our association continued. At various times he asked two famous directors to stop by my house and have me read parts of the show for them. One was Gower Champion, and the other was Josh Logan.

They both loved the show, which bolstered Merrick's confidence. Logan laughed loudly at the historical scenes, but he said he thought he was the wrong director for it. "Satire isn't really my thing," he told Donna and I later over dinner with his charming wife, Nedda. Josh was right. The things he had done on Broadway—*South Pacific, Camelot, Picnic*—and on the screen (he had directed movies as varied as *Mister Roberts* and *Bus Stop* with Marilyn Monroe) were of a different nature. Surely not satire. I was grateful to him for leveling. Gower Champion was a brilliant director and choreographer who had directed such successful Broadway musicals as *Bye Bye Birdie* and *Hello, Dolly!* for Merrick. (Later, the last thing he directed before his death was *42nd Street* for David Merrick.) But Gower saw it a whole different way than I did. Gower told me, "I see it done with no costumes at all. Just the men in dark suits and the women in black cocktail dresses." He was striding up and down in front of my fireplace. "Here and there a red sash . . . or at most a three-cornered hat for Washington, say, but stark! Just vague *impressions* of costumes. You see?"

I didn't see. I had always pictured it the way I figured all the fans of the record had pictured it in the theaters of their minds. Washington looking down at Betsy Ross with the flag draped over her lap, just the way the painting looks in the National Gallery. The only thing different being the dialogue I had created to come out of their mouths. Betsy Ross in a black cocktail dress and high-heeled pumps? Washington in a button-down shirt and a Brooks Brothers suit? Not likely. Marge Champion, to whom he was married at the time, sat on my couch with Donna and just smiled at Gower. It was hard to tell what she was thinking. Was the man putting me on? I asked him if he was.

"No! I'm serious!" he said. "Costumes are too obvious."

I felt like asking him in that case why hadn't he staged *Hello, Dolly!* without costumes. But I politely told him, "Well, that's certainly something to think about all right," as we said goodnight.

I had always wanted to direct it myself, but I knew it was too much to bite off, since I was also appearing in it. So Merrick finally decided that I should codirect it with my old friend Jack Donohue. Donohue was not only a brilliant director but was also able to operate as a choreographer like Champion did. Years before I knew Donohue, I had seen shows he had staged on Broadway, like *Top Banana* with Phil Silvers. I had been impressed with the way he had moved dozens of people around with intricate, split-second timing to great comedic effect. He was also a top comedy producer/director in television, directing everyone from Red Skelton and Lucille Ball to Frank Sinatra, Dean Martin, and Jerry Lewis in their musical variety shows. I would direct the actors in the special subtle readings I try to get on all my records and commercials, and Donohue would be in charge of the overall staging. Also, his comedic input from years of work with practically every comedian in the book would be invaluable. We had mutual respect for each other as well.

We started to cast the show, but at that point it seemed to me that something very subtle started happening to David Merrick. I began to see some of the manifestations of the character flaws and strangeness I had heard about for years. He would tell you one thing on

Monday, then something entirely different on Tuesday. Frequently, the change would come from Monday noon to Monday evening. At first, I thought it was my imagination. One day, for example, I sat alone with him in the Polo Lounge at the Beverly Hills Hotel. He put his hand on my arm and pressed ever so slightly. I looked up into big brown eyes boring holes through me. After a moment he spoke. His words are indelibly printed on my memory pan: "Not since the days of George S. Kaufman will we have seen such scathing wit on Broadway," he told me.

I was bowled over by this comment from a man who gave out compliments very sparingly. "Really?" I said, fishing for more.

"Yes," he nodded. "We don't have that many true satirists working in the theater. We're lucky to have you."

Afterwards, I floated around the corner to my house, like a Hovercraft with glasses. Actually, my feet touched the ground at the exact moment on the third day when Merrick called to ask how I would feel about another comedy writer coming in to help "punch up" the comedy sketches.

I stood staring at the phone. The answer obviously was (1) he was kidding, or (2) I was going crazy.

Neither answer was correct.

The correct answer would come to me much later. Merrick had started to play games with my head.

I would find out that this was standard procedure with him. He would encourage a playwright, an actor, or director one day, then tear the person down the next. It was his warped way of keeping everybody slightly insecure at all times. That way he could deal with them.

When *Hello, Dolly!* opened out of town in Detroit, the constant infighting and bickering set in motion by

Merrick created a battlefield atmosphere. A friend of mine, Charles Nelson Reilly, was with the original company of *Hello, Dolly!* through all the turmoil in Detroit and Washington, D.C., and for several years of its run on Broadway. Reilly, a veteran actor and gifted director, played the part of Cornelius in the production. He told me that Merrick fired twenty-five people in the first twelve months of *Dolly*.

He ought to know. He was also the union steward who sent in paperwork to Actor's Equity each week.

"People would occasionally be fired in clusters. Some nights the audience would be staring at great gaping holes on the stage where dancers and singers had stood the night before. The company was so demoralized that they couldn't even bear to say the name of the theater. They'd just give a cabdriver the street address and sink into the vinyl upholstery. Merrick kept the composer, Jerry Herman, on pins and needles all the time by threatening to bring in another composer to punch up his score. (Sound familiar?)

On another show, *Inadmissible Evidence,* by the English playwright John Osborne, Merrick started the same mind games, playing the principals off against each other while the show was out of town in Philadelphia. Nicol Williamson, the star, had finally had enough. As the story was told to me by someone who was present, Williams after a matinee told Merrick he wanted to talk to him. He took him out behind the theater, told him off, and knocked him into a trash can. Then he said, "I quit!" and walked off down the alley. As one of Merrick's people helped him up, he supposedly said: "Get him back! I like his spirit." And they did.

Much later in New York, when our own relations became strained, I confronted Merrick and asked him if this story was true.

"Almost," he said. "He didn't actually hit me. He only shoved me."

"But what about these other stories?" I asked. "Your pitting of performers and directors against each other? Do you actually do that?"

Merrick smiled at me. "These things are usually a bit exaggerated, but . . ."

"But why?" I asked him. "Why would you put people through that?"

I will never forget his answer. The smile had disappeared, and his eyes bored in like lasers. "I only want the strongest to survive," he said.

Of course, I didn't have any of this insight to Merrick at the time. If I had, life would have been a lot easier. A few days after our meeting at the Polo Lounge, recalling what he'd said in a previous phone conversation, I told him that under no circumstances could he bring in an outside writer to "punch up" my material. He either had faith in me as a writer, or we could forget our association.

"Just a moment," he told me. "Who ever mentioned bringing in an outside writer? Certainly not me. You wouldn't want to fool with that script. Let's just get this show on its feet. All right?"

I was thrown off balance by this complete turnaround. And not for the last time. I decided to pretend that we had never had the previous conversation and just go along with Merrick.

Things went along smoothly for a while, and then Merrick started his old tricks again. After many more creative differences I decided to take a walk. After all this mental anguish I put the musical on the shelf for a while, and I became more and more involved with the advertising part of my life. Finally, I managed to put the whole frustrating experience out of my mind. In the meantime, people all over America came up to me constantly asking whatever became of the additional volumes of my "USA" project?

About a year went by. During that time, I managed to record a different Capitol album called *Freberg Underground,* which had nothing to do with American history. One day, before the album had been pressed, I sat in the den at home, proofreading the liner notes for the album, which Capitol had sent over. And which, to this day, are engraved in stone in the back of the *Underground* album. In a small box in the middle of the copy, I had decided to refer to the "USA" series. The headline I had written read SAYYY, WHATEVER HAPPENED TO VOLUME II OF . . . "THE UNITED STATES OF AMERICA"?

"I'm glad you asked that question," I went on to say. "Here is what has happened until now: 'Stan Freberg Presents the United States of America' was released in 1961 after one year of writing, and thirteen continuous weeks in the studio recording it. After a full weekend off, I crawled to the typewriter and started writing Volume II. Shortly after that, a famous Broadway producer with a large black mustache appeared at my door requesting the rights to produce it as a Broadway musical. He said the material was 'brilliant, irreverent, brave, disloyal, outrageous and very funny.' Or words to that effect. In the face of that sort of flattery I succumbed and set to work. 'Meanwhile,' he said, 'don't release any more recorded versions of this. Not until the Broadway show opens.'

"Four years and several creative disagreements later, here is where it stands: The musical, which will encompass Volumes I, II, and III (from Columbus to World War I is as far as you can go in an evening), is finished. Meanwhile, none of this new material has been recorded into the subsequent volumes, pending the long delayed Broadway version. Will we ever resolve our differences and produce the show? Will I go ahead and record Volume II anyhow, in response to thousands of requests? Watch this space for further developments!"

I sat, pencil in hand, proofreading the above material, as I said. Then, as God is my witness, just as I got to the line about the famous producer with the large black mustache, Frances appeared at my den door. She was wide-eyed with amazement as she pointed to the blinking hold button on my phone:

"You're not going to believe this! David Merrick on line one!"

Since our last phone conversation almost a year before had been somewhat less than pleasant, I couldn't imagine why he was calling me. I also wondered which of the two Merricks to expect. I took a deep breath and picked up the phone.

"David?" I said. The familiar deep voice flowed like warm molasses into my ear.

"Hello Stan . . ." he said. "I'll tell you why I'm calling. I was just wondering if we could get our little musical on its feet now. Don't you think it's time we did?"

Ahh. It was the nice Merrick. I said nothing for a moment. Then I told him, "Listen, David, you may not believe this, but just as you called, I was proofreading the notes on the back of a new album." I referred to the fact that a famous Broadway producer had held up the other albums and . . . but he wasn't interested in that and chopped me off.

"Let's just cut through all this. For one thing, I've had to cancel a show I had booked into the National Theater in Washington. I thought we could open it in

Washington, D.C. Perfect! Don't you think?" Once again he had cast the hook, and I bit hard.

"Washington, D.C., eh? Well, that certainly does sound like a great town for a historical exposé."

"Historical exposé!" Merrick said, chuckling. "I like that! That's how we'll bill it in the ads. 'A Historical Exposé.' Done, and done! That's one nice thing about having an ad man as the author and star. I'm sure the advertising campaign you'll create for the show will be marvelous." (He was slowly but surely reeling me in now.) "Anyhow, I've got a theater standing empty in Washington in three months. *You* want to do it, *I* want to do it. Let's just *do* it. All right?"

I was almost all the way in now.

"Only if I can do it the way it's written," I said.

"Absolutely," he answered. "You have my word. Nobody will ever again question your material as long as I'm the producer." His voice was rich and hypnotic, now soothing my stomach muscles and novocaining my brain. "Come on! Let's go. We're in complete agreement. All right?"

"All right," I said. "Why not?"

"Done, and done!" Merrick said.

After I hung up, I dialed Donna at our office.

"You're not going to believe this," I told her, "but I just got back up on the horse with Merrick."

"You're right, I don't believe it," she answered. "But in case it's true, when do we leave for New York?"

I remember that before I could answer her, I was racked with intense stomach pains. It would not be the last time.

# 21

## *"Take Lincoln Out of the Civil War— He Doesn't Work"*

OVER THE NEXT FEW WEEKS, DONNA AND I WRAPPED up the current commercial production and got ready to leave for New York. I got the script into a final form, grateful in the knowledge that nobody was going to mess around with my words but me. My lawyer in New York, Lawrence Green, was into negotiations with Merrick's lawyer on a last couple of contractual differences, and the world looked sweet indeed.

One night, just before Donna and I left for New York, we had Merrick at our house to hear a couple of songs I had added to the score. One was called "Shoot if You Must (You Are Kidding I Trust)," for Barbara Freitchie to sing in the Civil War part of the show. She sings it to a gentleman from the War Department who has asked her to stick her old gray head out the window with a Union flag, "with the possibility of getting shot at but look at the press we'll get!" Needless to say, she is not thrilled with the idea.

The other was a song for a scene with Thomas Edison later in the century. In my version of history, Edison has invented a "lifetime bulb" that will last for decades. A business tycoon is there in his lab to straighten Edison out. The song he sings to him is a satire on the pitifully poor quality of many American products and the "throwaway" mentality that is responsible for most mass production in this country.

The song is called "Planned Obsolescence." "That's the thing to shoot for," the man tells Edison. "A lifetime bulb is against the scheme of things. Almost un-American!" Merrick and the ubiquitous Delynn laughed loudly and applauded as I finished with Paul T. Smith once again at my piano. A few moments later, Merrick, Delynn, Donna, and I stood outside saying goodnight. Because of the significance of the scene, I remember every detail. It was a perfect California night, with a cool breeze blowing away the heat of the day. The moonlight had painted the Spanish walls of my house even whiter, and the smell of night-blooming jasmine was delicious. I have an old French streetlight uprooted from Paris where it used to operate on gas at the turn of the century—electrified now and transplanted to just outside my front door. Merrick stood directly under my streetlight, its silvery beams bouncing off his head. He was dressed to kill as always: dark blue double-breasted pinstripe fresh from his London tailor, white fingers of his breast-pocket hankie pointing to the stars.

"What is that wonderful smell?" he asked my wife.

"Night-blooming jasmine," she told him. "It's that bush right over there."

"Marvelous. I only smell it in California," he said.

The crickets filled in the small talk for a while. Then he turned to me.

"Well, the next time we meet will be in New York. It sounds to me like the show is all ready now."

"I just want to do a little more work on the score," I told him. "A little polish on a couple of songs . . ."

He held up his hand like a cop stopping traffic. "Leave it alone!" he commanded me.

"Leave it alone?" I asked him.

He took a step forward and put one fatherly hand on my shoulder.

"Leave it alone, and we'll win the Pulitzer," Merrick said. Nobody dared to speak. I was filled with emotion at such incredible praise from Broadway's biggest producer.

"See you in New York," he said, as he kissed Donna's hand and strode down my walk. The perfect gentlemen.

ABOUT THREE WEEKS LATER, I WAS SITTING AT DINNER with Merrick in New York. He had invited Donna and me along with a few other guests to a Sunday evening outing at Lüchow's, a legendary New York restaurant that featured rich German food and an earsplitting beergarden orchestra. Donna and I were ensconced at the Algonquin Hotel by then, trying to get the show cast, and Merrick wanted us to get out and "have a little social life," he told us. But Donna couldn't go, so I took Bill Andresen, who had just flown in from Los Angeles. At the table were about twelve people, including Jerry Herman, the composer of *Hello, Dolly!;* Clay Felker, the brilliant editor and innovator who had created *New York* magazine and is now editor of *Manhattan, Inc.;* Pamela Tiffen, the actress to whom Felker was then married; Mike Nichols; Gloria Steinem; and a few other beautiful

New York trendsetters. The German oompah-pah band was deafening, I remember; suddenly, they mercifully took a break. In the comparative silence that followed, Merrick picked his moment. He cleared his throat loudly. Then he asked me the following question: "How's the score coming?"

For a moment I considered the possibilities: (1) he was putting me on; (2) he had simply forgotten that he had told me two weeks ago to leave the score, and especially the music, alone. Of course. That was it. The man had a lot on his mind. "I haven't done anything further on it at all," I said. "Besides, we've been casting and uh . . ."

A few people at the table were leaning into our conversation. Merrick notched his voice up a couple decibels: "It seems to me . . ." he boomed, "that score needs a lot of work!"

I hardly knew what to say. Was I going crazy? In my embarrassment, I had forgotten the games Merrick played. I decided to remind him of our previous conversation in a roundabout way. "Gee, I don't know," I ventured. "A friend of mine told me to leave the score alone, and who knows, we might win the Pulitzer." This was the moment he had waited for. Merrick's table knife had been poised in the air, a foot above this plate. He dropped it now with a great *crash!* The impact of heavy silver on bone china caused not only our entire table to look up, but half the restaurant had now swung their heads around to gawk at the startling sound. In that beautifully programmed millisecond of silence, Merrick's voice sliced through the big echoey room like a Wilkinson Sword through butter:

"Win the Pulitzer?" he bellowed. "Do you think the Pulitzer Committee is tone deaf?!"

I have been asked how I felt at that moment. Not

great, is how. It may not be one of the most humiliating moments of my life, but it comes close. At first I was sure he was kidding, but a palpitation later, I knew he wasn't. What does one do in that brief moment of total deflation? Stand upon your chair and shout to the entire restaurant: "Just a moment! Excuse me? A couple of weeks ago, this man—David Merrick—stood outside my house and told me my musical was all ready to go! He said to leave it alone and . . ."

No. One cannot do that. So in the time that it took for everyone to stop staring at me and start talking again —about an hour and a half is what it seemed—I said nothing. It was only when the German orchestra returned to finish turning my brain into jelly with their unbearable Bavarian bund music that I remembered that Merrick probably hadn't actually meant it for real. He was simply starting to manipulate my head again. He was Uri Geller in a large black mustache, bending my mind like it was a soup spoon. Years later I recounted this story to Marge Champion, who told me, "Of course. The man has no conscience."

Back at the Algonquin, I lay on the bed in a fetal position, recounting the painful story to Donna. I was sure I had developed a bleeding ulcer on the cab ride home. Donna was saying, "If only I'd been there, I could have spared you all that."

"How?" I wanted to know.

"Easy," she told me. "The moment he asked you, 'How's the score coming?' I would have given you a kick under the table you would not soon forget and answered him myself: 'Just fine, David,' I would have said. 'Just fine.' And that would have been the end of it." And I knew that she would have. And that *would* have been the end of it. But she *hadn't* been there to kick me—so Merrick had.

*Stan Freberg* ✍

The next day we were hard at work in the St. James Theater reading actors, and I tried to forget the painful dinner at Lüchow's. I have never returned to that restaurant, and to this day, when I am treated to either *Wienerschnitzel mit Spatzel* or German music, I double over with cramps on the spot.

Dorothy Loudon, the marvelous Tony Award–winning comedienne, became available, and we all loved the way she played Queen Isabella and Betsy Ross. So, to my great delight, she joined our company. The next week, Merrick and I were having a drink together in the Algonquin lobby at cocktail time. After a few moments Alan Delynn dropped by, and Donna came downstairs and joined us. By now I had managed to build an imaginary steel wall around my stomach, when in Merrick's presence, so that no sudden spears or arrows could pierce it. (Later, I refined this mental trick to a larger illusion. I imagined myself completely encased in a bulletproof glass booth—like Adolf Eichmann had sat in during his trial in Israel—so that all negative or counterproductive comments bounced off the glass, without doing any permanent damage to the creative center in my brain. It worked pretty well, but I sustained a few mental concussions before I arrived at the glass-booth trick.) The thing was, you had to throw up the armor pretty fast, because Merrick suckered you in with sweetness, then struck like a diamondback. Or a cobra. A cobra with a mustache, where seconds before there hadn't been a snake in sight. He was smiling, I remember, chuckling over some amusing comment of mine, just as though "the Lüchow's Incident," as I had come to think of it, had never happened. Suddenly, he asked about the size of the orchestra. "How many men do you see in the pit?" he said, peering over his martini.

Was this a trick question? Probably. Just in case, I touched the computer key in my brain, and the steel wall booted up around my stomach. Donna's foot was pressing against mine now, no easy thing to do under the Algonquin's tiny lobby tables. *Be careful!* her black Ferragamo pump said to my Bass Weejun. *Be alert!* I swizzled my Dubonnet on the rocks. "Well . . . do you like the way my album sounds?" I asked him. He narrowed his eyes. "Marvelous," he said. "Just wonderful." "Wonderful, yes," Delynn was mumbling, bobbing his head in agreement. I paused, there in the mine field. Then I took another step:

"Well, that's . . . let's see . . . nineteen men," I told him. Merrick's eyebrows shot up. Delynn's eyebrows shot up.

"Nineteen men?" Merrick boomed.

I could hear Donna inhaling deeply, then holding it in. Merrick's face settled into a wide grin. The smile of an uncle who has just come to visit with a toy in his pocket. "Well, what's wrong with that?" he asked. Delynn shrugged an all-purpose shrug.

Donna and I exhaled. "Actually," Merrick continued, "that's a rather small band. I have over thirty in the pit for *Dolly.*"

"Well, that's probably because you have a string section," I said. "These Billy May orchestrations are for brass, woodwinds, and rhythm, but no strings."

Merrick shrugged and checked his watch. "Sounds fine to me. Nineteen men it is. Done and done."

We waited for a last-minute strike of the cobra. On the way out, Delynn winked at me and made a circle with his thumb and index finger, as though he and I together had somehow brought it off.

Twenty-four hours later, Donna, Bill, and I sat in

Merrick's office above the St. James Theater, going over a few things. Merrick's office is rather small, made smaller by a baby grand, and features fire-engine-red walls, red carpeting, and a red ceiling. The only window is covered by heavy red drapes. After a few minutes in there, you begin to feel the symbolic heat of all that redness, like you are having a bad dream with the walls slowly closing in. Merrick, it is said, has a hidden control under his desk with which he can shut off the air-conditioning (though I cannot prove this.) If an actor or agent is giving him a hard time, the legend goes, he not only kicks off the cool air but can make the heat pour in. Secret switches aside, after a few minutes in this oppressive cell, hard-to-deal-with actors or agents are reduced to sweating masses of jelly. They begin to feel that they are truly in hell and soon agree to anything in order to escape the tyranny of the red room. I wasn't aware of any of this hearsay, however, and merely knew that I was starting to feel very claustrophobic in there.

"Oh, by the way," Merrick suddenly said. "How many men did we agree upon for the orchestra again?" An easy question. I knew the answer and saw no need to drop the armor around my vital organs. "Nineteen," I answered brightly.

"Nineteen men in the orchestra?" he said. "Surely you're kidding! I couldn't go for anything over ten or possibly twelve."

*Whafff!* The cobra had struck without warning, and my undefended stomach went into spasms. "But David!" I said, struggling to get out of his red overstuffed sofa. (Was it a trick sofa too?) "Just yesterday you said nineteen men would be fine!"

Merrick opened his arms to the world in a wide shrug. "I said that? When did I say that?"

Donna, who thought she had seen it all, stared at

Merrick for a moment with her mouth slightly open. Then she recovered. "In the Algonquin, David. Yesterday. Don't you remember?"

"Where?" Merrick asked. A puzzled look now. I had managed to escape the poofy red sofa and was on my feet.

"In the Algonquin lobby! You said nineteen men! Done and done!"

Merrick turned to Delynn. "Alan? Do you recall my agreeing to anything even close to nineteen men?"

Delynn was tipped back in his chair, his eyes rolling upward. "Not me, David," he told the red ceiling.

Donna was trying to catch my eye. *Don't play into his hands!* the look was projecting. But it all went over my head. "Ten men! That's a small Lester Lannin *dance* band for somebody's bar mitzvah!" I was shouting. I remember thinking that I might faint. I was breaking out in a heat rash. "Say, is it hot in here or what?" I asked.

I looked at Merrick's face, chalk white against his red walls. Not a drop of perspiration. Every slick black hair in place. "It feels comfortable to me," he said.

The man was a phenomenon. *Definitely* not of this world. Donna stood up, taking my elbow. "Stan will call Billy May. He and Stan will see if the instrumentation can possibly be a little smaller. We'll see." Bill had taken my other arm, trying to calm me.

"I don't *want* it smaller!" I was yelling. "What are you talking about?"

Sweat was pouring off me. I felt Donna's fingers digging into my arm, as she and Bill moved me toward the door.

"We'll talk to you tomorrow," Donna told Merrick as we escaped into the cool air of his outer office and then the sanctuary of Forty-fourth Street waiting below.

Walking back to the Algonquin, Donna said, "We

had to get you out of there. Don't you see? You were playing right into his hands. Confrontation is all he lives for."

"But is he *kidding* about the size of the band? Could the man be serious?" I said. We were sidestepping winos and panhandlers, threading our way out of the theater district across Broadway toward the hotel.

"Maybe. . . . Maybe not," Donna told me. "I've worked with a lot of strange people in show business, but this guy is really something else. Hard to figure out. . . ."

"We've heard the stories; now we're seeing the movie," I said. "Listen, were you hot in that room?"

"Are you kidding?" Donna said. "It was *un*believable. I'm dripping wet. We'll be lucky if we don't get pneumonia coming out into this cold air."

Later in the afternoon, there was a knock on our door at the Algonquin. I opened it and Alan Delynn breezed in, his Burberry collar flipped up rakishly, British necktie loosened ever so nonchalantly. Then it was a playful chuck in the ribs for me and a quick air kiss for Donna as he made himself at home, just as though the previous verbal battle in Merrick's office had not taken place. Although the atmosphere was strained, I ordered him a drink from room service as he stretched out on the sofa, maneuvering a satin pillow into the small of his back. Finally, after minor chitchat, he cleared his throat and frowned at Donna and me.

"By the way, ahhh . . . I hope you understand why I can't back you up on some of these things," he said, swirling the ice cubes in his drink. "I always have to agree with David."

"Why?" I asked him. He gave us a kind of crookedy smile.

"That's my role," he shrugged.

• • •

That night I called Billy May in California. I went through the whole scene. After his initial outrage at what Merrick was putting us through, Billy agreed to see if he could cut the arrangements down, and we hung up. In a few minutes he called back.

"Okay, Stanley, here's the best we can do," he said. "Fifteen men. I cut two brass, one reed, and the guitar. So that's four rhythm, four reeds, three trumpets, only two trombones, but we need the two French horns for your joke. Plus, I've added them to the brass section all the way through." I thanked him and told him I'd try the fifteen men on Merrick.

The next day Donna and I were back in Merrick's office. This time we had dressed lightly underneath with warm coats that we shed instantly after we sat down in the red inner sanctum. It did no good. I was burning up before I hit the couch.

I programmed the steel wall to drop down around my solar plexus, took a deep breath, and looked him in the eye. "I spoke to Billy May," I said, "and although it's against our better judgment, we think we might be able to get by with fifteen men in the orchestra. But no less! That's it."

Merrick leaned back in his black executive leather chair. A dramatic stage wait, and then:

"Fifteen men? I thought you wanted *nineteen*?"

"Nineteen??" I said. "Well . . . of course, but—"

"Why would you settle for fifteen, if it was against your better judgment?" Merrick said to me.

"Heyy," I answered with a wobbly smile, "Nineteen it is then. Fine by me. Done and done."

There was silence for a moment. Then to keep the conversational ball rolling, I went on: "It's just that . . ."

Donna's knee was pushing hard against my leg. *Shut up!* the knee said. *Quit while you're ahead, for God's sake!* I couldn't be stopped. " . . . it's just that *you* had mentioned a smaller band possibly."

Merrick leaned forward and laced his fingers.

"*I* had mentioned a smaller band?" He chuckled deep in his throat. "I don't know what you're talking about. I'm the one who okayed the nineteen men. You must be imagining things." Deep in my brain a theremin began to play. It was that strange shimmery instrument used to underscore old Hollywood suspense movies like —*Gaslight!* Merrick was playing *Gaslight* on us!

Over the theremin's shimmery music I heard the buttery voice of Charles Boyer. "The lights? But I didn't notice the lights dim."

Ingrid Bergman's voice came in now, trying to hold tight to her sanity. "But they did! Oh, please tell me you saw the lights dim!"

"Nonsense. You're not well, that's all. It's just your imagination. Come lay down for a while."

Merrick's voice, I realized, had the same deep hypnotic quality as Charles Boyer, but without the French accent. I was caught in a scene from *Gaslight!* Merrick must be trying to drive Donna and me crazy the way poor Ingrid Bergman was driven to the brink by Boyer. As my mind snapped back to reality, I heard the calm voice of my wife: "Nineteen men was always my understanding too, David. So I don't know what Stanley's raving about, but I'm with you. We'll lock that in. Now. Dorothy Loudon was a *wonderful* idea of yours—marvelous—we're almost set on the two second leads, and we'll be talking to you about that by the end of the week. We have to run now, so nighty-night." The woman was a wonder. She had somehow bridged into a different subject and concluded the meeting. Now she was reaching her cheek for a quick kiss from Charles Boyer as he stood up and was guiding me in the small of my back toward the elevator.

During this period, Merrick had two straight plays fold on Broadway, after extremely brief unsuccessful runs. One was a play by an English playwright called *The Astrakhan Coat,* and the other was *We Have Always Lived in the Castle,* directed by Garson Kanin. On the heels of the successful *Hello, Dolly!* these failures threw Merrick into a black mood. He didn't like the feeling of anything but raging success. Donna and I flew back to Beverly Hills for a long weekend to spend some time with our daughter Donna Jr., then about nine years old. For company she had Frances, plus the nanny she'd had since birth, Sweety Magnolia. Still, it wasn't like Daddy and Mommy. But she was a trouper, who had gone to sleep on many a recording-studio couch while her parents finished editing, only to be awakened in the wee hours so she could go home and catch a couple more hours sleep in her own bed, before getting up to go to the Westlake School for Girls.

She was very fast with a line. Once when Merrick was at our house, we brought her downstairs to meet him.

"This is David Merrick, Donna," I said. Merrick stood up and shook her hand solemnly. "Do you know who I am?" he asked her. She stared up at him with her angelic little face.

"Yes I do," she said. "You're the mean man who keeps my daddy working all the time, so he has no time left for me." It got a pretty good laugh from everyone but Merrick. He rolled his eyes toward the rest of us. "Someone else, to hate me," he said. We returned to New

York on Columbus Day. I was reminded of a brief joke on my album, as well as in the show, when Columbus arrived in America.

**COLUMBUS:** (TO INDIANS) Well, if you'll lead us to the nearest bank, I'll get a check cashed, and start the country.
**INDIAN:** You out of luck today. Banks closed.
**COLUMBUS:** Oh? Why?
**INDIAN:** Columbus Day.
**COLUMBUS:** I see. (AHEM) We going out on that joke?
**INDIAN:** No . . . we do reprise of song. That help.
**COLUMBUS:** But not much.
**INDIAN:** Not much, no.
**INDIANS:** *Yo ho ho and a buckskin sleeve!*
*Now the white man's here,*
*I guess it's time to leave.*
*But why go to war*
*And fight like a jerk?*
*Perhaps we can pick up*
*Some kind of work*
*In an Indian extravaganza*
Wyatt Earp *or* Bonanza.
**COLUMBUS:** *Don't call us pal,*
*We'll call you.*
**FERDINAND:** *Step aside, pal,*
*Meet the new*
*Big cheeses of this round, round world!*

As Donna and I were ushered into the red room that Columbus Day afternoon, Merrick was on the phone. "What do you mean the sets won't fit into the theater?" he was shouting. We started to go back out, but Merrick gestured us to sit down. "Put him on the phone!" he was saying. We found out later that the sets for some show out of town were too big to fit through the stage doors. This dilemma did not bring joy to David Merrick. He was seething into the phone:

"How can you build a set that can't fit into the theater?" Merrick had a point. The excuses from out of town were falling on deaf ears now. He stood at his desk with a large blue vein pulsating at his temple—his usually calm face twisted into a snarl. The room was heating up badly. Donna whispered that maybe we ought to go, but Merrick heard her and held up his hand. I examined him. Had he sprouted tiny horns? No. Just tufts of hair standing up in outrage.

"Fix it, and fix it fast, or you'll never work again in this town, and that's my promise to you!" *Slam!* He hung up and whirled on us, his hands trembling: "Goddamn scenic designer idiot!"

I decided to try changing the subject.

"Well, we're back in town. Heh, heh. We flew in on Columbus Day just to put us in the mood."

Merrick's face looked as if it was returning from an out-of-body experience. He stared at me for a moment as though trying to place me. Then he sat down and smoothed his hair into place. "I suppose that's some vague reference to your show," he said. "*Another* goddamned musical to worry about."

"Look, you have your hands full here," Donna said. "Let us come back tomorrow when you've got this crisis off your hands."

"My whole life is a crisis," Merrick said. His secretary entered then, hesitantly. "Oliver Smith is here," she said. Oliver Smith, the distinguished art director of *West Side Story, Hello, Dolly!* and other Broadway hits, entered behind her.

"Look, David, I'll come back another time . . ." he said.

"No, no," Merrick told him. "This is Stan and

Donna Freberg. I want you to hear Stan's new show, and see if you have some ideas on the sets."

At the mention of the word "sets," a tic started in Merrick's check. A bad sign, and Smith knew it well.

"How about tomorrow?" Smith said. "This is not the best of times . . ."

"Besides, I don't have the script with me," I added.

"I have the script right here," Merrick said, producing the thick book. Donna and I had been edging toward the door, but now Merrick herded us back with his arms. I looked around the red room. The window? Forget it. The red velvet drapes were tightly pulled. Trapped! I hadn't even started, and I was wringing wet. How could I read comedy material under these tense, traumatic conditions? And why? A scenic designer doesn't need to hear the sketches read to him. He could read the script himself. Or later, he could come to a read-through with the actors and get a *much* better feeling for the show. But I decided to be Mr. Good Guy and play along. Read a few pages.

"How much of the show would you like me to read, David?" I asked.

"All of it," Merrick said.

"*All* of it???" I looked down at the five-pound manuscript.

"I want to hear it again myself," he said.

"But you've heard it so many times . . ."

"Sing the songs, too," he told me.

"How can I do the songs without a piano pl—"

Merrick buzzed his secretary. "Send the piano player in," he said. The rehearsal pianist I had been working with a few days earlier walked in, with my lead sheets under his arm. He gave me the slightest of shrugs and sat down at the baby grand up against Merrick's red wall.

I looked at Donna. Her eyes were shut. Sometimes, you just had to play the game.

"I want Oliver to get the full flavor," Merrick said.

I couldn't believe I was going to have to read and sing under these adverse conditions. But I opened the script to page one. Out of my peripheral vision, I saw Oliver Smith sneak a tiny glance at his wristwatch. When a man looks at his watch before you've even *started,* you know you're in trouble. But to his credit, he sat through act one, which took about an hour, and laughed heartily. Merrick didn't laugh, but then he had heard it all many times. After that, the red room and the humidity had done their worst, and I begged off. Merrick finally relented and released his wilted hostages, who stampeded to the elevator before he changed his mind.

When we got back to the hotel, I weighed myself on a bathroom scale. I had lost ten pounds in an afternoon.

"It's called 'The David Merrick Diet,' " my wife said.

I finally convinced Merrick to cast Peter Leeds and Jesse White, the actors who had done the original album with me, in the show. "Let them pay their own airfare to New York," he said. "Is it my fault they live in Los Angeles?"

Merrick was known to merely tolerate actors anyhow, under the best of conditions. Now, with the troubles he had been having in the theater, he became more sadistic than ever in his attitude toward performers, as though they were somehow responsible for his recent setbacks.

The final blow to Merrick's sensibilities during this blue period came when his second wife divorced him. The woman was nobody to fool around with herself. She took out an ad in *The New York Times* that was satiric, sexist, and hilarious. It was also terribly embarrassing to

Merrick. In huge black type it read, NOT RESPONSIBLE FOR ANY DEBTS OTHER THAN MY OWN. [SIGNED] MRS. DAVID MERRICK.

Going into preproduction, I saw less and less of Merrick in person. Mostly, we talked on the phone, between my hotel and his office. It was easier that way. One day I said to him, "I've written a part for you in the show."

"Not likely," he said. "Do you think I would demean myself by actually walking out on the stage with common actors?"

"Well," I said, "It was just a thought."

He cleared his throat. "All the same," he asked me, "what historical character did you see me playing?"

"Benedict Arnold," I told him.

A small chuckle came over the phone.

"Anything less than that, Freberg," Merrick said, "and I would have been very disappointed in you."

At times like that, David Merrick seemed almost lovable. Almost.

Later, in a face-to-face meeting at the Algonquin with Merrick, he broached the subject timorously. "Ahem. . . . Did you actually write a scene for me? Playing, ahh . . ."

"Benedict Arnold?" I said. "Yes, I did. Would you like to hear it?"

"You really have a script?" His eyebrows were up.

"I rummaged around my suite and came up with a couple pages of a first draft on yellow paper.

"Not that I would ever do it, you understand," he said. I read it to him, then I looked up, expecting Merrick to lash out at my audacity. By this time I had learned to lower the complete bulletproof glass booth around me and was beyond being wounded.

He was preening his mustache, displaying just a faint smile. A Xerox of a smile, actually.

"It's tempting," he told me. "Maybe I'd just do it opening night in New York, then let someone else play me."

That was the remarkable thing about Merrick. He had a perfect understanding of his image. He knew how he was disliked by many people—indeed, he tried hard to live up to the image. Playing a despicable person like Benedict Arnold on the stage could have been the culmination of a career devoted to playing someone very close to being that treacherous in real life. I had managed to lift his spirits for a few moments, but he was soon back in a black mood the next day. He had begun to retrench slightly. I heard he was trying to get out of a couple of other commitments for shows, but he continued moving ahead with *my* show. Then something happened that had never happened up till then: He began to personally tamper with my script. For all the other maddening things he did, he had stayed in the background pretty much. As he began to panic during this depressed period, all that changed. By now, we were rehearsing at the St. James beneath Merrick's office. We had to get out by late afternoon, because *Hello, Dolly!* was in the theater every night.

We were blocking one afternoon, working on the Civil War section. Dorothy Loudon was playing Mary Lincoln, and I was playing Lincoln. A few people from Merrick's organization were sitting in the center section of the theater down front, with Jack Donohue and Donna. They were all laughing loudly at the lines. Suddenly, David Merrick strolled into the theater. He sat down in front of the other people. Gradually, the Merrick people moved away from behind where he was sitting and over to the right side of the theater. It was as though he had brought some kind of radioactive material in with him, and people wanted quickly to put distance between him and themselves. Whatever he was radiating, it was not good vibrations, and his people sensed it instantly. Indeed, a pall had fallen over the theater. Delynn told me later: "We knew David was in a terrible mood. That's why we all wanted to be as far away from him as possible." At any rate, no one laughed again that day. The other actors and I continued to block and rehearse, although it was a bit unnerving with no more laughs coming over the footlights. Demoralizing, to say the least. Finally, we took a break, and Merrick walked down to the edge of the orchestra pit.

"Stan?" he boomed. Then he crooked a finger at me. The theater grew silent. I walked to the footlights. "Yes, David?" I smiled. He was about to turn the St. James Theater into Lüchow's restaurant, but I was so preoccupied with the show that I failed to see it coming. Merrick's voice lashed through the theater. Here's what he said:

"Take Lincoln out of the Civil War—he doesn't work!"

I tell audiences this line today, and people scream with laughter. Nobody was laughing that day. Could the man be serious?

"You're not serious," I said.

"Yes, I am," he told me. "The Lincoln character is unnecessary. Just drop him." It was Alice in Wonderland again, where nothing made any sense. I walked down the rabbit hole, into the audience with Merrick. "The Lincoln *character*," he had said? I tried to reason with him. "Look, David, ahhh, Lincoln is not a character in a fictitious play. This may be a satirical comedy, but everything is historically accurate. You can't just drop Lincoln out of the Civil War! People will notice!" I said.

"No, they won't," he said. "They'll never miss him. Oh, sure, *you'll* miss Lincoln, I'll miss him, a few history teachers maybe. But the average person . . ." He shrugged it off.

I suddenly figured out where I was. I was in an insane asylum, trying hard to hold a rational conversation with one of the inmates, but losing ground. Merrick's hypnotic talents were going to work on me. *Don't look at his eyes!* I thought to myself. *DON'T LOOK AT HIS EYES!* But he had the ability to wear you down. I couldn't believe I was having this conversation, and yet I found myself actually trying to rationalize his suggestion: "Well . . . let's hypothetically say that we *did* leave Lincoln out of the Civil War," I found myself saying. "Surely we'd make some mention of it in the playbill." He continued to stare at me. "In a little black box," I said. "We could say: 'The producer wishes to point out that Mr. Freberg has somehow left Abraham Lincoln out of the Civil War. We wish to apologize for this oversight.' "

But Merrick was shaking his head slowly back and forth with his eyes shut—a grim look around his mouth.

"No! No apologia!"

Apologia? Merrick the lawyer was throwing the Latin term for apology at me. I looked over at Donna, who was giving me the *cut!* signal from television, dragging her index finger across her throat. *Cut off this conversation,* she was signing me.

Suddenly, Jack Donohue was beside me. "Let's pick it up where we left off, son," he said to me, pointing to his watch. "We can discuss this later, right, David? We've got *Hello, Dolly!* hard on our heels."

The rest of that day is a blur, except for one final

suggestion of Merrick's later as we were walking up the aisle toward the lobby. "Let's take Barbara Freitchie out of the Civil War, too, and move her back to the Revolutionary War era," he said.

"Ummm, why would you want to do that?" I asked the inmate.

"We don't have any strong women in the Revolutionary War," he said.

"What about Betsy Ross?" I asked him.

"She's good . . . so we can leave her where she is," he said benevolently, "but we need another strong woman back there."

I stopped and looked at Merrick. "David," I said, fighting to be calm, "we can't rewrite history. Barbara Freitchie was a real person who lived in the 1860s. She grabbed the Union flag and stuck her head out the window when she saw General Stonewall Jackson marching up the street in the middle of the Civil War! You can't move her back almost a hundred years!"

"Why not? We can do anything we want in the theater!" he was yelling. We were outside The Saint James now, and Merrick's hair was windblown. He seemed to have lost some of his powers outside the aura of the red room. His eyes flicked up toward the window of his lair above, then back down. He was staring straight at me now. A small smile began.

"Would you like to come up for a moment? Perhaps we can . . ." Donna and Jack were pulling me away from the magnetic pull of his eyes.

"Stan's exhausted," Donna was saying. "I'm going to make him go to bed early and order room service. We'll talk to you tomorrow, David. Have a good night."

And the three of us whirled away from him into the wind, moving swiftly up Forty-fourth Street around the hookers and the street vendors with light-up yo-yos, toward the sanctuary of the Algonquin.

THAT NIGHT, AS I LAY ON THE BED WITH A RED-HOT burning sensation from my throat to my intestines, waiting for a painkiller to relax the knot in my stomach muscles, I noticed my wife moving briskly around the suite. I wondered if I was having a heart attack from David Merrick. A doctor who had examined me a couple of weeks earlier back in Beverly Hills had told me I was suffering from obvious stress from *something*. He had told me my heart was in good shape, but not my stomach. "Duodenitis. You're right on the brink of an ulcer," he had told me. "You can't let things get to you like this!" Easy for him to talk. Donna was . . . what? Throwing clothes into suitcases!

"What are you doing?" I asked her.

"I'm pulling you out of here," she said. I sat up.

"You're what?"

"You heard me. It'll never work with this man. The timing is all off. He's gone through a bad period, and he's panicking. If we'd come back here and done it with him a year ago, even six months ago, when he wasn't having so many problems . . ."

"He was just as strange then."

"Strange, yes. But not maniacal. You can't tell what he'll try and do to your show next."

"I'm protected by the Dramatists Guild!" I reminded her.

"Hah! Don't make me laugh!" Donna said, hurling dresses into a suitcase. "He'll run over any agreements like he was a Brink's truck. He's not a lawyer for nothing."

Brink's truck? Actually, I pictured him more like a Sherman tank in a pinstripe suit, rolling over my script.

"But what about our contract?" I said. "How can we just walk away?"

"That's the best part," Donna said. "Merrick kept insisting that you sign the contract first. But Larry Green told us, 'No! Wait till Merrick signs first, and then sign.' So in the meantime nobody signed. You can walk away with your work under your arm. You think you can help me pack now?"

"How do we know we can get a plane in the morning?" I said.

"I called American while you were napping. We're confirmed to L.A. nonstop at noon." She stepped over and put her arms around me. "I know what this means to you," she said, "but it isn't worth it. Believe me, it's better this way."

Much later, after we'd finished packing, we lay in bed, exhausted. I held Donna in my arms and tried not to think about Merrick any more. I was running a fever, and I felt like someone had been beating me all over with a baseball bat. One thing was for sure: Both I and my beautiful wife had aged several years from the whole experience. Just before we drifted off to sleep, I suddenly felt great sadness. My *United States of America* had nearly opened on Broadway. But this thing of beauty—conceived several years before with such great expectations—had ended up stillborn because of the tyranny of David Merrick. Donna was drifting off. I shook her gently.

"You're sure we should leave?" I said. "We can handle Merrick."

"Sure we can handle him," she answered. "But consider this—suppose—just suppose—we open on Broadway, and by some miracle you *haven't* had a bleeding ulcer or a heart attack from the stress of working with this man . . . what good will it be? Because in the end it *won't* have been the way you saw it in your head."

The woman was right, of course.

The next morning, our bags were by the door. Tony and Little Mike, the Algonquin bell captains, were on their way up in the elevator. The only person who had no idea we were walking away from David Merrick was David Merrick. I picked up the phone to dial him. Then I thought of a better idea: On the way to the airport—though it was out of the way—I would have the limo swing by F.A.O. Schwartz, the toy store. I would run into the game department, where they sold little steel balls for replacements in the Labyrinth game. Donna would not be wild about this stunt, as it could possibly make us miss our plane. But it would be worth it. Already I could see the final scene playing in my head: the limo waiting for me at the curb in front of The Saint James Theater, Donna checking her watch with aggravation but humoring me while I run upstairs to the red inferno for the last time. I dash into that infernal place, and The Prince of Redness looks up from his desk:

*Don't look at his EYES!* I tell myself.

"Stan?" he begins. "What . . ."

I make myself look at the lower half of his face only. "I'm leaving, David. We're on our way to the airport," I tell his mustache.

"What do you mean?"

"You're trying to rewrite history and my musical too. You're playing *Gaslight* with us all the time. I can't take it anymore."

"*Gaslight*?" Merrick stands up now. "What are you talking about?" he demands. I accidentally lock onto the brown eyes for a moment, but wrench away just in time.

"It'll never work with you and me. We're both too strong. And I have to do it my way or not at all. I'm sorry it couldn't have been, David."

I reach into my pocket and pull out the Labyrinth balls.

"A little good-bye gift. Open your hand," I say.

He pauses cautiously for a moment, then obeys me. I shove the little steel balls into his hand.

"What's this?" he asks, staring at them.

"Just a little something for those cold nights up on the bridge," I tell him.

Whether or not he recognizes himself as Captain Queeg in *The Caine Mutiny* is not immediately apparent. But he is already starting to manipulate them—in lieu of me—in his hand.

"You'll be back," he tells me as I turn and walk from the red room.

"No, I won't," I say.

"They all say they hate me . . . but they all come back!" he shouts. I say nothing more, in reply.

As I get to the elevator, which will take me to my long-suffering wife waiting below in the car, the building is suddenly strangely silent. Except for the distant *click-click-click* of someone manipulating two small steel balls in the palm of his hand.

I realized that this meant my being dropped from David Merrick's Christmas card list. We had received the same card from him for a few years. It pictured a Santa Claus in a red suit, dangling from a hangman's noose. "Merry Christmas from David Merrick," it read. Nice. Try explaining that sometime to your eight-year-old daughter as she stands blinking at the card. Ah, well. The Christmas card should have tipped me off if nothing else.

In the basement of my house today is a bird cage,

on a stand. Inside, sitting on the perch, is a papier-mâché bird, constructed by a well-known sculptress friend of mine named Kim Stussy. The bird seems to be wearing a pinstripe suit and has the face of a familiar Broadway producer with a serious black mustache. There is no newspaper placed underneath the Merrickian bird. Instead, a large picture of that same well-known Broadway producer smiles up from the bottom of the bird cage.

# 22 ✍

## *"Funnier Than* Cleopatra*!"*

AFTER MY HARROWING RIDE ON THE MERRICK MATterhorn, I didn't want to think about putting myself through *that* again. I had walked away with my work intact, but not my stomach. I went on a bland diet and tossed *The United States of America* into a drawer in my desk. It had been the kind of ordeal that could have easily turned a man into an alcoholic. Fortunately, I don't imbibe much, unless you count the odd glass of Dubonnet or occasional rum Lifesaver. Instead, I drowned myself in the advertising work that had been stacking up.

Soon after returning from New York, I was hired by Stanley Kramer to create and produce the advertising campaign to promote his new movie, *It's a Mad Mad Mad Mad World.*

This was not the first movie ad campaign I had done. A few years earlier, I had been hired by Frank Sinatra to create the ad campaign for his *Sergeants Three,* a United Artists film starring Frank, Sammy Davis, Jr., Dean Martin, and in fact the whole "rat pack" of Sinatra cronies. Howard Koch, Sinatra's executive producer at the time, confided in me that the picture was simply a remake of the original *Gunga Din*—but done as a western. He told me, however, that this was a fact better left unsaid. But as he ran a rough cut of the picture for me, I knew I couldn't resist. Sitting in the dark, there in the screening room, I blocked the whole campaign out in my mind. I knew it would employ the old "more honesty than the studio had in mind" technique. After the screening, Koch and I went in to see Frank in his production offices. Sinatra has always been a great booster of mine, but when I told him what I wanted to do to promote *Sergeants Three*, he just stared at me. He was in the middle of preparing to shoot *The Manchurian Candidate*, which he not only starred in with Laurence Harvey, but produced as well. God knows he was probably preoccupied.

"What do you mean you want to kid the fact that it's a remake of *Gunga Din*?" Frank asked me.

"Here's how it might work," I said. "We have an announcer walk up to people on the street and say to them, 'Excuse me, but have you heard that Frank Sinatra has remade *Gunga Din* as a western?' Then I'll cut to the person, who will slowly shake his head and say, 'I'm sorry . . . I can't accept that.' "

Frank looked at me for a minute and then laughed. "I like it," he told me. "It's honest. It might work."

Two weeks later, about fifteen people from United Artists tromped into my Sunset Boulevard offices. I read them the spot I had ad-libbed for Sinatra but with an ending that went like this: After the announcer, played by me, had confronted a number of people—a woman hurrying down the street, a man popping out of a manhole—who couldn't accept the fact that *Gunga Din* had been remade as a western, I would walk over to Dean Martin and Frank Sinatra. They would be in Civil War uniforms leaning against a fence.

**FREEBERG:** (TO MARTIN) They can't accept it.
**MARTIN:** (TO SINATRA) They can't accept it.
**SINATRA:** Yeah, well . . . (HE SHRUGS)
**MARTIN:** (TO SINATRA) Maybe we should have remade *Ben Hur* as a western . . .
**SINATRA:** Next time.

CUT TO THE MOVIE LOGO

**FREBERG:** (VOICE-OVER) *Sergeants Three*, starring Frank Sinatra, Dean Martin, and Sammy Davis, Jr., opens Friday. Try and see it! Try and accept it!

When I finished reading the commercial to the UA marketing people and assorted brass, I was once again greeted by "the long pause." Nobody had said anything, let alone laughed. They quickly informed me that the whole approach was wrong. "We don't want to bring up the fact that it's a remake of *Gunga Din*," one of the UA vice presidents told me with a grim set to his mouth. "That's not for the public's information."

"I'm sure they'll figure that out, a few minutes into the picture," I told him. "We might as well get it out of the way up front. Better they hear it from us. Look, movies might be ready for a little 'truth in advertising.' I think it'll work if anything will."

"Well, I don't," another man said. "You want me to be frank? I hate it."

Howard Koch spoke up. "Frank doesn't hate it. He loves it. He's the producer, and this is the campaign he wants to go with."

One of the UA brass asked me if I could give them a few moments alone. I went outside. When I came back in, Koch was smiling, but nobody else was. After I sat down, one of the glum United Artists men told me they would reluctantly go ahead with the radio and television campaign.

In one TV spot I used a clip from the movie showing Sinatra killing Indians left and right. I cut to a new shot I made with the great Indian character actor Iron Eyes Cody and another Indian.

**IRON EYES CODY:** (STARING OFF AT SINATRA) Who is that?
**SECOND INDIAN:** It is "the thin one."
**IRON EYES CODY:** What he thinks he doing?
**SECOND INDIAN:** He remake *Gunga Din* as a western.
**IRON EYES CODY:** (SHAKING HEAD SLOWLY) Mmmm . . . me no accept that!

After a two-week advertising blitz the movie opened successfully. According to Koch, the campaign was responsible for helping the four-million-dollar movie gross about forty million dollars.*

At any rate I'm sure Stanley Kramer was aware of this success story, plus other movie campaigns I had done, like the one for the last Hope and Crosby road picture, *The Road to Hong Kong*. This had also been for United Artists, but by this time all was forgiven and they were treating me like a favorite nephew who had somehow finally straightened out.

Donna and I had been invited to lunch by Kramer, who was, of course, the producer and director of *Mad*

* Howard Koch later went on to become the head of Paramount Pictures and the highly successful producer of such films as *On a Clear Day You Can See Forever* and *Airplane!*

*Mad World*. We joined him in the dining room at Universal, where he was still shooting for UA. As he told us about the movie, which starred Spencer Tracy and just above every comedian alive, I realized that it was a radical departure for Kramer, who usually directed and produced much more serious movies, like *On the Beach, High Noon,* and *Judgement at Nuremberg,* and later *Guess Who's Coming to Dinner?*

Kramer told us that he didn't want the usual studio ad campaign full of promotional clichés. I told him, "You mean like 'It's the slap-happiest, rib-tickling-est laugh-a-thon of the year!' "

Kramer winced and held his head. "Precisely!" he said. Then he hold us that he wanted me to create original material, so that UA didn't end up just using TV spots made from clips from the movie. Kramer and United Artists agreed to put the broadcast-advertising fate of *Mad Mad World* in my hands, and I set to work at the typewriter.

I created several radio and television spots, but one of the things that leaps out in my memory is standing at one end of a Universal sound stage with *my* camera crew, waiting for Kramer to finish directing the actors with *his* camera crew, so that on a brief break Sid Caesar, Mickey Rooney, or Milton Berle could run down to the other end of the sound stage, where I was all lit, ready to direct them in a thirty-second commercial. It was a frantic way for me to have to shoot. But in order to get the main stars into my TV spots, I not only had to have close proximity to them but be there constantly ready to grab the actors as Kramer finished with them.

One day, as I was standing on the set, I saw Kramer staring at me. Finally, he came over to me.

"You want to be in the picture?" he asked.

"Sure. Terrific," I said. "What do you want me to do?"

Thirty minutes later, I had been fitted with a policeman's uniform and was playing a scene with Andy Devine as my police chief. Later, as Kramer had to edit the movie down from it's original four-hour length, most of that scene was cut; and now you have to look fast to see me.

Kramer agreed to give me a whole day to film a sixty-second TV spot. But it turned out that only Kramer, my crew, and I knew that we had planned for a normal eight-hour shooting day. The stars had all been told by Kramer's publicity man that they'd "be out in an hour." While we were still lighting, I started blocking with what had to be the most stars I had ever directed in one commercial: Sid Caesar, Milton Berle, Ethel Merman, Mickey Rooney, Phil Silvers, Buddy Hackett, and Jonathan Winters. After we had rehearsed for an hour, trying to get it down to time, and hadn't made a shot yet, my actors began looking at their watches and getting antsy. They told me that the publicity man had told them they'd be out in an hour. I threw myself on their mercy and explained that normally I take one day per commercial, sometimes longer. And this spot was a complicated one. I told them it wasn't Stanley Kramer's or my fault that they'd been lied to about the time, but what could we do? Everybody was milling around grumbling, grousing, and checking their watches.

Finally, Milton Berle leapt up onto a chair and said: "Listen! Hold it! Stan Freberg is an artist at what he does, right? He didn't get to where he is by sloughing things off anymore than *we* did. How can he make a great commercial if we don't take the proper amount of time to do it right? I was due at the Friars Club for lunch, but

I'm going to cancel that now! If this commercial will help sell this movie, then that's good for all of us, right?" Everybody cheered Milton's speech, including Kramer, who had just walked in. Then they all ran to the phones to rearrange their day, and that was the last I heard of anybody leaving. But then the trouble *really* started.

The plot of the commercial was this: As Phil Silvers says, "Be sure and see *It's a Mad Mad Mad Mad World,"* four of the actors hold up little wooden cutout MADS, one at a time. Whereupon they all set to arguing with each other.

**HACKETT:** You got a problem here. You got seven actors and only four "Mads." (HE GRABS THE "MAD" FROM BERLE.)

**BERLE:** That's not my problem . . . All I know is I'm holding up one of the "Mads." (HE GRABS HIS "MAD" BACK.)

**MERMAN:** You mean you wouldn't give your "Mad" to a lady?

**BERLE:** To a lady maybe . . . not to you.

MERMAN SWINGS HER PURSE, CLOBBERS BERLE, AND GRABS THE "MAD" OUT OF HIS HAND. THEN MICKEY ROONEY AND CAESAR GET INTO IT, FIGHTING OVER A "MAD."

**ROONEY:** I think it's important that—

**CAESAR:** The importance of the importance is not important to me.

**WINTERS:** Shut up. Gimme one of those. (HE GRABS PHIL SILVERS'S "MAD," AND THEY TUSSEL WITH IT, ETC.)

In other words, I had taken the main theme of the movie—greed—and transferred it to the commercial. The stars were fighting over who would hold up one of the four MADS, the same way they did over the treasure money in the movie.

Arguing about the four MADS helped drive home the name of the movie, through all the bedlam. The problem was, none of them had ever adhered to the discipline of a precise sixty-second television commercial. I was shooting with three cameras, but one of them was making the "master shot" of all the stars together. It had to be on time and perfect so that I could intercut the other shots into it, but everyone ad-libbed and kept departing from the script. Off to one side, Milton's gag man was walking around with an index file drawer full of jokes for all occasions, feeding Berle fast one-liners that had nothing to do with the script. The man who had championed me was now innocently starting to torpedo me. I finally sweet-talked Milton into sticking to the script.

Then Winters started ad-libbing, throwing everyone's lines off. Jonathan has been a friend for thirty years, since we were both on the *NBC Comedy Hour*, and he is one of the most hilarious performers on earth. But right now he was demolishing the delicate structure and rhythm of an ensemble piece. I might have bought it but he was causing the commercial to run overtime. Donna told me we were now coming in at thirty seconds long on her stopwatch.

I gave everybody a brief break and walked back to Stanley Kramer. He said, "Now you know what I've been going through for the last six months shooting the movie. You have seven comedians here who all think that the idea is to top each other, instead of sticking to a script. They did the same thing to me in the beginning. The first day of shooting was in Palm Springs. It was 110 degrees. I had a terrible time with everybody ad-libbing.

Milton's gag writer walking around with that file drawer, just like they're doing to you here."

"What did you do?" I asked Kramer.

"At the end of the first day," he said, "I stood up on a camera truck and called the cast together. They were all exhausted, sweat pouring off them. Wiped out, really. They all thought they had given the greatest performances of their lives. But I said to them, 'Ladies and gentlemen, I'm not going to print anything we shot today.' They all looked at me like they hadn't heard me right, because what I was telling them was that all their work would never see the light of day. It was all for nothing. But I had to get control. I said, 'I'll see you here tomorrow morning at eight o'clock, and we'll do it all over again. If you stick to the script, maybe I'll print something. Good night.' "

"What happened the next day?" I asked him.

"They were all meek as lambs, and believe me, in that desert heat they stuck to the script."

"Any suggestions?" I asked. Kramer told me, "Yes. You have to be tougher on these people. Watching you work, it seems to me that you don't have the proper degree of arrogance."

This was a revelation. There are many people around the advertising business who might be inclined to tell you that Freberg has more than enough arrogance. But I knew what Kramer meant. It reminded me of a line once uttered by the director William Wyler, when asked what one ingredient it took to become a great director. Without batting an eye, Wyler said, "The willingness to be intensely disliked."

I finally got my stars on their chalk marks, but before I could roll the cameras, Jonathan Winters was off on a tangent again. He had unexpectedly launched into a speech about the injustice done to American Indians over the years. He was not going for laughs—this was a straight lecture with no apparent connection to the script. I told him I couldn't agree more, but could we just get the commercial in the can and then I'd be happy to discuss the Indian plight. "That's right, put it off!" Jonathan said. "Sure. That's what people have been doing for a hundred years! Lemme tell you . . ."

He told us all for several minutes, as the cast stood in position under the lights and I attempted to bring him in from the tower to no avail. Suddenly I felt someone at my elbow. Stanley Kramer had eased up next to me. He deftly transferred Jonathan's attention from me to himself. Then he walked right into Winters as he babbled on, slowly forcing him to back up a step at a time until he had manipulated him back onto his chalk mark. Suddenly, Kramer reached up in the air above Jonathan's line of vision. His eyes followed Kramer's hand above his head. Then Stanley pantomimed drawing an imaginary theatrical curtain down . . . down . . . down in front of Winters's face, all the way to the floor. As Jonathan stopped in mid-sentence, there was absolute silence. Then Kramer turned and bowed to me as if to say, "It's all yours." I had the distinct impression that he may have done this before with Winters. While we had Jon back on earth for a few moments, I quickly nodded to my assistant. We rolled the cameras, and I gave them "action."

After a few more takes the byplay was working exactly right, and it was funny. Then, as we neared the end of this first perfect take, Buddy Hackett unexpectedly dropped his pants. Believe me, nobody laughed. Least of all the other stars, who realized that he had ruined the shot and now, after all that work, they'd have to do it over again. Ethel Merman looked like she was going to slug him with her purse. I held on to my temper and quietly told him we'd have to go again from the top.

Hackett said, "What's the difference? Can't you cut out the part where I dropped my pants?"

I told him he knew perfectly well I couldn't chop off the end, because this was a "master shot." It had to be perfect.

"Then leave the part with me dropping my pants in," Hackett said.

"Even if I could get it on the network," I told him, "what has dropping your pants got to do with the plot of the commercial with everybody fighting over the MADS?"

It took another seven takes before we got back to where we had been, and I got a perfect take in the can. Then I started making close-ups.

It was one of the longest days I can recall on a sound stage. I walked back to Stanley Kramer, who told me, "If you'd killed Hackett, there wouldn't be a jury that would convict you. Look at my hair! I was only *partly* gray when I started this movie."

The commercials went on the air, and the movie opened to great business. *Mad Mad World* may not have been the most socially significant movie Stanley Kramer ever made, but it made the most money ($100 million to date).

I went on to do two other ad campaigns for Stanley Kramer movies: *Bless the Beasts and Children* and *Ship of Fools*. But Kramer's and my favorite commercial for him was the last one I came up with for *Mad Mad World*.

20th Century–Fox's epic bomb, *Cleopatra*, had just opened to terrible reviews and worse business. Elizabeth Taylor and Richard Burton, megastars of the movie, had pursued a behind-the-scenes romance, which drew the attention of the world press. The production of the Egyptian spectacle with thousands of extras dragged on for months and the costs soared to almost forty million dollars, before Darryl Zanuck, the head of Fox, stepped in and wrested control away from the director, Joe Mankiewicz, who had been hired when the original director, Rouben Mamoulian, had been fired. But it was a sinking barge, and Mankiewicz had done the best he could under the circumstances. All of it had been to no avail. It was not, shall we say, Elizabeth Taylor's finest moment, and the movie was roasted by the critics and the audiences. Into this environment was dropped the following commercial I had created for *Mad Mad World*:

**FREBERG:** Try and see *It's a Mad Mad Mad Mad World!* —Funnier than *Cleopatra!*

**MAN:** Wait a minute! I don't think we can get away with saying that.

**FREBERG:** No, listen! I've seen both movies, and *Cleopatra* is funny—don't get me wrong—but I have to say that *Mad Mad World* is a little bit funnier.

**MAN:** Yeah but—

**FREBERG:** Spencer Tracy, Milton Berle, Ethel Merman, Sid Caesar . . .

**MAN:** Hold it—

**FREBERG:** . . . Jonathan Winters, Phil Silvers, Mickey Rooney, Buddy Hackett. Every great comedian alive is in it.

**MAN:** It sounds hilarious, but we can't say that it's "funnier than *Cleopatra*."

**FREBERG:** Okay then, how about this: "*almost* as funny as *Cleopatra*"?

**MAN:** Well, *that* might be all right.

# EPILOGUE ✍

A conversation between the author's left- and right-brain personalities. The more practical left-brain persona is asking the questions.

**Q:** What do you mean, "Epilogue"? That only comes at the end of a book. How can this be the end of your memoirs? You're barely up to 1963.

**A:** I know. But this is just the end of the first half of my life. Think of it as having watched the first part of a two-part miniseries.

**Q:** What makes you think anybody will want to see part two?

**A:** That's a chance I'll have to take. I was once able to talk Jeno Paulucci into using the following line for his canned Chinese food: "Always buy *two* cans of Chun King chow mein; one for now . . . one for when you're hungry an hour later."

**Q:** Isn't that a little arrogant? Are you suggesting that readers may be "hungry" for more Freberg?

**A:** I don't know if I'd be so presumptuous as to use the word "hungry." At the very least, it is my hope that people may be "mildly curious" enough an hour later to entertain the thought of buying a second can of Frebergian memoirs.

**Q:** Suppose they *did* want to buy the second can an hour later—theoretically speaking, mind you. Where is it right now?

**A:** Still in my word processor.

**Q:** It's finished though?

**A:** Nearly. It will be by the time this book is in the stores.

**Q:** You're sure this isn't going to be like waiting for Volume II of *Stan Freberg Presents the United States of America?*

**A:** Trust me. For one thing David Merrick hasn't come around wanting to turn my memoirs into a musical and asking me to hold up on the second book.

**Q:** Hmm. Okay. You're sure you don't want to just go ahead and finish your memoirs right here in this book?

**A:** Surely you're kidding. I've got at least two and a half decades more to cover. If I did what you're suggesting, people would be discouraged from picking it up in the bookstore. The sheer bulk alone would put them off. It would be like lifting two Sunday *New York Times* at once.

**Q:** Aren't you exaggerating?

**A:** Not at all. Gore Vidal's *Lincoln* would be a pamphlet by comparison.

**Q:** How come other authors are able to get their lives down in one volume?

**A:** Winston Churchill took *six* volumes to get his memoirs of World War II *alone* down.

**Q:** Are you comparing Stan Freberg with Winston Churchill?

**A:** You said it, not me.

**Q:** But you haven't included some of your most famous advertising campaigns in this book. Like . . .

**A:** I've already told you about that a few hundred pages back. In my introduction I said I had to cut this first book off as I had barely entered the world of advertising.

**Q:** But what if I bought this book thinking I was going to read the inside story about your controversial airline campaign? The one that enraged the airline industry?

**A:** Next book. I hope to include the original full-page "Sweaty Palms" airline ad just as it ran in *The New York Times*. It will fold out, rather like an aeronautical *Playboy* centerfold.

**Q:** Does your publisher know about this?

**A:** They do now. The book will have a couple of other surprises as well.

**Q:** Like what?

**A:** Sorry. We're into an area of national security now.

**Q:** Okay, look . . . is the next book going to have a lot of laughs?

**A:** One can only hope.

**Q:** The Prunes! Before you sign this book off, aren't you going to at least tell us about your famous adventures with the Prune People?

**A:** "The Prune People"? That sounds like a science-fiction movie.

**Q:** You know what I mean. "Today the pits . . . tomorrow the wrinkles!"

**A:** All in the next book. Don't press.

**Q:** It sounds like the next book is going to be mostly about your advertising escapades.

**A:** That's what I keep trying to tell you. Furthermore, that's mostly what I've been involved in over the years that follow this book. I've tried to stay chronological.

**Q:** What kind of book are you going to do after the *next* book?

**A:** I may put out *The Gregorian Chant Workout* book. Mental aerobics—you never get up from your Lazyboy recliner chair—while singing the top forty Gregorian chants. We're talking low-impact aerobics here. Of course, now that I've tipped my hand, Jane Fonda will no doubt beat me to it.

**Q:** Are you serious, Mr. Freberg?

**A:** You never can tell with me.

**Q:** Any last comments about advertising to sort of set us up for the next installment, before we close the back cover?

**A:** Maybe a few parting words. You may be sorry you asked.

**Q:** I'll bet.

**A:** In the next of these missiles from Beverly Hills, I will detail not just more of my adventures in the ad game, but the difficulties I have had over the years in getting companies and their agencies not to take themselves so seriously. The more honest, lighthearted approach I suggested circa 1956, and before, did not easily see the light of day, as you may have gathered in this book, starting with the Loch Ness Monster chapter.

Some advertising people are slow learners. Nevertheless—they eventually got the idea. Sort of.

But if there is any humor in advertising today, it is no thanks to the advertising establishment. When I began creating my own brand of commercial in that hard-sell and deadly serious era, there was practically no one doing funny commercials—this being the ice age of humor in advertising. There were only my friends Bob Elliot and Ray Goulding doing their brilliantly droll commercials for Young & Rubicam in New York, and me on the West Coast. An off-the-wall trio, to say the least. And the serious ad practitioners just viewed our work as mostly an irritant. A few funny commercials that would occasionally surface. They didn't realize that as far as I was concerned, it was a "movement." But as soon as they figured it out, they proceeded to throw up every barricade they could to discourage me. "Paranoid," you say? A man who later became the head of a major New York agency once wrote an article, which was printed in *Advertising Age* magazine, urging agencies to join him in a "Stop Freberg!" movement.

I can't speak for the difficulties encountered by other people over the years, only my own obstacle course.

But I am a survivor. One notch up from Che Guevara, it would seem.

Slugging my way through the swamps and undergrowth of darkest Madison Avenue, I have come out the other side only slightly scathed.

Somehow recovering from the advertising-agency knives thrust deep into my back, I healed fast, and lived to create another day.

Long before the Saatchi brothers started sucking up the agencies of the world into their giant power vacuum, poisoned bamboo stakes were set for me in the tiger pits of J. Walter Thompson and Fuller Smith & Ross.

Safes and grand pianos teetered on the high-rise window sills of BBD&O and Kenyon & Eckart, as I walked, oblivious, below.

Nevertheless . . . I am still here.

A few flesh wounds perhaps—here and there a cut tendon—and yet I limp, undaunted (well, hardly daunted), to my private drummer; my sense of humor dented, but intact.

**Q:** I'm sorry we'll have to stop now.

**A:** You're the one who invited this outpouring.

**Q:** Why don't we just pick it up in the next book?

**A:** What an interesting idea.